HAUNTINGS

New Light on the Greatest True
Ghost Stories of the World

Peter Underwood

First published in 1977

Google Map

peterunderwood.org

Underwood Publishing

*For my friend and fellow
searcher after truth
Tom Perrott
Chairman of the Ghost Club*

CONTENTS

Title Page
Dedication
Illustrations   1
Line Drawings   3
Acknowledgments   5
Introduction   7
The Ghosts of Hampton Court   10
The Drummer of Tedworth   42
The Ghosts of the Wesleys   77
The Haunting at Hinton Ampner   105
Glamis and its Ghosts   135
The Mystery of Amherst   161
The Ghosts of Berkeley Square   206
The Cheltenham Ghost   226
The Mystery of Versailles   266
The Borley Hauntings   286
Select Bibliography   328
About The Author   333
Books By This Author   335

ILLUSTRATIONS

The rooms at Hampton Court Palace occupied by Mistress Sybil Penn

Hampton Court Palace: the west front where an unidentified ghostly female figure has been seen

Fountain Court at Hampton Court Palace, once haunted by the ghosts of two cavaliers

The Flower Pot Gates at Hampton Court Palace where a police constable saw a group of people disappear

The Old Court House, Hampton Court, once the home of Christopher Wren

Part of the frontispiece to Joseph Glanvill's Saducismus Triumphatus (1681), a contemporary artist's impression of the 'Drummer of Tedworth'

Zouch Manor, North Tidworth

John Mompesson's account of the 'Drummer of Tedworth' manifestations, 6 December 1662

Epworth Old Rectory

The Revd Samuel Wesley, Rector of Epworth

Aerial view of the present Hinton Ampner House, showing the site of the former 'haunted' manor

The tree-lined approach to Glamis Castle, long known as Scotland's house of mysteries

Glamis Castle: inside the main entrance showing the

stairway to the clock tower

Glamis Castle showing what may be the cause of some of the strange noises repeatedly heard at Glamis

Glamis Castle: the chapel where a 'Grey Lady' has been seen

The haunted house at Amherst, Nova Scotia, scene of the 'Great Amherst Mystery'

Walter Hubbell, actor and author of The Great Amherst Mystery

The haunted house in Berkeley Square

St Anne's, Pittville Circus Road, Cheltenham

The Grand Trianon, Versailles

The Petit Trianon, Versailles

Borley Rectory: probably the earliest photograph of 'the most haunted house in England'

Borley Church, where many strange happenings have been reported in recent years

The interior of Borley Church, dominated by the massive Waldegrave tomb

The site of Borley Rectory from the roadway

Borley Church: the bricked-up north doorway

LINE DRAWINGS

Plans of Hampton Court Palace: the State Apartments and Grounds, based on plans published by Her Majesty's Stationery Office for the Department of the Environment

Position of the present Zouch Manor, North Tidworth and probable site of the original 'haunted' Mompesson house

An artist's impression of Epworth Old Rectory at the time of the disturbances, based on an old print

Plans of Epworth Old Rectory, the home of the Wesleys

An artist's impression of the sixteenth-century Hinton Ampner Manor House, based on a sketch by Ralph Stawell Dutton

Speculative plan of the vanished Hinton Ampner Manor House, based on crude plans in the possession of Ralph Stawell Dutton and on information in narrative form

Plan of Glamis Castle based on Hubert Fenwick's *Scotland's Historic Buildings* (1974)

Plans of Daniel Teed's cottage, scene of 'the Great Amherst Mystery', Amherst, Nova Scotia

The 'Haunted Room' at 50 Berkeley Square

Plans of the Cheltenham haunted house, based on those in The Cheltenham Ghost

Sketch map of the Petit Trianon gardens, Versailles, scene of the famous 'adventure'

Borley: the site of the haunted rectory, 1976

Plan of Borley Church

ACKNOWLEDGMENTS

Ray Armes; Mrs C.C. Baines; Maurice Barbanell; Mrs I. Barry; Alan Bestic; Paul Bloomfield; Tony and Georgina Broughall; Ivan A.W. Bunn and The Borderline Science Investigation Group; G. Chesterfield and Robert Hale Ltd; Charles F.W. Chilton, MBE; Mrs Dorothy Collyer; Geoffrey Croom-Hollingsworth; the Revd Alan Daniels, MA, BSc; James Wentworth Day; Paul deVos; Ralph Stawell Dutton, FSA; the Revd W.Le Cato Edwards; Dr Joan Evans; Revd Keith A. Finnimore; Leslie J. Harris, Ancient Monuments (Presentation), Department of the Environment; Renee Haynes, Eleanor O'Keeffe and The Society for Psychical Research; Mrs Pamela Huby; Charles Hunter; James J.F. Kemp, Factor, Strathmore Estates; Richard S. Lambert; Bernard M. Little, FLA, Divisional Librarian, Salisbury; Andrew MacKenzie-. H. Berenice McKague; Lt. Col. (Retd) J. Macqueen, Garrison Adjutant, Tidworth Garrison; Maggs Brothers, Antiquarian Booksellers; Metropolitan Police Records Office, New Scotland Yard; Ian K. Neil, Assistant District Librarian, Forfar Public Library; Nigel Nettlefield; Peter Le Neve-Foster, MA, ARPS; Marion Neville; Michael Phillip Oakes; John Pickford; Mrs Pringle, Local History Librarian, Cheltenham Library; Colonel J.A. Russell and his staff; Richard E. Sandell, Hon. Librarian, Wiltshire Archaeological and Natural History Society; Professor John Taylor; Beverly True, Librarian, Cumberland Regional Library Board, Amherst, Nova Scotia; Chris Underwood; Steven White. The plans of Hampton Court Palace and grounds are based on copyright originals used with the permission of the Controller of Her Majesty's Stationery Office. Photographs for the jacket were taken in the churchyard at Bentley in Hampshire by kind permission of the rector, the Revd G.L. Russell.

INTRODUCTION

In an age of science, technology and materialism it is perhaps appropriate to take a long, hard look at some of the celebrated cases of haunting that have accumulated over the years; to discover whether it is possible to clear away some of the cobwebs of confusion and re-examine the evidence and the surroundings to see whether any prosaic explanation is possible.

After more than thirty years' experience of hauntings — talking to the people concerned, visiting the localities affected and not infrequently spending a night or several nights in 'the most haunted room' — I am no dyed-in-the-wool sceptic but neither am I convinced that everything that we cannot explain must be supernatural in origin. No one has ever seen a wireless wave but it is useless to deny that they exist.

Many cases of so-called hauntings can be explained without resorting to the supernatural, the supernormal or the paranormal. Some can be attributed to psychosomatic disorders, some to disturbed personalities, some to hallucinatory effects that are a necessity born of emotional difficulties, and there are other explanations for people seeing ghosts and experiencing ghostly phenomena. But there arfe also some cases of haunting that are reported by happy people who are healthy in mind and body and where strange happenings transcend all known laws.

Where this happens, and it does happen, the phenomena reported is often identical to that reported from every part of the world and in every civilization since the beginning of recorded history. There is irrefutable evidence, for example, that tragic and violent happenings can leave behind 'something' that is perceived through one of the five senses by certain people hours, days, years, even centuries later.

It was therefore, I hope, with something like an open mind that I set about re-examining these ten celebrated cases of haunting and in only one instance can I be said to have anything like a vested interest. The famous hauntings associated with Borley Rectory, 'the most haunted house in England', have interested me for many years. I first visited Borley in 1947 and today I possess a very considerable collection of memorabilia, miscellanea and evidence pertaining to the case; perhaps I should not have had a chapter on Borley but how can you write a book that is devoted to all the famous cases of haunting without including Borley, the most famous of all?

Otherwise the re-examination of such cases as the Great Amherst Mystery, the Drummer of Tedworth, the Visions of Versailles and all the others has been an enjoyable journey of exploration and discovery. Sometimes it seems the key to the mystery is within my grasp, at other times the solution eludes me; but certainly the majority of the cases here discussed are a little less of a mystery to me now than when I began.

I acknowledge with gratitude the help I have received from the people listed and I am always interested to hear from anyone who has something original to say about these or any other case of haunting — or who has a ghost of their own...

Peter Underwood
The Savage Club
Fitzmaurice Place, Berkeley Square, W1

THE GHOSTS OF HAMPTON COURT

The rooms at Hampton Court Palace once occupied by Mistress Sybil Penn, beloved foster-mother of Edward VI. The ghost of Mistress Penn is said to have been seen and heard many times hereabouts

Fountain Court at Hampton Court Palace, once haunted by the ghosts of two cavaliers. When their remains were discovered and buried elsewhere, the disturbances ceased

Hampton Court Palace: the west front. An unidentified ghostly female figure, a strange, distraught form with long hair blowing in the wind, has been seen both here and inside the palace

The Old Court House, Hampton Court, once the home of Christopher Wren, whose phantom footsteps are said to echo here each 26th February, the anniversary of his death. A ghostly page-boy was also seen at a garden party here in June 1929

The Flower Pot Gates at Hampton Court Palace, where a police constable saw a group of people disappear

THE GHOSTS OF HAMPTON COURT

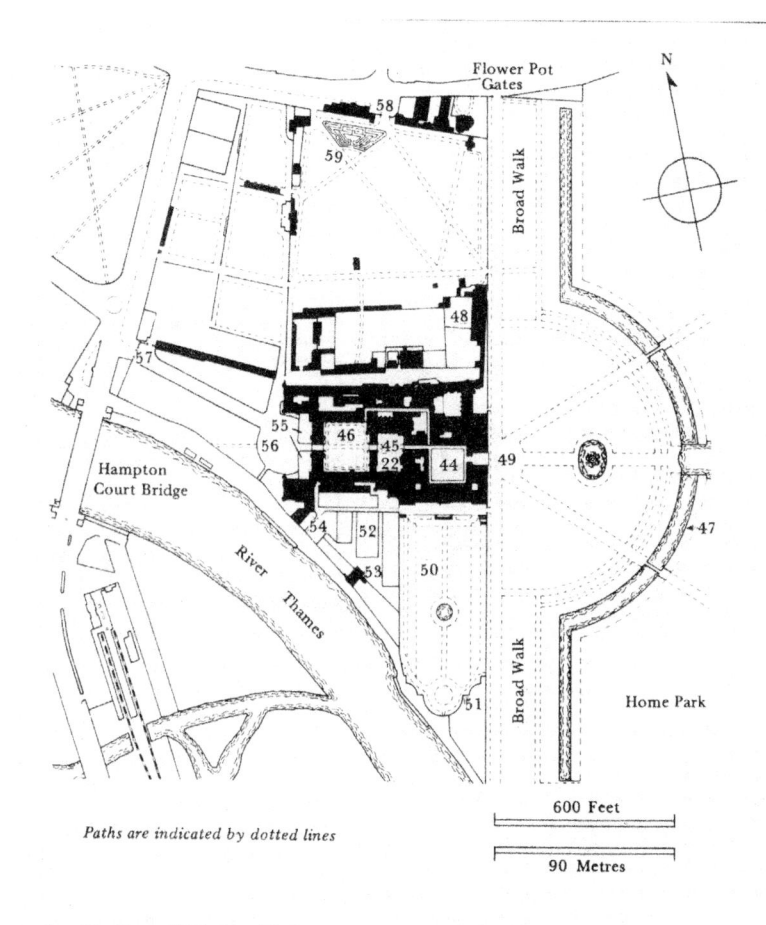

1	King Henry VIII's Great Kitchen	20	Anne Boleyn's Gateway
2	Cumberland Suite	21	Wolsey Room
3	Horn Room	22	Mistress Penn's Rooms
4	Cellars and Kitchens Entrance	23	King's Staircase
5	Great Hall	24	King's Guardroom
6	Great Watching Chamber	25	King's First Presence Chamber
7	Round Kitchen Court	26	King's Second Presence Chamber
8	Haunted Gallery	27	Audience Chamber
9	Royal Pew	28	King's Drawing Room
10	Chapel Royal	29	King William III's Bedroom
11	Prince of Wales's Bedroom	30	King's Dressing Room
12	Prince of Wales's Drawing Room	31	King's Writing Closet
13	Prince of Wales's Presence Chamber	32	Queen Mary's Closet
14	Prince of Wales's Staircase	33	Queen Mary's Gallery
15	Public Dining Room	34	King George II's Private Chamber
16	Queen's Presence Chamber	35	King George II's Private Dressing Room
17	Queen's Guard Chamber	36	Queen's Bedroom
18	Queen's Staircase	37	Queen's Private Chamber
19	Approximate site of Silver Stick Gallery, above Queen's Staircase	38	Queen's Drawing Room
		39	Private Dining Room

Plan of Hampton Court Palace and Grounds

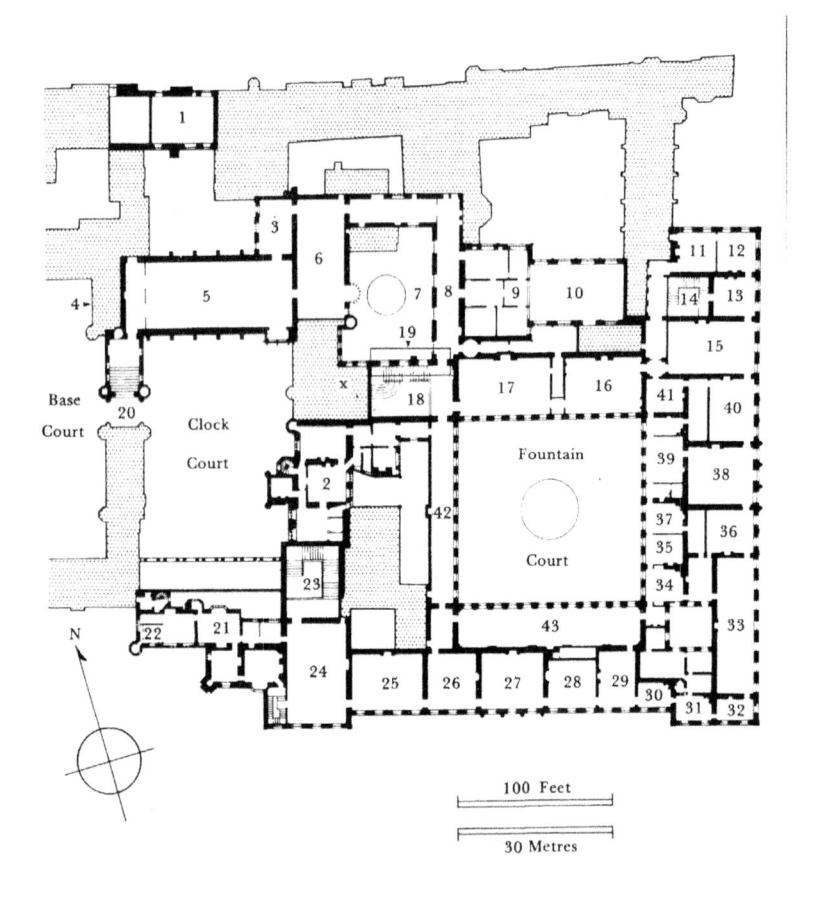

40   Queen's Audience Chamber
41   Queen's Private Chapel
42   Communication Gallery
43   Cartoon Gallery
44   Fountain Court
45   Clock Court
46   Base Court
47   Canal
48   Tudor Tennis Courts
49   East Front
50   Privy Garden
51   Tijou's Wrought Iron Screen
52   Pond Garden
53   Banqueting House
54   Great Vine
55   Moat
56   West Front
57   Main Entrance (Trophy Gates)
58   Lion Gates
59   Maze

x   Approximate position of elaborate Tudor doorway on second floor where the ghost of Jane Seymour is said to emerge

Hampton Court Palace: the State Apartments

At least a dozen different ghosts have been reported from Hampton Court, the great palace that Cardinal Thomas Wolsey built in the reign of Henry VIII. This country house on the bank of the majestic Thames was planned and furnished by the most powerful man in England with a magnificence that rivalled, if it did not surpass, a royal palace. When the King stripped Wolsey of all his power, the former Lord Chancellor of England, in a desperate bid to regain favour, presented his manor, its buildings, furnishings and plate to the King; but Wolsey's days of glory were over. While he was arrested on a charge of high treason — he died on his way to London — the King was already enlarging the house that was to become one of the most luxurious palaces in the kingdom and the home, successively, of five of his wives — Anne Boleyn, Jane Seymour, Anne of Cleves, Catherine Howard and Catherine Parr.

Henry VIII's son Edward VI was born at Hampton Court and the merry monarch's daughters Mary I and Elizabeth I each held court there; James I presided over a conference at the great house approached by the river; Charles I lived there as King and, for a short while, as prisoner during the Civil War. Charles II restored the palace that had been damaged and the royal possessions sold by order of the Protector, Oliver Cromwell. There was more rebuilding during the reign of William and Mary when Sir Christopher Wren was commissioned to redesign and add to the existing buildings. Queen Victoria first opened the State Rooms of the palace to the public while nearly a thousand rooms on various floors of the palace form 'grace and favour' apartments, granted by the sovereign to the widows or children of distinguished servants of the Crown.

There is a theory that thought fields can become attached to inanimate objects and that such objects — perhaps in particular walls and stonework — can retain a psychic influence that is perceptible to certain people. It may be that the chance of such a process taking place is enhanced by concentrated thought, vivid, dramatic or tragic events and powerful and intense personalities; if so, Hampton Court had every chance of becoming a haunted as well as a beautiful but brooding palace, and its claim to have more ghosts than any other place on earth may well be true. Ernest Law, the historian of Hampton Court Palace, considered the ghost of Mistress Sybil Penn, foster-mother of Edward VI, to be among the best authenticated historical ghosts, but the best known ghost at Hampton Court is probably that of Catherine Howard, the shrieking phantom of the Haunted Gallery.

Folklorist and researcher Christina Hole has told me of the 'many residents' of the palace who have heard the terrified screams of Queen Catherine in the Haunted Gallery, a fact she later published in her review of England's ghosts [Christina Hole, Haunted England (Batsford, 1940), p. 60]. The story goes that on 4 November 1541, the Queen escaped from her guards after she had been arrested at Hampton Court: she rushed towards the chapel to make a last appeal for her life to the King, only to be taken back, sobbing for mercy and shrieking with terror, to her room which she was only to leave when she was taken to the Tower where she was beheaded on 13 February 1542. Before her marriage Catherine had had several lovers, including Francis Dereham to whom she had been betrothed. After becoming Queen she occasionally met two of her earlier lovers; when this came to the knowledge of the King and the relationships were admitted, both men were executed. Afterwards there was fresh evidence of alleged infidelity after marriage and then Catherine must have known that her only hope of avoiding execution was her husband's mercy. According to tradition, the King was at his devotions and although he could hardly have avoided hearing Catherine's frantic pleas, he piously continued with his worship and sealed Catherine's doom. Christina Hole says terrified screams have been heard by many residents, apparently emanating from the Haunted Gallery and occasionally a figure in white, with loose-flowing hair, has been glimpsed, noiselessly gliding along the same panelled gallery.

A century ago this gallery was locked and used as a storage room for pictures. At the time some of the nearby rooms were occupied by residents, one of whom used to maintain that she had been awakened in the middle of the night by horrifying shrieks for which she never discovered any explanation; she did notice that it was usually late autumn and altogether she said she had heard the screams perhaps twenty times. Once, a friend, spending a few days at the Palace as her guest, said she too had been awakened by similar sounds which she said, without any prompting, seemed to come from the direction of the Haunted Gallery.

There is another story that when the Gallery was first opened to the public an artist was busy sketching some of the beautiful tapestry that used to hang in the gallery when he was astonished to see a hand with a ring on one finger appear on the tapestry. He hurriedly sketched the hand and the ring with its unusual jewel; later this ring is said to have been identified as similar to one known to have belonged to Queen Catherine. Whatever the truth of the stories about Catherine it has to be remembered that she went to Hampton Court in 1540, a lovely young girl of eighteen and the bride of a fat, lame and ageing man; perhaps it is not altogether surprising that she behaved little better than a harlot, both before and after her marriage.

At the foot of the great Queen's Staircase a low-roofed corridor — containing the rooms to which Queen Catherine was confined — can be seen on the right-hand side. To these rooms Catherine was dragged back, her shrieks and sobs mingling with the echoing chanting that emanated from the chapel, her first steps to the execution block. Those who say they have seen and heard this famous ghost in the Haunted Gallery include Mrs Cavendish Boyle and the Lady Eastlake, as well as many servants. All agree that the figure has long and flowing hair and that it invariably disappears so quickly that there is no time to observe it closely. In recent years one of the occupants of an apartment at the palace, situated near the Haunted Gallery, told a 'ghosthunter' that she had witnessed the shrieking figure so often that she took it as a matter of course, but to me this sounds suspiciously like a person telling someone what they want to hear.

Another well-known ghost is that of Jane Seymour, Henry's third wife, who bore him a son and died a week later. Her ghost, a figure 'dressed' in white, perambulates Clock Court, having emerged from the stately entrance to Catherine of Aragon's Rooms in the Queen's Old Apartments, perhaps where she had been discovered sitting in amorous dalliance on the King's knee. The figure of Queen Jane wanders noiselessly about the stairway and the immediate vicinity of the Silver Stick Gallery, carrying a lighted taper: it is said that she always appears on the night of 12th October, the anniversary of the birth of Edward VI. Jane was a tragic figure. She married the King, produced a male heir to the throne and died, all within the space of a twelvemonth, so it might be considered plausible that something of the happiness, the sadness and the deep emotion that was crowded into that year could survive the death of the physical body. Indeed it has been reported that quite recently some servants gave in their notices because they had been frightened by the sight of a 'tall lady, clad in white, with a long train and a shining face', gliding without a sound down stairways and passing through closed doors, carrying a lighted candle, white and slender, with a flame that never flickers.

Oddly enough, no one seems to have verified the precise location of this oft-quoted part of the haunted palace. On my behalf the Department of the Environment consulted their historians and I am informed (18 October 1976) that in the last century the Silver Stick Gallery was the name given to the grace and favour apartment situated in the attic storey, above the Queen's Staircase. The apartment consisted of about twelve small rooms facing north over Round Kitchen

Court and south over the roof of the Communication Gallery, leading off an unlighted central corridor. The partitions have since been removed, creating once again a single large attic space, and the name has fallen out of use, although the designation appears to be an old one. It probably belonged originally to a sixteenth-century gallery in the same area, part of the portion of the old Tudor palace demolished by Wren to make way for his new Fountain Court in 1689.

Another famous Hampton Court ghost is Anne Boleyn. The phantom has been recognized from a portrait that hangs in the palace, the blue dress shimmering in the light of late afternoon as the figure glides noiselessly along corridors that once Henry's second wife, the vivacious and charming former maid of honour, must have known and loved during her few short years of happiness. Palace servants at the end of the nineteenth century reported seeing the figure of Anne wandering, disconsolate and downcast, among the rooms and passages where once she walked as Queen.

There is, however, better evidence for the ghostly activities of Mistress Sybil Penn, foster-mother of Edward VI, Henry VIII's only legitimate son. As his nurse the sound of her voice and the whirr of her spinning-wheel must have been some of the first sounds heard by the baby prince. Mistress Penn seems to have been much loved; certainly the sickly Edward would never forget his old nurse and Elizabeth granted her a pension and residence at Hampton Court where both she and the queen suffered an attack of smallpox. The Queen recovered, although she was marked for the rest of her life, but the old servant died and was buried at nearby

St Mary's Church, Hampton. It would seem that she rested in peace until the church was wrecked in a thunderstorm and pulled down in 1829. During the course of demolition the grave of Sybil Penn was desecrated and, although the handsome, full-length effigy and most of the tomb were removed to the new church, the outrage coincided with reported disturbances at the palace at Hampton Court, the place she had known so well during her lifetime.

At first two occupants of grace and favour apartments, occupying rooms not far from those once used by Mistress Penn, complained that they were constantly being disturbed by the sound of a whirring spinning-wheel and a woman's muffled voice that seemed to emanate from the wall qf one of the palace rooms in the south-west wing. Little notice was taken of these complaints but, during the course of subsequent alterations, a hidden and forgotten chamber was broken into containing, amid several relics of the days of Mistress Penn, an old and much-used spinning-wheel. It is probable that it was the actual instrument used by the old nurse during her lifetime, but the discovery did not bring the haunting to an end.

The rooms of the wing that Mistress Penn must have known for many years began to be frequented by a female figure in a long, grey, straight dress with a hood or close-fitting cap, a figure that was recognized by officers and staff at the palace as resembling the stone effigy on Sybil Penn's tomb. There are several stories of this figure emerging from rooms once occupied by the devoted nurse, of the same figure vanishing inexplicably, and of quiet and unhurried footsteps being heard in her old rooms. Indeed Christina Hole, writing in 1940, said the footsteps were still heard and the ghost still seen occasionally by residents and servants at the palace [ibid, p. 55.]. One sentry is reported to have deserted his post after seeing a grey form apparently pass through a wall, while servants have told of mutterings, loud crashing noises, stealthy footsteps and of awakening in their apartments, usually just after midnight, and finding the rooms bathed in 'a ghastly, lurid light'.

Princess Frederica of Hanover, who knew nothing about the reported appearances of the ghost of Mistress Penn, said she once found herself face to face in the palace with a tall and gaunt figure, seemingly clothed in a long grey robe with a hood. The figure stood silent and still, with its hands held out as though taking charge of a baby. Before it had disappeared Princess Frederica had been struck by a likeness between the mysterious figure confronting her and the effigy of Mistress Penn that she had seen. This Hampton Court ghost is sometimes known as the Grey Lady.

Other witnesses for the ghost of Mistress Penn include a resident, Lady Maude. She told Winifred Graham, the novelist, that a guest of hers had just arrived at the palace and was seated at a dressing table in the bedroom when a tall and gaunt woman in a long grey dress entered the room. Thinking that she must be a housekeeper or servant of some kind, the guest asked, 'Will you please switch on the light?', the switch being situated near the doorway. There was no response and the visitor turned to see the figure glide silently through the half-closed door. Lady Maude was emphatic that there was no person answering such a description in her employ at the time and there is no doubt that the description fits the Grey Lady ghost that is Mistress Penn.

Hampton Court also boasts a White Lady, a figure that haunts the area of the landing stage. This vague and indistinct form seems to disappear almost as soon as it is seen and, consequently, it has never been identified. It has been reported by dozens of visitors to Hampton Court and a number of anglers who saw the figure collectively one midsummer night.

Fountain Court used to be haunted by the ghosts of two cavaliers who were glimpsed from time to time, in daylight as well as at night, by those residents whose apartments overlooked the court in the heart of the palace. One resident, Lady Hildyard, collected together contemporary evidence for the pair of phantoms and sent it to the Lord Chamberlain, complaining also about strange rapping noises and other unexplained sounds. The letter was passed to the Board of Works who promptly did nothing. Shortly afterwards, however, workmen excavated parts of Fountain Court for the purpose of laying new drains and, during the course of this work, the remains of two young cavaliers were unearthed, having been buried just below the paving stones. Subsequent research suggests that they were the mortal remains of Lord Francis Villiers and another Royalist officer who were killed in a skirmish between the forces of the King and those of Parliament; after they were removed and buried elsewhere there were no more reports of strange noises or unexplained figures in Fountain Court.

Even the grounds of Hampton Court seem to be haunted and there are stories of various ghosts being encountered in several parts of the beautiful palace precincts. In February 1907, a policeman (PC 265 T) reported seeing a group of people walking towards him along Ditton Walk. As they came nearer, apparently chatting and laughing among themselves — although, looking back, he could not remember hearing any sound except the slight rustle of the ladies' dresses — he noticed that there were eight or nine ladies in long evening dresses and two or three men, also clad for a formal dinner. The constable, an experienced officer with some twenty years' service to his credit, turned and opened the gate for them as they drew nearer but when he turned back they had all altered direction and were heading towards the Flower Pot Gate on the road to Kingston. As he watched, the group formed itself into a kind of procession, two deep, led by the men and then, to the policeman's utter astonishment and while he was still watching them, the whole group vanished completely. One moment they were there, lifelike and looking absolutely natural and normal; the next moment they had completely disappeared. The official report of this incident is still preserved in the station occurrence book.

Producer-actor Leslie Finch told me that after a costume performance of Twelfth Night, performed at Hampton Court Palace, he was walking towards one of the palace doorways, at the back of the old part of the building, in the company of Lady Grant who had a grace and favour apartment, when he saw a misty, grey figure in Tudor costume approaching them. He thought the figure must be one of the actresses and, since she seemed determined to walk straight into them, he moved to one side to give her room to pass. As he did so he experienced a sensation of sudden coldness and said afterwards, 'My skin went stiff like parchment and I felt a shiver but apart from that it was not at all an unpleasant experience'. He resumed his place at the side of Lady Grant, who looked at him a little oddly and asked what had caused him to suddenly move in that way. He then discovered that Lady Grant had not seen the figure that had seemed so natural and lifelike to him although, at the moment that it had passed, she too had noticed a sudden coldness in the air.

During the 1966 season of Son et Lumiere, at Hampton Court, a member of the audience wrote accusing the organizers of breaking the rules by introducing an actor into the production. The writer had seen the figure of Cardinal Wolsey walking through one of the gateways of his beloved palace. Christopher Ede, the producer, referred to the incident in his contribution to the 1970 programme, saying, 'For that one member of the audience at least the magic had worked'.

Among the well-authenticated ghostly happenings at Hampton Court there is the experience of a lady resident who, in her young days, had a devoted friend; after the sudden death of her first husband, the friend married a German count and left Hampton Court to live with him in Hamburg, taking her little daughter, Maud. One night when she was about to retire to bed the lady who had remained behind at Hampton Court saw, climbing the wide staircase opposite the door of her apartment but making no sound whatever, the figure of a lady dressed entirely in black except for white kid gloves. As the face of the figure became visible the testifier recognized her friend and, as the apparition drew nearer and nearer to her, she shrieked and then fell to the floor in a faint. When she recovered there was no sign of the figure but a few days later she received a letter informing her of the death of her friend. She hurried to Germany where she learned from Maud that her friend had requested, on her deathbed, that she should be buried in black, with white kid gloves, the parting gift from her dear friend. The Baroness had died in Germany on 9th November, and it was on that date that the ghost was seen by her friend at Hampton Court Palace.

Twenty years ago I talked with Baroness von Kovatch (Sonia Kavori) when she was a member of The Ghost Club. She lived for a time at Hampton Court Palace and never ceased to be fascinated by the massive and rambling building with its eerie corners, secret staircases, hidden passages and endless corridors. She saw her first palace ghost in the cloisters beside the ancient tiltyard, having gone down to post a letter one evening at twilight. At first the yard appeared to be deserted and then, as she reached the overhanging shelter of the cloisters, she saw a figure dressed in 'period clerical robes and hat', walking towards her at an unnaturally rapid pace. At the same time as she saw the figure she felt the atmosphere change: instead of the warm, humid air of a summer evening, suddenly there was an overwhelming clammy coldness that intensified as the figure drew nearer. The Baroness felt suddenly frightened for she saw that the figure seemed to be walking several inches above ground level! She noticed, too, that the clothing or outline of the figure seemed indefinite and she described the whole appearance, except for the piercing eyes, as 'nebulous and cloudy in character'. After the first feeling of chill and alarm had somewhat subsided, she became convinced that she had been privileged to catch a glimpse of the ghost of Cardinal Wolsey.

Baroness von Kovatch was always very interested in the various ghosts purported to walk at Hampton Court. She told me that she had often watched for the pallid form of Jane Seymour with a lighted taper in her pale hands, but she had never seen this royal ghost. The Baroness often attended services in the chapel where, in the Royal Gallery over the lower door, King Henry VIII had knelt and prayed while the anguished screams of his doomed Queen echoed through the chapel. My informant told me that she had talked with several other residents of the palace who had heard faint screams and laboured breathing in the vicinity of the chapel and the adjacent corridor, but she never heard these sounds herself. What she did often experience was an awareness of invisible forces that jostled and whispered and quietly laughed in many parts of the palace. Frequently she would hear the sounds of a crowd of people talking together, the voices rising and falling in happiness or gossip, apparently emanating from a room ahead or around the corner of a corridor. But when she passed into the next room or turned the corner of the passage, the sounds would cease or, more rarely, flee before her into another room or around another corner. She told me that her nights were rarely disturbed, apart from the occasional sound of a swishing skirt or the whispering of many voices, or footsteps; all these sounds soon ceased to trouble her and later she took them for granted.

However, there was an experience one night that she could never forget. For at least four nights out of seven, week after week, she heard footsteps pass along the corridor outside her bedroom at midnight. She began to wonder whose footsteps they could be. Was there a rational explanation for that tap-tap-tap of high heels that hurried past, always to be followed a moment later by the shuffling tread of an old man? The Baroness made many inquiries, both within the palace and outside, but she obtained no satisfactory explanation for the sounds that she heard so regularly; she determined to sit up and establish whether anything visible accompanied the noises. She opened her bedroom door far enough to conceal her presence and waited in the darkness. At the usual time the footsteps sounded in the distance and with her heart in her mouth she heard the sound of hurrying high heels tapping their way towards her. She forced herself to remain concealed and saw, coming towards her along the dark passage, what appeared to be a faint cloud of luminous matter that formed itself into the figure of a small woman 'who seemed to spread an aura of anxious terror about her'.

She made her apprehensive way towards the King's Staircase where the figure faded or dissolved and there was silence.

Then came the shuffling footsteps, slow and laboured. Baroness von Kovatch felt an icy chill as they passed only an arm's length away and she thought she saw a darker shadow in the darkness of the corridor. The dank smell of an open grave assailed her nostrils, but she saw nothing with any degree of clarity. These footsteps also faded away at the head of the King's Staircase.

The Baroness had something to tell me about most of the palace ghosts. She said that the sound of a spinning-wheel was heard whenever the ghost of Mistress Sybil Penn appears in the room in which she lived, and where she has been seen sitting with a great dog lying across her outspread skirts, forever watching, it seems, for a child that never returns. Whenever a child is about to die within the palace, her ghost is seen leaning over the ailing child's cot, watching with piercing but not unkindly eyes as it passes from life to death.

Anne Boleyn's ghost, I was told, frequents the Witch Hazel Avenue, leading from the King's Staircase to the Banqueting Hall, and she has also been seen in the audience chambers. Her ghost has become rare in recent years but her scheming, ambitious and immodest personality is strongly felt in many parts of the palace.

Baroness von Kovatch also related to me a curious affair that was never explained. She had in her employ a woman who came once a month to wash down the King's Staircase and since, at that time, Queen Mary used to visit the palace every Friday, it was necessary to ensure that this job was done properly. The woman who did this work was strong and healthy, as she had to be since, at every three steps, she had to return to the kitchen quarters and change the dirty water in her bucket. One day she took her bucket as usual to the head of the stairs, in the passage that led past the Baroness's apartment, and worked her way down as far as the fourth step. She did not return for a change of water but no one thought about the matter until she had been on the staircase for about three hours. At last someone started to make inquiries. Had anyone seen her? No, no one had seen the woman that day. Yet her coat and hat were hanging where she had evidently left them when she had arrived and the bucket she usually used and the scrubbing brush were missing. She was eventually found kneeling on the fourth stair of the King's Staircase, the scrubbing brush still in her hand, the other hand supporting her and she was quite dead. No one ever really knew what had killed her but the look of horror and shock on her face, that was raised towards the steps above her, told their own story: the Baroness von Kovatch told me she and everyone who saw the body had no doubt that the woman had died of fright. About a month afterwards and at monthly intervals thereafter the sound of scrubbing was sometimes heard, in daylight, from the head of the King's Staircase and it was a long time before another permanent cleaner could be found to scrub down the haunted stairway. There is an old tradition, the Baroness told me, that the King's Clock in Clock Close stops when a death in the palace is about to take place and, indeed, she told me that she had known this happen on three occasions while she was at Hampton Court. And the ghosts of the romantic youths, Dereham and Culpepper, who dallied with Anne Boleyn and so suffered agonizing deaths, still haunt the little-known byways and narrow passages of the palace; tortured spirits, perhaps, whose pain of mind and body has left something behind that can survive for more than four centuries.

One day in February 1975, my wife and I visited Hampton Court Palace at the invitation of two residents, a mother and her daughter, who occupied beautiful grace and favour apartments. There, over tea, we were told that the rooms we were sitting in used to be, and perhaps still are, haunted. Things had become so troublesome at one stage that the rooms had been blessed but only the lower, living quarters, which were thought to be the more haunted; both our friends told us, however, that it was the stairway and upper rooms that they had found to be most affected by strange noises, possibly the remnants of a more extensive haunting years ago. Many, many times, unexplained footsteps (usually ten in number) have been heard climbing up the stone stairs towards these apartments. Usually the footsteps were assumed to be those of a real person but, at the same time, the person hearing the footsteps had the frightening impression that she must on no account open the door.

In one of the bedrooms, we were told, one of the occupants had repeatedly found herself suddenly thrown against the bedroom door. She had noticed that this often happened if she chanced to be in the bedroom when she heard the footsteps on the stairway. After she has been hurled against the bedroom door she has realized each time the footsteps cease and then she feels that it is safe to open the door. There is never anyone there and, indeed, no figure has ever been seen to be connected with the footsteps, as far as is known.

A few months before our visit the daughter had been doing some work in her room upstairs one evening and, a couple of hours later, came down to the drawing room, which is situated partly beneath her room. Her mother was in the drawing room when her daughter entered and she immediately asked, 'Well, does it look nice?' Unable to understand what she meant the daughter was then told that her mother had presumed that she must have been moving the furniture about and altering her room to judge from the extraordinary noises that had been going on — sounds that suggested heavy furniture being dragged across the floor of the room above. Needless to say the daughter had been working and had caused no noise whatever, nor for that matter had she heard any noise.

When Lady Ironside was resident at the palace she had a ghost which she never saw. On one occasion a few friends came in for drinks and, as she was about to welcome a new arrival, she directed an earlier guest upstairs to a room where she could leave her coat. When this visitor reached the room to which she had been directed, she was somewhat surprised to see a man lying full-length on the bed. She decided that he must be a servant taking a nap, perhaps during his time off work and not realizing that that particular room would be used for cloaks; most surprising of all was the fact that the man lay there, completely uncovered, fully dressed and with very muddy boots. However she said nothing, enjoyed the drinks party, collected her coat and was somewhat relieved to find the man no longer in the room. Months later, after Lady Ironside had left the palace, she was talking to this particular friend and she chanced to mention that during her stay at Hampton Court Palace she had not seen any ghosts, not even the one that was supposed to haunt the wing where she had apartments. The ghost was that of a cavalier who was seen resting in one of the bedrooms, complete with muddy boots.

The Birdwood Apartments, on the south side of the Great Gatehouse, have long been reputed to be haunted. It is here and elsewhere in the palace that the ghost of Mistress Penn has been seen many, many times. She appears in the form of a little woman dressed in grey who politely says 'Good Morning'. Many of the inhabitants of Hampton Court have seen this ghost and there is nothing frightening about her. The ghost of Mistress Penn seems, in fact, to have become confused with the haunting associated with the Birdwood Apartments, named after a previous occupant. A curious creaking and spinning noise was heard for years, apparently emanating from the walls. During some renovations a wall was discovered containing an old spinning-wheel with the step worn away by constant use. Some people associated this discovery with the ghost of Mistress Sybil Penn who, of course, must have worked hard for the infant prince, later Edward VI, for many years. But we were informed that there is good and recent evidence to show that the find had nothing to do with Mistress Penn, and that the strange creaking and spinning noise was heard several times after the spinning-wheel had been found. It is not commonly known that a male human skeleton came to light at the same time. It seems likely that the creaking and spinning noises — and the human remains — are associated with a misshapen servant at the palace who, once upon a time, was responsible for raising and lowering certain machinery, a servant whose ghost has been heard and seen in the apartment where once he lived, worked and died.

Another ghost associated with the west front'of the house is that of a woman in a flowing dress and long hair blowing in the wind. This strange, distraught and rather frightening figure runs out of the main entrance beneath the Great Gatehouse, across the bridge over the false moat, turns to the south towards the river and then suddenly halts in her tracks and looks frantically first one way and then the other. Then she runs back through the Great Gatehouse and into the palace where she has been seen to appear in one particular apartment. The present occupant of that apartment happens to be a woman who sleeps in the nude and on three occasions the guard at the main entrance has been startled to find a naked and terrified lady appealing for his help because she has woken up in her room and seen the ghost of a woman sitting on her bed. The figure that is seen is said to resemble that of a woman who committed suicide — or was pushed — from the window of an apartment (perhaps the apartment in which the ghost is seen) into the 'moat' below. This tragedy happened many years ago when the moat was composed of thick mud and the lady is said to have drowned in the mud of the false moat. Several of the palace wardens have seen this ghost.

A phantom monk is said to appear at the rear of the palace but he puts in precisely three appearances once every twenty years. He was last seen by a visitor about twelve years ago. She thought it rather odd that a monk should be standing where he was and when she saw him a second time she approached the figure, whereupon it vanished. She then learned that a resident of the palace had also seen the figure shortly before she first saw it. No one knows who this figure is or why he reappears every twenty years; nor does he appear to keep to any special dates. It has been suggested that he may have belonged to the old monastery that formerly occupied the site before Wolsey built the red-brick palace that was to bring happiness and misery to scores of people.

The comparatively recently opened Cumberland Rooms were haunted when they were last occupied, only a few years ago. The sound of piano playing, footsteps and doors opening and closing were all repeatedly reported before the rooms were opened to the public. Today they have a sense of peace and of 'having been lived in' that is not apparent in much of the palace that is open to the public. A most attractive suite, it is not surprising that the Cumberland Rooms harbour something of a previous occupant's thoughts and actions. From one of these windows some red brickwork can be seen in a courtyard far below. During some repair work remains of the previous property that stood on the site of Wolsey's palace were discovered and when the repairs were complete, the workmen resurfaced the old parts with red bricks so that they could be distinguished from the later stones. It is such thoughtfulness and affection for one of the most historic, beautiful and ghost-ridden buildings in England that could preserve the ghosts of Hampton Court for all time.

It is interesting to speculate on the possibility that certain areas may become potential centres of psychic power and, should the essential elements be present, hauntings or other psychic phenomena may take place. Existing evidence suggests that this may well be so and it is a fact that additional psychic activity, distinct from the main haunting, is to be encountered at Cheltenham [see chapter 8] and Borley [see chapter 10], possibly at Versailles [see chapter 9] and certainly at Langenhoe [see Peter Underwood, Nights in Haunted Houses (1994)] where the whole area around the haunted church seemed to be saturated or charged with psychic power. At Hampton, too, there are a number of other hauntings, one at least apparently connected with Hampton Court Palace.

Penn Place, once the home of Mistress Sybil Penn, one of the more frequent ghostly visitors to Hampton Court Palace, was at one time (and perhaps still is) haunted by a 'lady in grey'. It will be recalled that the ghost of Mistress Penn is invariably described as 'clothed in grey' and indeed the phantom has come to be known as the 'Grey Lady'.

A few years ago the well-known artist Eric Fraser entertained my friend Dr Peter Rowe and I at Penn Place, told us about the ghost and showed us the haunted room. It seems that delightful Penn Place probably incorporates parts of the original house in which Mistress Penn died. When Eric Fraser's daughter was two or three years old — and could hardly have known anything about the ghost of Mistress Penn at Hampton Court Palace — she said casually one morning: 'I've seen a nice lady in a grey dress. She came to my room last night and I didn't mind.' After that the little girl told her parents on several occasions: 'I saw the grey lady again last night.' In all the child mentioned seeing the figure perhaps half-a-dozen times although, of course, she may have seen the form when she did not tell her parents. After a while she no longer referred to the subject and it is possible that the grey lady at Penn Place, in common with certain other apparitions, is only visible to some children.

A stone's throw from Hampton Court Palace, across the busy roundabout, stands the mellow Old Court House where Sir Christopher Wren (1632-1723) lived during the years that he supervised the rebuilding of parts of the old palace. In the low, oak-panelled front dining room on the ground floor phantom footsteps are reportedly heard each 26th February: the great architect died on 26 February 1723.

The Old Court House was occupied for many years by Norman Lamplugh who did all in his power to restore the house to the gem it had been in the eighteenth century; perhaps his success in this direction was rewarded by the visitation of a ghost from an earlier age. One Friday in June 1929, Norman Lamplugh gave one of his not infrequent garden parties. In the middle of the hot afternoon Norman's brother Ernest and a friend of the family were standing chatting on the first landing of the staircase when the friend, the Comte de l'Hopital, noticed a little boy of about eight threading his way through the groups of guests dotted about the lawn. He knew that no children had been invited to the garden party and he mentioned the matter to his companion who joined him in idly watching the boy wend his way across the sunlit lawn towards the house. They both agreed afterwards that the boy appeared to be quite normal in every way although he was dressed in what appeared to be the black-and-white costume of a page boy at the time of Charles II. The two men agreed that the boy wore breeches and doublet of black velvet, long white stockings and shiny black shoes with big silver buckles; and they watched with interest as he approached the house and entered the front door.

Unhurriedly, but with the confidence of someone who knew exactly where he was going, the boy crossed the hall and began to climb the stairs towards where the two friends stood. To make room for him to pass it was necessary for them to stand to one side on the landing and this they did while the boy passed on up the stairs, taking no notice of the two men. Later they were to learn that Ethel Lamplugh, Norman's sister, also watched the figure walk up the stairs from outside the drawing room. The boy went on up the stairs, watched by three pairs of human eyes, and at the top of the house disappeared into a room which had only the one door. When the boy did not reappear, a search was made but the room into which he had gone was found to be deserted; nothing more was seen of the boy and the mystery was never solved.

My old friend Alasdair Alpin MacGregor told me that he was among those who had heard footsteps at the Old Court House one 26th February. On that date in 1937 he, Norman Lamplugh's niece, Mrs Helen Done and her daughter Carol heard footsteps, the sound of something brushing along a wall and the 'creak-creak' of boards on the stairway, as though a procession of people were walking upstairs.

There are other ghosts at Hampton Court Palace including those of Archbishop Laud, various unidentified Tudor wenches and servants, and even the redoubtable Henry VIII himself but reports of these ghosts appear to be as unsubstantial as the forms they represent. However, neighbouring Bushey Park, The Dittons and East Molesey have more credible apparitions, hauntings, poltergeist activity and inexplicable happenings of a psychic nature. Perhaps sufficient has been recounted to establish the possibility if not the probability of meeting ghosts at Hampton Court Palace.

It could be suggested that such ghosts as those reported at Hampton Court Palace, where there is an undoubted atmosphere and feeling of history and past events, are caused by 'something' affecting the optic nerve fibres in such a way that the one-way valves suddenly become unable to cope with the nervous impulses being relayed to the retina. It might be possible to imagine a picture that would be transmitted to the brain that would be received and accepted as real and genuine as any normal image formed on the retina. A number of psychical investigators feel that such an explanation for some ghosts is not beyond the bounds of possibility: it is a sobering thought that some at least of the ghosts of Hampton Court Palace, and possibly those elsewhere, can be explained in terms of visual projection.

THE DRUMMER OF TEDWORTH

Part of the frontispiece to Joseph Glanvill's *Saducismus Triumphatus* (1681), representing a contemporary artist's impression of the 'Drummer of Tedworth' producing his disturbances above the house of John Mompesson

Zouch Manor, North Tidworth, long regarded as the house (much altered) where the famous 'Drummer of Tedworth' manifested in 1662-3

strangeness of y[e] thing, & indeed had we not been stren-
-gthened by y[e] grace & power of God, wee must have
sunk under it; for many passages have been very ter-
-rible, but y[e] same God that hath hitherto defended us
I doubt not, will continue his goodness to us; & upon
that confidence doe resolve to keep my house as long
as I can take any competent rest, & those smites doe
not return, unless I may understand from you, that
you take it to be my duty to leave my house for a
time as some have perswaded me; wherefore if you please
to send your opinion in that particular, or what else
you conceive may be fit for me to doe in y[e] case, I
shall wth thankfulness receive it. I have acquainted
my worthy friend y[e] President of Magdalens, that I have
given you this account (w[ch] is very rude & much short
of w[t] hath been here acted) and I humbly desire you
to let him see it, from whom, as well as from yourselfe
either seperatim or conjunctim, it would be great
satisfaction to me to receive what rules or directions
you shall vouchsafe me; and I shall be carefull to
follow: and soe wth my hearty thankes to your selfe,
& my owne & my wifes service to my Cosen your wife
I take my leave & rest

Dec[ber] 6th

Y[r] faithfull kinsman & real
Serv[t]
    Jo Mompesson.

A page of John Mompesson's first-hand and contemporary account (dated 6 December 1662) of the 'Drummer of Tedworth' manifestations

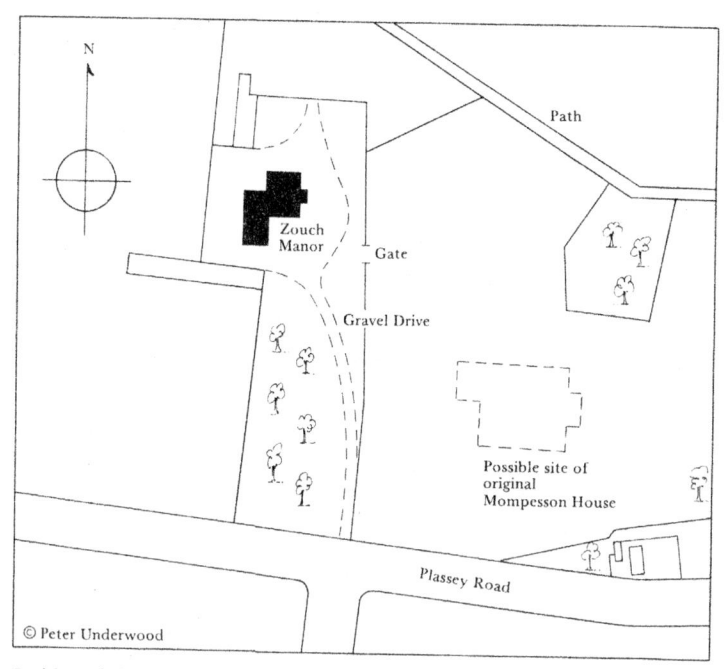

Position of the present Zouch Manor, North Tidworth, in the middle of Tidworth Army Camp

The 'Demon Drummer of Tedworth' has been referred to as 'a classic — if not the classic — amongst poltergeist cases' [Harry Price, Poltergeist Over England (Country Life, 1945), p. 44.] but a re-examination of all the available evidence three hundred years after the events leads one to suspect the possibility of a more prosaic explanation. However, let us look at the traditional account of the Tedworth poltergeist and the origin of the story.

There is some confusion about the dates of these remarkable occurrences but it would now appear that the Revd Joseph Glanvill (1636-80) is incorrect in giving the date of March 1661 as the commencement of the disturbances and that in fact they took place between March 1662 and April 1663. At all events, in the spring of either 1661 or 1662 (most probably the latter) a rogue and vagabond who had been wandering about the countryside annoying people with his violent solicitations for alms and disturbing the peace by the noisy beating of a large drum, happened to be in Ludgershall in Wiltshire at the same time as a Mr John Mompesson, who has been described wrongly as a magistrate although he may have been a Justice of the Peace.

John Mompesson, whose residence was The Manor House, Tedworth (now North Tidworth — the change in the spelling is accredited to a War Office misprint), noticed the itinerant drummer and the noise he made and, since he chanced to be staying in Ludgershall (then Ludgarshal) with the Town Bailiff, Mompesson mentioned the matter to him. He was told that for some days the town had been troubled by the idle drummer who had even demanded money from the Town Constable to whom he had shown, when challenged, a Pass and Warrant that apparently gave him authority to travel the country, playing his drum to obtain alms. The Constable suspected the documents to be forgeries but, without proof, he had no option but to allow the man to continue with his noisy drumming.

John Mompesson decided to have a look at the drummer's Pass and Warrant himself and without further delay he had the man brought to him. The man, a shifty individual, gave his name as William Drury of

Uscut (now Uffcott, where the surname Drury is not unknown among the local inhabitants). He said he had been a soldier under Cromwell and was on his way to Portsmouth, having possession of a Pass and Warrant, 'under the hands and seals of two of His Majesty's Justices of the Peace for the County' which enabled him to pass without let or hindrance and allowed him to collect any money that he might require by means of playing his drum.

On examining the Pass John Mompesson found upon it the names of two of his fellow Justices of the Peace for the county of Wiltshire, Sir William Cawly and Colonel Ayliff — men whose handwriting he was familiar with. He had no hesitation whatever in declaring the Pass and Warrant to be counterfeit. He immediately ordered the man to be arrested and to appear before the next sitting of the Justices, to be further examined and punished — and he instructed the rogue's drum to be taken away from him. The rascal Drury immediately confessed that he had manufactured the false Pass and Warrant and readily submitted to being apprehended but he is said to have earnestly and strenuously begged Mr Mompesson to allow him to keep the drum with him. This was refused; however Mompesson tried to be as fair as he could and he told Drury that if he was satisfied by Colonel Ayliff (whose drummer Drury said he was) that he had been an honest man, he would see that the drum was returned to him. Accordingly the drum was deposited at the house of the Town Bailiff. Drury was left in the charge of the Town Constable who seems to have been a gullible sort of man since he was so impressed by the scoundrel's plausible talk that he let the fellow go!

A month later, when John Mompesson had presumably forgotten all about the matter — including the fact that the drum was still at the Town Bailiff's house at Ludgershall — and was preparing for a journey to London, the drum arrived at his house, at that time one of the country's outstandingly beautiful buildings [See John Britton, The Beauties of England and Wales (London, 1814), Volume XV, pp. 396-7], surrounded by a large park. The house, according to Harry Price [Poltergeist Over England (Country Life, 1945), caption to plate facing p. 46] has been much altered but still exists while Arthur Mee [Wiltshire, The King's England (Hodder and Stoughton, 1939)] states 'the ancient home of the Mompessons has gone and a new house stands in its stead'. My own researches suggest that the present house, bearing little resemblance to the Mompesson mansion, occupies a nearby site although some of the original stone may have been used. The former Manor House is now known as Zouch Manor and is the property of the Army, being occupied by Colonel J.A.P. Russell, and forming part of Tidworth Army Camp. Monuments and records to the Mompesson family are to be found in the local church and churchyard.

On the return of her husband from London, Mrs Mompesson, who was expecting a child, told him that soon after he had left and 'that idle fellow's drum' had been lodged in the house, a 'hurling' or commotion or tumult had been heard in the air over the house and when it went away the sound of a beating drum had been heard. Other reports suggest that she was in a somewhat nervous state and greeted her husband with the news that the whole household had been 'much affrighted' during his absence by night thieves and they greatly feared that the house was being broken into. John Mompesson comforted his wife and they all enjoyed two peaceful nights and then, apparently, Mompesson himself heard the sounds that had so disturbed his household.

He was aroused from his sleep by a great knocking at the doors and outside walls of the house and his first thought, too, was that a gang of thieves was about to break in. Quickly arming himself with a brace of pistols he searched the house and then opened the front door, whereupon the knockings ceased there and began at another door. Throwing open that door, the sounds again ceased from that quarter and seemed to sound upon the walls around the corner. Quietly Mompesson walked round the house but found nothing to account for the noises which had by this time diminished to 'a strange noise and a hollow sound'. Yet he had no sooner returned to bed than the noises increased to a loud thumping and drumming which seemed to come from the top of the house. These heavy and distinct sounds continued for 'a good space' and then, by degrees, 'went off into the air'.

Thereafter noises described as 'thumping' and 'drumming' were 'very frequent', usually being heard for five nights consecutively, followed by three nights of peace. Mostly the sounds seemed to originate from the outside walls of the house which, at that time, were mainly wooden in structure. It was noticed that the noises always began just as the Mompessons (and possibly, but not necessarily, the rest of the household) were about to drop off to sleep and this would be so whether they were early in going to bed or late.

After some four weeks the noises seemed to move indoors and to concentrate inside the room containing William Drury's drum. Thereafter disturbances took place, according to reports, four or five nights out of seven each week, within half an hour of the household (or householders) retiring to bed and continued until about two o'clock in the morning. The sign of its arrival continued to be a hurling or commotion in the air above the house while the signal for its end was the sound of a beating drum 'like that at the breaking up of a military guard'. In the Revd Joseph Glanvill's first published account of the case [Philosophical Considerations Concerning the Existence of Sorcerers and Sorcery (London, 1666). There is an enlarged account in Glanvill's posthumously published Saducismus Triumphatus (London, 1681)] John Mompesson is stated to have maintained that the mysterious noises continued to emanate from the room containing the drum for a period of two months (taking us, presumably, to the end of July 1662) and during this time Mompesson is said to have slept in the affected room so that he might observe it. He reports that in the hours before midnight the noise was inclined to be very troublesome but that after about two hours all would be quiet. About this time, according to his sworn deposition of 1663, John Mompesson burnt the drum in an effort to stop the disturbances.

Then occurred one of the more puzzling features of this curious case for Mrs Mompesson was 'brought to bed' and it was noticed that there was very little noise while she was in labour or for any of the three weeks after the birth, that is, until she had recovered her strength. The sceptic might be forgiven for suggesting that she had other things to think about. However after this 'civil cessation' as Glanvill calls it, the disturbances returned with renewed vigour, in fact with more violence and variety than before; now the noises seemed resolved on following and annoying the younger Mompesson children, two girls of perhaps seven and nine years of age. These children complained of a beating noise and vibration of their bedsteads, so violent that they expected the beds would fall to pieces at any moment. It is reported that anyone taking hold of the bedsteads at these times would feel no vibration, as one would if the bedsteads were hit, but the beds would shake 'exceedingly' and the sound of a drum would beat a tattoo, 'Roundheads and Cuckolds go dig, go dig' and 'several other points of war', as well as any drummer — tunes that William Drury was known to beat...

After the prolonged drumming there would be a loud scratching noise which seemed to originate underneath the childrens' beds, 'as if by something that had iron tallons'. Sometimes the girls would be lifted up in their beds and it would follow them from one room to another. Things became so bad that John Mompesson and his wife sought where best to put the children so that they might rest undisturbed and, having observed that an attic had never been troubled during the disturbances, they removed the childrens' beds to this attic, put the girls to bed while it was still daylight and all was quiet for a while. But before long the disturbances began in the attic and 'were with them as before'.

The months passed with the drumming and other noises continuing to disturb the Mompesson household and in particular the two little girls. Then, on 5 November 1662, 'it' kept up 'a mighty rouse' and a manservant, noticing that two of the floorboards in the childrens' room seemed to be moving, asked aloud to be given one of the floorboards, whereupon the board lifted itself and came to rest within a yard of the astonished man. He then asked for the board to be put into his hand and, when that was done, he thrust it back whereupon it was driven to him again and so forth, up and down, to and fro, for at least twenty times. This is stated to have happened in full daylight and in the presence of a room full of people, the tug-of-war continuing between the servant and his invisible adversary until John Mompesson ordered the man to desist from 'such familiarities'. Afterwards a 'sulphurous smell', which those present found very offensive, lingered for some time in the room. (The word 'sulphurous' used at this time and in this context could equally have referred to an 'infernal', 'bad' or 'ill-disposed' smell and could well have had a very ordinary and mundane explanation in a small room full of people.)

That night the Mompesson home was visited by a local minister named Clegg, and various neighbours and friends were also present. During the course of the evening the minister led the company in prayer, kneeling beside the beds of the children where the noises were especially loud and troublesome. When the praying began the noise seemed to go away into the attic above but it returned as soon as the prayers stopped and then, in full view of the whole company present, chairs walked about the room by themselves, the childrens' shoes were hurled high over the heads of the astounded visitors and 'every loose thing moved about the chamber'. Suddenly a piece of one of the bedsteads flew towards the minister and hit him on the leg, 'but so favourably that a lock of wool could not have fallen more softly' and it was noticed that the bedstead piece stayed where it landed, without rolling or moving in the slightest.

In an effort to give the children some rest, John Mompesson and his wife now arranged for the two younger girls, who seemed to be the most persecuted, to be lodged at a neighbour's house while the eldest daughter, aged ten years, was taken into John Mompesson's own bedchamber. Within a month (presumably during December 1662) the disturbances would begin as soon as the child was put to bed and during the three weeks that the drumming noise was centred in J ohn Mompesson's bedchamber it was noticed that the noises seemed to possess some kind of intelligence. 'It would exactly answer in drumming any thing that was beaten or called for . . .' Somewhat similar circumstances, some two hundred years later, marked the birth of modern spiritualism.

Soon the younger children returned home, but when the room they had been occupying was required for visitors, their parents recalled that of all the rooms at the Manor House, that used as a parlour had always been free of any manifestations, so the children were put to bed there. However, 'their persecutor' soon found them, worried them by continually plucking at their hair and night-clothes but otherwise caused no disturbance.

When the trouble was at its height and the noises at their loudest (and sometimes, apparently, the noises were heard a considerable distance away across some fields and they are even reported to have awakened some of the villagers, 'none of which live very near the house') it was noticed on several occasions that no dog in the house would move. No matter how boisterous, vigorous and loud the noises and disturbances might be, the dogs would stop in their tracks and remain motionless until the volume of the disturbances lessened. Several times servants reported being lifted bodily with their beds and gently let down again, without any harm or discomfort, but on other occasions 'something' would lie like a great weight upon their feet so that they were unable to move.

Towards the end of December 1662, the drumming noises began to be less frequent and a new sound was heard, a noise that sounded like the jingling of money. It was immediately recalled that only the previous day, Mrs Mompesson's mother had said to a neighbour, who had talked of fairies sometimes leaving money at houses they visited, that she thought it would be a good idea if they left some at her daughter's home, to make amends for all the trouble there...that night, it is reported, there was 'a great clinking of money over all the house'.

After this manifestation the disturbances 'desisted from the ruder noises' and confined themselves to silly and less troublesome pranks such as one of the little boys being 'hit on a sore place upon his heel, with the latch of the door — the pin that it was fastened with being so small that it was a difficult matter to pick it out'; the throwing of clothes about the room of old Mrs Mompesson (John Mompesson's mother) and hiding her Bible in the ashes. The observant John Mompesson noticed that the Bible was lying face downwards but open at the third chapter of St Mark's Gospel, where there is mention of unclean spirits falling down before Jesus and of His giving power to the twelve apostles to cast out devils. It is only fair to point out that the same chapter tells of the healing of a withered hand, the choosing of the twelve apostles and the shewing of who are the true brothers, sisters and mothers: none of these incidents is in any way applicable to the Tedworth disturbances. The next night John Mompesson strewed ashes over the floor of his mother's chamber in an effort to discover what impressions, if any, would be left by whatever might be causing the disturbances. In the morning he found, in one place, the 'resemblance of a giant claw' and in another place, the mark of a smaller one, some letters (unspecified but which 'they could make nothing of') and elsewhere a number of circles and scratches in the ashes.

The disturbances then seemed to turn their attention to one of Mr Mompesson's servants, John, 'a stout fellow and of sober conversation'. This man, for several nights, endured the nuisance of 'something' trying to pluck the bedclothes from his bed so that he had to fight hard to retain them. Sometimes they would be wrenched from his grasp by a superior strength and end up in a heap on the opposite side of the room — and on one occasion his shoes were thrown at his head. Once or twice he felt himself forcibly held, 'as it were bound hand and foot'; but on those occasions when he was able to reach for his sword and brandish it, the 'spirit' ceased its hold on him.

Shortly afterwards the son of Sir Thomas Bennett (who had once employed William Drury as a workman) came to Tedworth Manor House and spoke with John Mompesson, relating to him some unspecified thing that had happened or taken place during the (unspecified) period that the drummer had been in his employ. This visit seems to have infuriated whatever was molesting the Mompesson household for no sooner were they all in bed that night than the loud and violent beating of a drum was heard. Young Mr Bennett rose from his bed and called his manservant who was sleeping with the Mompesson's manservant, John. When Mr Bennett's man had left the room John said he heard a rustling noise within the chamber and the sounds of someone dressed in silk approaching his bedside. He reached for his sword but found it held fast by some invisible force and it was only with great difficulty and much tugging and wrenching that he managed to get the weapon into his hands. As soon as he had done so all evidence of an invisible presence or force left the room and the servant came to the conclusion that whatever it was that plagued the household was afraid of a sword.

Early in January 1663 the sound of singing was often heard, apparently emanating from the chimney or fireplace, suggesting that this noise also originated above the house and that it entered through a physical opening, the chimney. About the same time mysterious lights were reported in the house; one from John Mompesson's chamber seemed blue and glimmering and caused 'great stiffness' in the eyes of those (unspecified) who saw it. Immediately after this light was seen 'something' was heard mounting the stairs and the sounds suggested a person climbing the stairway without shoes. A similar light was then said to be seen four or five times in the room occupied by the younger children and the maids affirmed that they had seen doors open and close without anyone being near them on at least ten occasions. When the doors were opened a noise 'was always heard as might be made by a dozen people entering the room, although nothing was visible. Afterwards sounds would be heard within the room that suggested several people were present and moving about; one especially was noticed that rustled as though dressed in silk and Mr Mompesson himself said he heard this particular noise on one occasion.

Once, when Sir Thomas Chamberlain of Oxford was present together with a number of other visitors, loud rapping noises were heard and one of those present called out, 'Satan, if the drummer set thee to work, give three knocks and no more' whereupon three distinct knocks sounded and no more. Nor were further knocks, made as a test, answered on that occasion, although when the same gentlemen asked for five knocks and no more later that night, if the drummer were really responsible, five knocks duly sounded and then the house was quiet for the rest of the night.

An hour before dawn on 10 January 1663, a drum was heard in the vicinity of John Mompesson's bedchamber but sounding from inside the room, as though somehow beat on the outside of the room itself; then the noise seemed to go away to the other end of the house where some guests were staying. It played outside their door 'four or five several tunes' and then 'went off into the air'.

Next night, when a practical and hard-headed blacksmith from the village slept with John the manservant, both men reported hearing a noise within the room that sounded as though a horse was being shod and, more frightening, something invisible, 'as it were a pair of pincers', kept snipping at the visitor's nose most of the night.

One morning John Mompesson rose early to prepare for a journey and, hearing a great noise emanating from the room below where the children were sleeping, he armed himself with a pistol and ran down. When he was nearly at the door he heard a voice crying out, 'a witch, a witch' — words that had been heard within the house previously — but when he opened the door all was immediately quiet.

Another night, after seemingly having got into Mompesson's bed and annoyed him by interfering with his feet, something apparently transferred itself to the bed of one of his daughters, in the same room, where it passed from side to side, lifting the girl up as it passed underneath. Father and daughter endeavoured to thrust at it with a sword but it was quick and agile enough to avoid each thrust, darting from one side to another under the child. At length it disappeared to be replaced the following night by a heaving and panting noise, putting one in mind of a dog out of breath. The girl took up a bedstaff that lay to hand and this was swiftly snatched from her hand and thrown to the other side of the room. Hearing the sounds of a disturbance various members of the family and servants came into the room which was soon filled with a 'bloomy and noisome smell' (not perhaps so very surprising and in all probability easily explicable). What is interesting is the reported rising of the temperature of the room: it became 'very hot', although there was no fire in the room and it was the middle of 'a very sharp and severe winter'. Whatever it was continued to pant and scratch under the bedclothes for an hour and a half and then it 'went into the next chamber' where it 'knocked a little' and made a noise like a chain rattling. This continued for the following two or three nights.

By this time the affair was the talk of the country and when it reached the ears of the king, Charles II sent Lord Falmouth to report on the matter. At the same time the queen sent Lord Chesterfield for the same purpose but few disturbances were reported during their one night's visit and the Royal Commission returned to London sceptical of the whole affair.

Now Dr Joseph Glanvill came on the scene, a distinguished divine and philosopher, chaplain to Charles II, a Fellow of the Royal Society, a reporter of witch trials and collector of ghost stories but a practical and careful investigator although, apparently, something of a sceptic in these matters. He wished to inquire into the authenticity of the Tedworth phenomena which were causing considerable comment far and wide. As he recounts [Saducismus Triumphatus (London, 1681)]: the famous drumming sound and 'ruder' noises had ceased by the time he went to Tedworth but he collected information about most of the past happenings first hand from the people immediately concerned and from others who had been present. Glanvill in fact arrived at a time when the happenings centred on the Mompesson children.

As soon as the youngsters went to bed, Glanvill was

told, things happened, and so it was the first night that the important visitor was in the house. The children went to bed about eight o'clock and almost at once a maidservant came down from the children's room to report that 'it was come'. Glanvill, his companion (a Mr Hill) and John Mompesson immediately went up to the room and on the way heard 'a strange scratching' apparently emanating from the room containing the youngsters. On entering the room Glanvill perceived that the sound originated in fact from the bolster of the children's bed and seemed to be located where the bolster met the mattress cover. The scratching was described by Glanvill as being as loud 'as one with long nails could make upon a bolster'.

The bedstead affected was occupied by 'two little modest girls', judged by Glanvill to be between seven and eleven. (Why, one wonders, did he not establish their exact ages from their father who was, according to Glanvill, beside him in the room?) Glanvill goes on to say that the children's hands were outside the bedclothes and he was satisfied that the little girls did 'not contribute to the noise that was behind their heads'. Indeed they seemed quite used to the noise and perhaps because there were grown-ups in the room with them, they were not 'much affrighted'. Glanvill stood at the head of the bed and after a moment, when the scratching was at its height, thrust a hand behind the bolster at the spot where the scratching seemed to originate. Immediately the scratching ceased there and was heard in another part of the bed. Yet, as soon as he took his hand from behind the bolster, the noise returned there.

Having been informed that on occasions the haunting entity would imitate noises, Glanvill decided to try this out and when there was a moment's silence, he scratched on the sheet five times; immediately five scratchings sounded from behind the bolster. Glanvill scratched seven times; seven 'paranormal' scratches sounded. He scratched ten times and was rewarded with exactly ten scratches from the region of the bolster. Now he searched with hand and eye under and behind the bed, turning up the bedclothes, grasping and removing the bolster, sounding the wall at the head of the bed and making all inquiry that he could think of to discover any trick, contrivance or common cause of the sounds. But he discovered nothing that might have accounted for the noises. Unfortunately he does not say whether he took the elementary precaution of ensuring that all the children and all the adults in the room were under observation; nor did he attempt to eliminate those unconnected with the noises by removing those present one at a time. There was certainly more that he might have done to establish or disprove the objectivity of the phenomena at that particular time but he was a guest and, presumably, this was his first personal experience of the Tedworth haunting (not that he was any more original, thorough or painstaking in much of his later inquiries into the case). In fact, within the short time that he had been at Tedworth and very soon after coming to grips with one of the manifestations, Glanvill was saying, 'So that I was then verily perswaded and am so still, that the noise was made by some Daemon or Spirit...'

After the scratching had continued for half an hour or so it 'went into the midst of the bed under the children' and there seemed to pant very loudly like a dog out of breath. Glanvill put his hand to the place and felt the bed bear up against his hand, as if something within had thrust it up. (Were the children's hands still visible, one wonders, and their legs controlled?) The intrepid investigator grasped the feather mattress to feel whether there was anything within and again he looked 'under and every where about' to discover if there might be a dog or a cat or any creature in the room, as did the other adults present, but all to no avail. Yet the panting noise was so strong that 'it shook the room and windows very sensibly and so it continued for half an hour' while Glanvill and his friend stayed in the room — and as long after, we are told.

During the time that this panting noise was heard Glanvill noticed something moving inside a linen bag that hung against another bedstead in the room and, thinking that a mouse or rat might be the explanation, he watched his opportunity and stepped forward to catch the bag by the upper end with one hand. He drew it through the other hand without releasing his grip but found nothing, and he was quite convinced that there was no body near enough to the bag to cause the movement or indeed, he adds revealingly, if there had been, 'no one could have made such a motion, which seemed to be from within, as if a living creature had moved in it'.

Later Glanvill recounts that he and his companion occupied the room where the 'first and chief disturbance' had taken place and they slept soundly and well all night but, just before dawn, both men were awakened by a great knocking, apparently just outside the door of their room. Glanvill called out several times, asking who was there, but the knocking continued without answer and at last he called out: 'In the name of God, who is it, and what would you have?' to which a voice answered, 'Nothing with you'. Thinking it must be some servant mistaking the room, both men returned to sleep but when he mentioned the matter to Mr Mompesson next morning, they were assured that no servant slept anywhere in that part of the house or had any business there; furthermore the servants were not up that morning till Mompesson himself had called them, which was certainly after dawn had broken. All the servants confirmed that this was so and affirmed that the noise had not been made by them. Glanvill remarks that previously John Mompesson had told them that the disturbances frequently went away in the middle of the night and came again early in the morning, perhaps about four o'clock; and he supposes this could well have been the time of the knocking.

Later that morning Glanvill records that his manservant came to tell him that one of his horses — the one he had ridden to Tedworth — had been found 'all in a sweat' and looked as though it had been ridden all night. Accompanied by his friend, Glanvill went down to see for himself and sure enough found the horse in the condition described to him. On inquiry as to how the animal had been used, he was assured that it had been well fed and attended as usual, the servant being his normal one and always very careful about the wellbeing of horses in his charge.

Glanvill decided to try the horse out and he rode it very gently over a plain down for a mile or two, and all seemed well until the horse suddenly went lame.

The horse returned to the home of the Mompessons with some difficulty, and died within two or three days, with no one being able to imagine what ailed it. Glanvill sensibly admits that this incident may have a rational explanation, perhaps being the result of an accident or 'some unusual distemper', but he adds that 'all things being put together, it seems very probable that it was somewhat else'.

Recounting further experiences of John Mompesson, Glanvill says that on one occasion the master of the house saw some wood move by itself in the fireplace of a room where he was alone. Having a pistol in his hand he discharged a shot into the moving wood which thereupon ceased to move, and afterwards he found several drops of blood on the hearth and in various places on the stairs but none, apparently, between the fireplace and the stairs. The pistol shot seems to have brought some peace to the Mompesson household and for two or three nights thereafter, Glanvill was told, there was 'calm in the house' but then the disturbances began again, seemingly centring around the latest addition to the family, 'newly taken from nurse'. This child was so tormented, it seems, that it could get no rest for two nights together, and when a candle was placed in the room, it would be mysteriously carried away lighted up the chimney or thrown underneath the bed. The infant seemed to be terrified by something that repeatedly leapt upon it, and it was hours before the child could be comforted enough to be lifted and taken out of the room. This episode caused the Mompessons to arrange again for the children to sleep away from home.

The very next night Mompesson heard 'something'

come up the stairs towards his room at about midnight. He heard it reach his door and knock, but he made no movement and no response, and then he heard 'it' proceed up a further couple of stairs to his manservant's chamber. In the morning this servant said that he had awakened in the middle of the night to see a figure standing at the foot of his bed; he could not see the exact shape and proportion but he had no doubt about a great body with two red and glaring eyes which were fixed upon him steadily for some time and at length disappeared. It would be interesting to know whether, as seems likely, Mompesson recounted his experience during the night before the manservant related his; if so it must appear likely that the somewhat obvious story of the manservant might have been invented on the spur of the moment with the thought (probably correct) that it would interest and please his master. Mompesson's own experience might easily have had a quite normal explanation but it seems unlikely that he made any inquiries before discussing the matter with his manservant and, by the time that story had circulated, the person who was actually responsible for the footsteps may well have decided that discretion was the better part of valour.

Another night, Mompesson told Glanvill, 'it' purred like a cat in the children's room. At the same time the bedclothes and the children themselves were lifted up bodily from the beds and six men could not keep them down. It is surely significant that nothing of this sort happened before Glanvill arrived and one cannot help wondering whether the 'six men' is an exaggeration of the category that would include his account of a voice saying 'a witch' more than a hundred times. Perhaps this is treating Glanvill a little harshly for, according to his report, the children were then removed from the room and it was intended to rip open the mattress to see what might be inside; but they had no sooner brought another bed into the room than the second bed was 'more troubled than the first'. These disturbances continued for four hours, we are told, during which time the children's legs were beat against the bedposts so often that the youngsters were forced to sit up in bed all night; when they did so first their chamberpots were emptied into their beds and the rooms were found strewn with ashes in spite of being watched 'never so carefully'. Nevertheless, many parents will recognize typical children's antics.

It is to be hoped that Glanvill is not being treated unfairly if it is suggested that a few further items — a 'long piked iron' that found its way into John Mompesson's bed, a 'naked knife upright' that was discovered in his mother's bed and 'porrengers filled with ashes', 'everything thrown about' and 'noise all day' — may be regarded as evidence of Dr Glanvill's zealous enthusiasm and determination to 'colour' the Tedworth story where he felt it was necessary to do so.

What are we to make of the final occurrences at Tedworth? At the beginning of April a gentleman visiting the Manor House found all the money in his pocket had turned black; John Mompesson, entering his stable one morning, found the horse he was in the habit of riding on the ground with its hind legs in its mouth and so fastened that several men had their work cut out to restore the horse onto its feet; seven or eight 'shapes of men' were seen who, as soon as a gun was discharged 'shuffled away together into an arbour'. Surely we have come a very long way from an itinerant drummer aggrieved by losing his drum and, possibly, a drumming noise being heard in the vicinity of the drum at the house of the man who took the drum away.

William Drury, the itinerant drummer, is the central, pivotal figure in the Drummer of Tedworth mystery, yet he is a shadowy and indistinct figure. As we have seen he evidently lived at what is now known as the hamlet of Uffcott. It would appear that he had been a tailor but, according to a letter from John Mompesson to the Revd William Creed dated 6 December 1662, he much preferred the wandering life of a man who lived by his wits. Posing as an itinerant drummer with a Pass and Warrant allegedly signed by two Justices of the Peace he was able to enjoy a life of freedom that was also a life of humbug, attending fairs, fetes and other convivial amusements where he could pick up enough money to see him on his way by beating a loyal tattoo. After slipping away from the custody of the Constable at Ludgarshal (leaving behind his drum, much to his annoyance) he does not seem to have stayed out of trouble for long and was soon in Gloucester Gaol for stealing. There is a story that he was visited there by a Wiltshire man who chanced to mention the strange happenings at John Mompesson's house at Tedworth that were the talk of the countryside. Drury, still doubtless nursing a grudge against Mompesson for taking away his drum, saw a chance of seeming to get his own back and he promptly claimed responsibility for the mysterious drumming. 'I have plagued him and he shall never be quiet, till he hath made me satisfaction for taking away my drum' Drury is supposed to have said, and upon this information he was tried for a witch at Sarum and was lucky to escape with his life, being condemned to transportation.

Here once again the story becomes uncertain and, although he was sent away aboard ship in accordance with his sentence, he somehow seems to have managed to return to England. There is a story that he used occult powers to raise huge storms that so frightened the sailors that the ship was put back to shore; at all events return he did. It is said that there were no reported disturbances all the time he was in custody and absent from England, but as soon as he was back in the country or at liberty, the disturbances returned. Unfortunately the confusion over dates and missing documents makes it impossible to substantiate or refute this statement.

Drury does seem to have served under Cromwell at one time, when it appears he was well known for his habit of talking in an elusive way about some intriguing books that he had acquired (most probably stolen) from 'an odd fellow' who, according to Drury, was known to be a sorcerer.

Mompesson, with the disturbances at his house then at their height, now accused Drury of causing the mischief by witchcraft and the vagabond was duly arrested and found guilty by the Grand Jury. But somehow he contrived to be acquitted by a Petty Jury and so disappears from history. A variation of the latter part of the story is that he returned to Uffcott and purchased another drum from a man named Farler, who had supplied him with the original drum, and somewhat rashly proceeded to beat it in the vicinity. As soon as news of this reached Mompesson he had Drury seized on a charge of witchcraft and, although Drury managed to obtain an acquittal, he was transported to Virginia on a charge of stealing and no more was heard of him.

John Mompesson's accusation of witchcraft against Drury is interesting in view of the fact that the Revd Joseph Glanvill relates a story to the effect that Mompesson's house was a rendezvous of witches! If the story has any foundation such an action by Mompesson, the respected country squire, could have had its purpose in diverting suspicion from the Mompesson home. Glanvill's companion when he visited the Mompessons, the man named Hill, maintained that a physician he knew by the name of Compton dabbled in 'strange matters' and Compton was convinced that the Mompesson house was a meeting-place for witches; he undertook to rid the house of all disturbances in return for the sum of one hundred pounds. But although Compton is said to have adequately demonstrated his magic powers to Hill, he does not seem to have been invited to Mr Mompesson's residence. Nevertheless Mr Compton sounds an odd, interesting and enterprising individual. It is only fair to say that while there is no more evidence now than there has ever been for suspecting Mompesson of anything underhand — and indeed he appears to have suffered in his affairs by having his name associated with the disturbances in his estate and in the general peace of his family — yet there were many people at the time who believed him to be an impostor. Ten years later, in 1672, Mompesson saw fit to make a sworn deposition [Produced in full as Appendix A in Harry Price's Poltergeist Over England (Country Life, 1945)] on the affair concluding with the remark: 'If the world will not believe it, it shall be indifferent to me, praying God to keep me from the same, or the like, affliction.' It is a document and a sentiment that proves nothing and, on balance, perhaps suggests an obsession or an abnormal obstinacy.

It is a strange, even a droll case and at this distance of time one is entitled to look at the many unsatisfactory elements in the story, from the viewpoint of a psychical researcher.

First, there is the confusion over the exact dating of the whole affair and it cannot be overlooked that the easiest way to avoid detection in any perversion of truth is to be inexact in the matter of times, dates and names, and so cause confusion. It is an artifice practised by schemers, politicians, swindlers and professional impostors since time immemorial.

Next, it is important to remember that the essence of many cases of haunting is to be found in the initial incidents, the first recorded phenomena. Afterwards, human nature being what it is, events tend to become exaggerated and distorted in the light of later happenings. This is why it is so important for investigators of spontaneous paranormal happenings to be on the spot at the earliest possible moment and to obtain firsthand reports of disturbances just as soon as possible after the events have taken place. It is interesting, to say the least, to notice that in the case of the Drummer of Tedworth the first recorded incidents were related to John Mompesson on his return from London by his extremely pregnant wife who said she had been 'much affrighted' during his absence by noises that sounded as though thieves were breaking into the house. It is a predicament that many married men have found themselves in, a situation that calls for sympathy, understanding and tolerance and under no circumstances ridicule, suspicion, derision or scorn. It must have been likely that the children heard about the noises that frightened their mother and noted (perhaps unconsciously) their father's apparently serious acceptance of the strange happenings. Three nights later Mr Mompesson was to be awakened by a great knocking at his door and then, apparently, from the direction of the outside doors, causing him to run round the house with a brace of pistols in his hands. When at length he returned to bed he was further disturbed by a 'thumping and drumming' noise, which seemed to come from the upper part of the house and, 'by degrees' ceased.

Similar noises continued intermittently, we are told, for several weeks although there was no disturbing noise to trouble Mrs Mompesson when she was in labour, or during the birth, or for three weeks afterwards. When it did return it was established that it occurred in the vicinity of the young children — who had probably enjoyed hearing the various explanations and descriptions of the noises and now enjoyed even more being the centre of the disturbances.

It could well have been about this time that the children first heard about the confiscation of the vagabond's drum; it is certainly significant that Mompesson readily admits that it was 'some time' before he connected the noises with the drum and when the imprisoned drummer apparently claimed to be causing the trouble; this could have been the hub or centre the children were looking for, upon which to build up a chain of various disturbances.

Psychologist and psychical researcher the late Dr Nandor Fodor has commented [Nandor Fodor, Encyclopaedia of Psychic Science (Arthurs Press, 1934), p.109.] that Glanvill was not apparently sure of the accuracy of his own observations since in at least one instance he did not refer to an incident at the Mompesson house in the first edition of his account of the case. If this is so one feels entitled to ask whether we can be certain of the accuracy of his observations on certain other aspects of the case. Certainly one is entitled to dismiss the suggested significance of some of the reported events which are related: for example the coincidence that Glanvill was awakened by a loud knocking at his door one morning and that same day his horse fell ill and died two or three days later.

Another point which has constantly to be borne in mind by investigators of haunted houses is the reliability of secondary evidence. In the case under discussion it must be remembered that John Mompesson was an important man and if guests were present when he or his wife said they saw or heard strange things, the guests may well have felt it wise to acquiesce or even elaborate on what was apparently happening. It will have been noticed that in the early days Mompesson states that the noises always began just as he and his wife were about to drop off to sleep and that this would happen whether they went to bed early or late. It might be suggested that, if children were responsible, they waited until they heard their parents go to bed before commencing their 'entertainment' so that they were less likely to be surprised in their actions.

Another unsatisfactory episode concerns the infant terrified by something that repeatedly leapt upon it so that it required hours of comforting before it could even be picked up and taken out of the room — nights of torment when the child (and others) had no rest. Most families have known nights when nothing seemed to comfort a fretful child and it seems highly irresponsible to attribute such a normal, if distressing and puzzling, incident to the paranormal. Equally the suggestion that something repeatedly leapt upon the child to cause it such distress must be speculation, pure and simple, since nothing was seen. A more likely explanation would be some physical upset like colic causing the child to retract and expand its abdomen.

John Mompesson's experience of hearing a great noise from the direction of the children's room early one morning and then a voice saying 'a witch, a witch' is elaborated or confused by Glanvill into Mompesson seeing a light one morning in the children's chamber and hearing a voice cry, 'a witch, a witch' not twice but 'at least a hundred times'. What on earth was he doing outside the door of the room containing his children while a strange voice from within repeated these words over a hundred times? One may well ask. In fact the inclusion of the report (from John Mompesson) that he heard a voice once say 'a witch, a witch' sounds suspiciously like a typical ruse of the time: to put the blame for anything apparently inexplicable on witchcraft and to blame some old woman or 'witch' in an effort to put an end to the trouble.

One of the least convincing accounts concerned John Mompesson seeing some wood moving in the hearth, firing a pistol at it, and afterwards finding some drops of blood on the hearth and in various places on the stairs. It seems highly probable that Mompesson, excited by the many puzzling happenings, mistook sunlight playing on the wood or some other simple explanation for actual movement of the wood and afterwards noticed for the first time some drops of blood on the hearth and on various parts of the stairs. Surely we are not expected to believe that something invisible bled when it was shot and slunk down the stairs, invisible and silent, still dripping blood...

I suggest that the impartial inquirer is entitled to consider the possibility that the so-called classic case of haunting, known as the Drummer of Tedworth, had little or no objective reality and that it was born out of the prenatal-postnatal imaginings of Mrs Mompesson, sympathetically accepted by John Mompesson. Once he had told his wife that he too had heard the noises (after two quiet nights during which his wife may have told him she again heard noises) he found himself trapped, as have so many people before and since, and he was forced to continue into a web of lies and deceit something that had begun as a sympathetic acceptance of his wife's imaginings, or even a light-hearted attempt at condolence. It must be remembered that, apart from John Mompesson, the whole affair rests on the evidence of Joseph Glanvill who first produced the story for the entertainment of Lady Conway and her friends at Ragley Hall in Warwickshire. This particular classic case of haunting falls apart when subjected to scrutiny and would appear on present day re-examination to be the result of exaggeration, conscious fraud and inexact and biased reporting.

Incidentally, there even may have been confusion as to the exact site of the disturbances. Harry Price, in Poltergeist Over England, published a photograph of Zouch Manor in North Tidworth and states 'It was in this house, in 1662-3, that the Drummer of Tedworth made so much noise.. while Ella Noyes in her Salisbury Plain (Dent, 1913) says that the 'great mansion house in the Park stands on the site of an old manor house of the Mompessons, who formerly owned the estate, and who were subjected in 1661 to a ghostly experience in the form of an invisible Drummer .. (she is evidently referring to the present Tidworth House in South Tidworth). I believe the Mompesson 'haunted' house stood on neither site. After consultation with the Garrison Adjutant at Tidworth Garrison (much of the area is government property and used by the army) I called at the present Zouch Manor, now the residence of Colonel J.A.P. Russell and part of Tidworth Army Camp. There I learned that locally there have always been doubts about the present house occupying the site of the Mompesson premises and, even allowing for extensive alteration over the years, the present structure is very different from the house shown in a contemporary print, even to the number of floors. Two members of the staff (with, between them, more than half a century of service at Zouch Manor) showed me the probable site of the old house, about a hundred metres southeast, where excavation in the past has brought to light ancient stonework, old crockery and even the remains of a tunnel.

I was interested to learn that the present Zouch Manor has been the scene of some strange happenings. Some years ago two ladies, in one of the ground floor rooms at the front of the house, were startled to hear, from the direction of the other ground floor front room, across the hall, the loud and prolonged sound of breaking crockery and rattling silverware. The two women knew that they were the only people in the house at the time and they were very frightened; in fact they were too terrified to come out of the room for some time. When they did so they were unable to find any cause for the noises they had heard; certainly all the crockery and silver in the room where the sounds had appeared to originate was intact and undisturbed. On another occasion a clergyman went down to the cellar for some reason and afterwards he always swore that while he was down there he had been touched on the shoulder and had seen a form of some kind which he could not explain and was in difficulties in describing. I was also told that a former occupant of Zouch Manor, a brigadier, became so intrigued by the story of the Drummer of Tedworth that he and some friends obtained a drum and went round the house, beating it, hoping to promote some kind of phenomena! Needless to say nothing happened and on that light note we will leave Tidworth and its seventeenth-century mystery.

THE GHOSTS OF THE WESLEYS

The restored Epworth Old Rectory, near Doncaster, as it is today

The Revd Samuel Wesley, Rector of Epworth during
disturbances at the parsonage, December and January 1716-17

An artist's impression of Epworth Rectory at the time of the disturbances

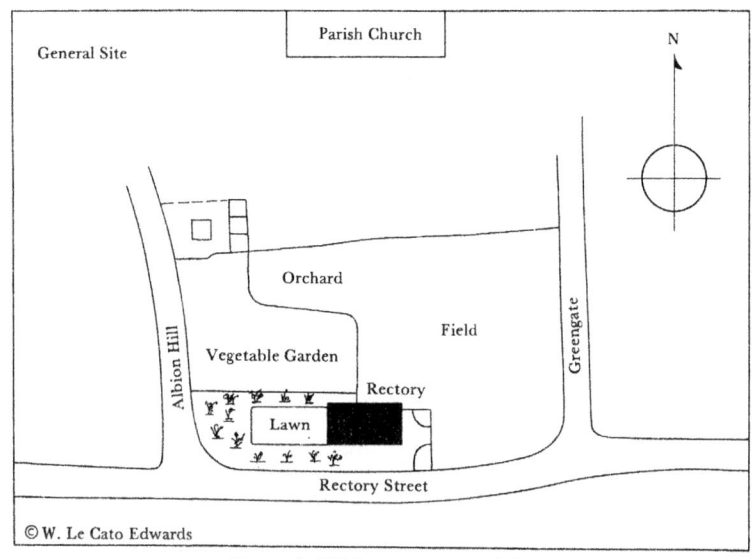

Epworth Old Rectory: general site

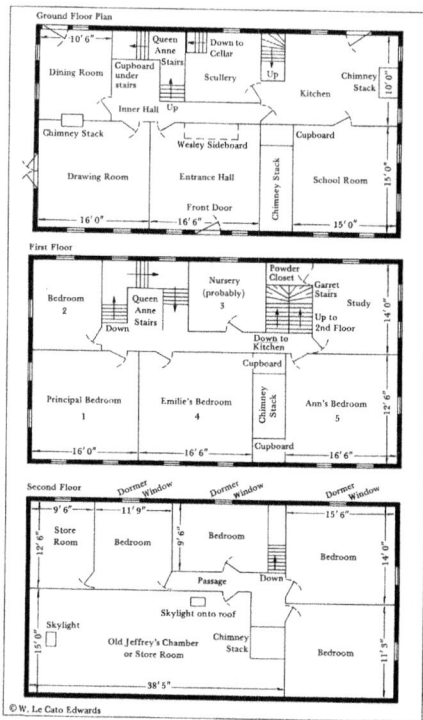

Epworth Old Rectory: plans

The haunting at Epworth Parsonage has been variously described as the 'most fully documented case in the history of the subject' [Frank Podmore, Modern Spiritualism (Methuen, 1902), Volume 1, p. 32]; 'one of the most famous cases upon record' [Sacheverell Sitwell, Poltergeists (Faber and Faber, 1940), p. 80]; and 'a classic — perhaps the classic of the early cases — amongst the best-authenticated ghost stories' [Harry Price, Poltergeist Over England (Country Life, 1945), p. 81]. It might also be described as a unique example of the 'explosion' of adolescent energy, the outburst or discharge of pent-up emotion, perhaps even the result of a reservoir of frustration. In the annals of psychical research there is considerable evidence to suggest that some cases of haunting stem from the unconscious mind of an unhappy, disappointed, overtaxed woman; there was such a woman at Epworth and in addition the wealth of adolescent energy may have resulted in the reported disturbances. Indeed whatever one may postulate as to the cause of the strange noises and even stranger shapes heard and seen by so many witnesses, it has to be accepted that we are faced with an account from the pen of John Wesley himself, who may have been credulous but can surely be depended upon to be truthful.

Although there is conflicting evidence about the actual dates concerned, the majority of the disturbances at Epworth seem to have been concentrated within the two months of November and December 1716, and they consisted primarily of noises: rapping, squeaks, creakings, groans, knockings, a winding noise and a gobbling sound, 'like a turkeycock'. The troublesome happenings nearly always began about 9.45 in the evening and occasionally apparitional forms were glimpsed including a little creature, like a rabbit, and another animal, presumably larger, that resembled a badger. Sometimes the knocks seemed to come at command; sometimes they would repeat a special knock of the Revd Samuel Wesley: 1 — 2 3 4 5 6 — 7; and sometimes they were said to follow one or another of the children about the house. At least two of the inhabitants were made aware of the strength and presence of some invisible power and the case is impressive on account of the wealth of contemporary and corroborative evidence in the form of letters that passed between various members of the Wesley family at the time the disturbances were taking place.

At that time, 1716, John Wesley was thirteen and then and later he was away from home so he had to depend upon the testimony of his mother, his brothers and sisters, his father and on the conversations he had with the Revd Mr Hoole, rector of nearby Haxey. From these sources the Revd John Wesley compiled a lengthy account for the Arminian Magazine (Volume VII, October, November and December 1784) which has long been the chief source of information concerning this strange case of haunting.

Who were the Wesleys who were to find themselves in the middle of a maelstrom of inexplicable energy and activity? Samuel Wesley had a distinguished ancestry, his forebears being traced back to the time of the Crusades [W. Le Cato Edwards, *Epworth, the Home of the Wesleys* (privately printed, n.d.), p. 9]. He was born in 1662 and lived through stirring times: during his young days he must have heard all about the Great Fire of London and the awful plague it followed; the painful deaths of the Scottish Covenanters who were damned by ministers of the established church 'to all eternity'; he would hardly have been unaware of the debauchery and bawdiness of the royal court or not known about the Test Act, passed in 1673, that forced the taking of the oath and the receiving of the sacrament, according to the Church of England, on pain of being debarred from public employment. The year that Samuel Wesley was sent to school in London — 1678 — saw the Popish Plot of Titus Oates and the brutal murder of Sir Edmond Godfrey whose body was publicly exhibited and whose funeral attracted an immense procession; and the Rye House Plot and the suicide (or murder) of the Earl of Essex, the execution of William Lord Russell and trials with the notorious Judge Jeffreys presiding — all happened before Samuel Wesley ended his schooldays. The Restoration of the monarchy brought to the English court the licentiousness and debauchery of the French court where Charles and his followers had spent much of their exile and, as several historians have pointed out, it is an unquestionable and instructive fact that during the years that the Anglican hierarchy was at its zenith, the national morals and virtue were at their lowest point.

It was a light-hearted age, frivolous, even wicked, yet it saw the emergence of some of England's greatest men — Samuel Butler, John Dryden, Thomas Otway, John Bunyan, Christopher Wren — and one of Wesley's schoolfellows was Daniel Defoe. Such were the contemporaries of Samuel Wesley, a boy whose father and grandfather had been occupants of church livings but yet had been Dissenters, and at first Samuel's sympathies were with them. He was still at school when his mother became a widow, but friends rallied round and helped; he had no doubt in which direction his life lay and before he went to Oxford he had heard most of the popular preachers of the day, including John Bunyan, and had taken down many hundreds of their sermons.

In 1683 Samuel Wesley left the Dissenters, the church of his fathers. His first winter at Oxford was one of the severest ever recorded; the Thames was frozen over and the ice so firm and strong that there were hundreds of shops and sideshows on it. Two years later Wesley published his first book, Maggots or Poems on General Subjects which included poems with such titles as, 'A Maggot', 'The Grunting of a Hog', 'To my Gingerbread Mistress', 'A Pair of Breeches' and 'Against a Kiss'. By this time King Charles II had died and James II had succeeded to the throne and, shortly afterwards, had visited Oxford, an event that has been said to have exercised an important influence on Wesley's subsequent career. At first Wesley may have been 'much attached to the interests' of the papistical monarch, but during a later visit by the King, his spirit 'rose in rebellion' against the royal arrogance; although he would never have actively worked against the King, he gave him no kind of support. When James ignominiously fled and William and Mary were proclaimed his successors, Wesley felt that he owed them the loyalty and obedience that he had paid to James and in fact he wrote the first defence of the government that appeared after

William and Mary's accession. He took his degree of Bachelor of Arts at Oxford in June 1688 and just seven weeks later he was ordained a deacon of the Church of England.

Susanna Annesley, who became Samuel Wesley's wife, was the daughter of Dr Annesley, 'one of the leading Nonconformist ministers of London' whose 'father was the cousin of the Earl of Anglesea' [L. Tyerman, The Life and Times of the Revd Samuel Wesley, MA, Rector of Epworth (Simpkin, Marshall, 1866), p. 119]. Samuel Wesley married Susanna about the year 1689 but where and by whom they were married there is no record; apart from a twelve-month separation they appear to have enjoyed a happy marriage, and certainly it was a fruitful one. There always seems to have been doubt and confusion about the innumerable children of the Revd Samuel and his wife Susanna, Sacheverell Sitwell going as far as to state that 'It is nearly impossible to determine the age of Hetty Wesley ... she may have been as young as fourteen or an old as nineteen'; or again 'equally confusing are the number of children in the Wesley household, and their names' [Poltergeists (Faber and Faber, 1940), pp. 82, 157]. Certainly matters are not made any clearer by the use of different names for the same children. Let us therefore sort out the children and the names they were sometimes known by. There were sixteen children altogether:

1690   Samuel (the eldest child, born in London)

1691   Susannah (the first of six children born at South Ormsby; Susannah died in 1693)

1692 Emilia (also known as Emily or Em)

1694 Annesley and Jedidiah (twins who died in infancy)

1695 Susannah (known as Sukey or Suky)

1696 Mary (also known as Molly)

1697 Mehetabel (known as Hetty; the first of nine children born at Epworth)

1701 Another set of twins born who also died in infancy

1702 Anne (referred to as Ann and also called Nancy)

1703 John Benjamin (known as Jack. The famous preacher and founder of Methodism, he is usually regarded as the first child born to the Wesleys after the estrangement that was due to their political differences)

1705 Yet another child born and 'smothered by its nurse and thrown dead into its mother's arms'

1707 Martha (known as Patty — her mother's favourite)

1708 Charles

1710 Kazziah (known as Kezia or Kezzy; the only child that grew to maturity and did not marry)

In 1696 (or possibly 1697) Samuel Wesley moved to Epworth, the capital of the Isle of Axholme and a place that was to become famous as the home of the Wesleys; yet if he and Susanna had not produced their famous son, John, who was, as we have seen, born at Epworth in 1703, it is unlikely that anyone would ever have heard of the Epworth haunting. John inquired into the matter and obtained a great deal of first-hand evidence, in particular a collection of statements from his mother, various sisters, the vicar of Haxey, a servant Robert Brown and an 'Account of Noises and Disturbances' from his father. It is from these statements that the following account of the haunting has been built up, but it should be clearly understood that the whole story came to light through the Revd Samuel Badcock (1750-88) obtaining (through Mrs Earle, daughter of Samuel Wesley, junior) a mass of Wesley manuscripts, some of which were subsequently published in the Arminian Magazine. The rest Mr Badcock passed to Dr Priestley, including a 'copy of Mr Wesley's Diary' and copies of various letters, all in the handwriting of Samuel Wesley, junior. These manuscripts were loaned to a friend and for a time were lost but at length they were found and published by Dr Priestley, whose account fills forty-seven octavo pages.

The first disturbances seem to have been knockings and rappings and were heard by Mrs Wesley during the evening after her son Samuel had quarrelled with his sister Susannah. Mrs Wesley was in her bedroom when she heard a loud clattering of doors and windows, followed by several distinct knocks, three in a row and then another three. She was not disturbed, however, thinking that some of the children must be responsible; later, similar noises were regarded as invariably heralding a family misfortune although no such inference was placed on the noise until the end of 1716; it was then that the noises became really alarming and 1 December 1716 might be said to be the date of the commencement of the Epworth phenomena.

During the morning of that day a maidservant, Nanny Marshall, had occasion to go into the dining room and, as she opened the door from the inner hall, she heard 'something that sounded like the groans of a dying man'; she was very frightened and her hair stood on end but she looked into the room and satisfied herself that there was no one there. That night Susannah and Anne (then aged twenty-one and fourteen respectively) heard a strange rushing sound while they were sitting talking together in the dining room. The noise appeared to come from the direction of the garden and to rush against the door opening into the garden, but nothing was to be seen to account for it. The noise was immediately followed by three loud knocks, and then another three and, half a minute later, yet another three, and these knocks seemed to come from above the girls' heads. The dining room, as can be seen from the plan, was situated at the same end although not immediately below, the principal bedroom, presumably occupied by the rector and his wife. Susannah, in a letter to her brother Samuel, dated 24 January [1717] says she and her sister established that no one was in the garden or in the room above at the relevant time. Shortly afterwards, Mary was downstairs with Susannah, after the rest of the family had retired to bed, except for Anne who was out (which is a little odd as Anne would only be fourteen at the time) when both sisters heard three bouncing thumps which seemed to come from under their feet and so frightened them that they promptly put away their work and went to bed... leaving young Anne to her own devices, apparently. A little later, they noticed an unexplained clicking of the latch (not poor little Anne, trying to get in, surely!) and a curious noise made by the warming pan — probably the result of their heightened imagination by this time. However, Mrs Wesley, in a letter dated 12th January, says that once the noises began they continued every night for a fortnight and were heard sometimes in the garret but mostly in the 'nursery or green chamber'; unfortunately we are unable to establish with any degree of certainty which room was alluded to by this description — it seems likely to have been a back bedroom in the centre of the house. At all events Mrs Wesley states, 'We all heard it but your father' and she adds, 'I am not willing he should be informed of it, lest he should fancy it was against his own death, which, indeed, we all apprehended.' It was in such an atmosphere of superstition that the Wesley haunting prevailed.

A couple of days later Emilia (then aged twenty-four) went downstairs at ten o'clock one night to wind up the clock and lock the doors, as was her usual custom, when she heard, 'under the staircase', presumably in the inner hall, the sound of some bottles being smashed. But when she looked nothing was broken and she could not discover anything to account for the noise. Another evening Emilia heard sounds resembling a sack of coal being thrown down but again, when she and Susannah (who described the noise as like a great piece of metal being thrown down) investigated together — the noise seeming to come from the kitchen area — they found nothing disturbed and the dog fast asleep!

On this occasion Emilia then retired but Mehetabel (aged nineteen), who always waited for her father to leave his study and go to bed, was sitting on the lower step of the garret stairs, outside her father's study, when she heard a sound and looking up the stairs she saw 'something' coming down the stairway towards her, something 'like a man in a loose nightgown' that trailed behind him. The sight so alarmed her (although it could easily have been a servant) that Mehetabel fled to her room. A little later (it may be significant to notice) a man-servant, whose room was in the garret, reported hearing a rattling noise and, when walking up and down the same stairway, he said he heard a gobbling noise, 'like a turkey cock'. It is reported that various noises were heard in all the nine or ten bedrooms and, most frequently, a loud knocking that began at the foot of the beds and progressed to the walls behind the beds.

Eventually the older girls told their father about the noises. 'He smiled but gave no answer', appearing to think that it was the result of tricks played by other members of the family — or by the girls' lovers; but thereafter he was careful to see that everyone was in bed before he retired himself. In front of her husband Mrs Wesley suggested that the noises might be made by rats and she sent for a horn to frighten them away. Emilia now christened the entity 'Jeffrey', for no good reason, but in spite of her many experiences she seems the least troubled by the disturbances and tells of laughing at the idea of a horn driving away the noises.

Then on 21st December strange and apparently inexplicable noises were heard, not only by Mrs Wesley, her family and the servants, but also by the rector who decided, or professed to believe, that they must be caused by someone outside the house and he sent the mastiff to 'rid them of the disturber of the peace'. The noises were in fact somewhat singular in themselves, nine distinct and loud knocks awakening Mr and Mrs Wesley and seemingly emanating (in spite of Mr Wesley's reaction) from the room next to their own; this could have been either Bedroom 2 or Bedroom 4 on the first floor. The rector did, in fact, rise from his bed and endeavour to discover the cause or reason for the noises but without success.

The following night six more loud and deliberate knocks were heard by everyone in the house and, two days later, at seven o'clock in the morning, Emilia fetched her mother and together they went to Emilia's bedroom where noises had been heard, first at the foot and then at the head of the bed. As mother and daughter stood at the foot of the bed, Mrs Wesley, in an effort to make some kind of contact with whatever had come into the house, knocked in answer and each time 'it' seemed to knock in reply — distinct and separate knocks, resounding from the area of the bedstead. Mrs Wesley looked beneath the bed and thought she saw something 'move and run and hide under Emilia's petticoats' — something that put Mrs Wesley in mind of a badger. We are not told Emilia's reaction; in fact, referring to the incident in a letter to her brother Samuel, Emilia says her mother saw something 'like a badger, only without any head that was discernible' and she adds, 'the same creature was sat by the dining room fire one evening, when our man went into the room, it run up by him, through the hall under the stairs. He followed with a candle, and searched, but it was departed. The last time he saw it in the kitchen, like a white rabbit, which seems likely to be some witch; and I do so really believe it to be one, that I would venture to fire a pistol at it, if I saw it long enough. It has been heard by me and the others since December.'

Two nights after the badger-like creature was seen by Mrs Wesley in Emilia's bedroom, the rector and his wife were awakened, shortly after midnight, by noises so loud and violent that further sleep was out of the question. Accordingly both of them set out to see what could be the cause of the disturbances that sounded for all the world as though several people were walking, and then running, up and down stairs — yet it seemed to originate from the room immediately above their own (that is, the large store room that became known as Old Jeffrey's Chamber on the second floor). Thinking the children would all be disturbed by the noise, Mr and Mrs Wesley carefully picked their way downstairs in the dark, to find a candle. Just as they reached the bottom of the 'broad' or Queen Anne Stairs, they held on to each other as a new and alarming noise sounded on Mrs Wesley's side; it was as if somebody had emptied a bag of money at their feet and as if all the bottles in the cupboard under the stairs (and there were many, adds Mrs Wesley) were suddenly dashed to pieces. They passed through the inner hall and into the kitchen where they found their pet mastiff whining and whimpering and 'more afraid than any of the children'. Finding a candle, they lit it and went to see the children whom they found to be fast asleep!

Next night Samuel Wesley persuaded Mr Hoole, the rector of the nearby village of Haxey, to spend the night at Epworth Rectory and the adults sat up till the early hours of the morning — and heard the knocking sounds 'as usual'. On this particular occasion the noise, apart from the knocks, resembled a carpenter planing wood; at other times it sounded like the winding up of a clock or the grinding of some kind of machinery, but most often three knocks sounded, then silence, then three knocks again and so on for hours at a time. Mr Hoole placed the knocks as coming first from upstairs and then in the rooms below on the ground floor. Quietly the two clergymen descended to the kitchen, whereupon the sounds seemed to come from above again. They went up the narrow stairs from the kitchen and, as they did so, heard rustling, as of a silk nightdress. Suddenly the noise seemed to come from Emilia's room and three knocks sounded at the head of the bed, followed by another three, and the same yet again.

More than once Mr Wesley observed that the children, although asleep, appeared to be restless and frightened in their sleep — trembling, sweating and moaning until the noise awakened them, whereupon it ceased. The rector comforted his children, saying he would stay in the room, and he settled down at the foot of the bed. When the children were asleep the noise began again. The rector pulled out a pistol and was about to fire at the place where the sounds seemed to originate when Mr Hoole caught him by the arm and said, 'If this is something preternatural you cannot hurt it by firing your pistol, but you may give it power to hurt you.' Wesley then put away his pistol and approaching the place 'whence the sounds proceeded' said: 'Thou deaf and dumb devil, why dost thou frighten children that cannot answer thee? Come to me in my study that am a man.' Instantly, we are told, the sounds rapped out Wesley's own particular knock, so loud that it seemed the board would be shattered. Finally one loud knock sounded on the outside of the house and then all was quiet for the rest of the night.

Several times the rector went outside, sometimes alone and sometimes in the company of others, to walk round the house and garden to see whether he could locate the origin of the noises. But he never saw anything suspicious or heard anything while he was outside the house.

The very next night, as he opened the door of his study, Samuel Wesley was thrust back with such violence that he was almost thrown down, and presently there was a knocking, first on one side of the chamber and then on the other. His daughter Anne was in the adjoining room and he went to her while the noise still continued and it was heard by both of them. Again the rector tried to communicate with the entity, speaking to it and asking what it wanted but he received no response. 'Spirits love darkness,' Samuel Wesley then told his daughter. 'Put out the candle and perhaps it will speak.' Anne extinguished the candle and her father repeated his request but the knocking continued unabated and he received no answer to his adjuration. He then suggested to Anne that two Christians must be 'an overmatch for a devil; go downstairs and it may be, when I am left alone, it will have courage enough to speak'. When she had gone Wesley suddenly had the thought that all the disturbances might be a sign that something had happened to his son, Samuel, who was away from home and he said out loud: 'If thou be the spirit of my son Samuel, I pray three knocks and no more.' Immediately all was quiet and the rest of the night passed peacefully. Only on one or two occasions did the rector hear two or three feeble squeaks, in apparent reply to his requests to tell him what it wanted, and never did he hear any articulate voice.

One night, when the noise was especially loud in the kitchen, apparently centred on a deal partition in the vicinity of the back or yard door, it was noticed that the door-latch repeatedly lifted itself up. Emilia tried to hold it fast on the inside but it still lifted up and the door pushed violently against her although outside nothing was to be seen.

The long separation between Samuel and Susanna Wesley came about because of political differences, Mrs Wesley being a violent Jacobite. It is interesting to notice that after a quiet period lasting twenty-seven days, on the morning of 24 January 1717, when the whole family were at prayers, they all heard knocks at the prayer for King George and the Royal Family, rising to a 'great noise' over their heads, whereupon some of the family called Jeffrey a Jacobite. Three times the rector says he was pushed by an invisible power, once against the corner of his desk in his study, once against the door of the 'matted chamber' and a third time against the right hand side of the frame of his study door, as he was about to enter.

The same day that sounds had disturbed family prayers, between nine and ten o'clock in the morning, the manservant Robert Brown was sitting by himself at the back kitchen fire when something came out of the copper hole, something that he thought looked like a rabbit. It turned itself round quickly five times but as soon as Robert took up a pair of tongs and went towards it, it vanished — 'to Robert's terrible dismay'. Robert also, apparently, saw the badger-like creature without any head, sitting by the fire in the dining room one evening; when he went into the room, it dashed past him, ran along the hall and disappeared. He followed with a candle and searched where the creature had vanished but he could find no trace of it or how it had dissolved from view.

Next day, 25th January, the Revd Samuel Wesley shortened family prayers in the morning, omitting the confession, the absolution and the prayers for king and prince and it was noticed that whenever he did this there was no knocking, but whenever he used the name of King George, it seemed almost to be a signal for the knocking to begin. This made Wesley, a staunch Royalist, so angry that he resolved to say three prayers each day for the royal family, instead of two. In reply he was astonished to see his plate dancing on the table where the family were dining; several times, too, the latch of his bedroom door was lifted.

It was observed that frequently the wind rose, as soon as the noises began, and whistled loudly round the house as long as the disturbances lasted. More often than not the noises seemed to begin at one corner of the nursery ceiling and the latches of doors were frequently lifted up, the windows rattled and whatever iron or brass was in the room, vibrated and clattered before the sound came into the room. Afterwards the sound sometimes appeared to be in the air in the middle of the room. There was very little actual movement of objects — except for the lifting of door latches, and once the door of the nursery was apparently thrown open when no one was inside. On another occasion a bed was lifted up when some of the children were playing cards; Anne protested, saying, 'Surely Old Jeffrey would not run away with her . . .' and then sat down on the bed again, whereupon it was lifted up a considerable height, several times successively.

There seems little rhyme or reason to the various reported happenings; even the apparitions are vague and unidentifiable; as we have seen, Mehetabel once saw something like a man in a loose nightgown on the stairs outside her father's study and Mary (aged twenty-one) was by herself in the dining room one evening when 'the door seemed to open' and someone entered in a nightgown which trailed along the ground. This odd form went leisurely around her and then vanished. Anne too was sometimes followed from room to room in daylight by something that pursued her and, in her own bedroom, went from one side of the bed to the other several times.

As time passed most of the family became accustomed to the noises and whenever a knock was heard, one of them would say, 'Old Jeffrey is coming; it is time to go to sleep!' If the noises were heard during the daytime, little Kezzy, just over six years old, would run upstairs in whatever direction the sounds seemed to originate and chase it from room to room, saying she wished for no better fun; the servants, on the other hand, seem to have been very frightened of the noises. Robert Brown was often so afraid that he would run downstairs, almost naked, not daring to stay alone to put on any clothes while Nanny Marshall, the maidservant, seems to have been more frightened than anybody.

Several friends of Samuel Wesley, fellow clergymen and laymen, advised him to leave the house but Wesley always said, 'No, let the devil flee from me; I will never flee from him'; and by the middle of January 1717, most of the noises and disturbances ceased although it was six weeks later that Samuel Wesley's plate 'danced', one or two doors opened by themselves and a few knocks sounded. Indeed thirty-four years later, Emilia, by then Mrs Harper, speaks of Old Jeffrey still visiting her and more than a century later the then rector of Epworth, in London with his family, said that his absence from Epworth was due to a repetition of the noises that disturbed Samuel Wesley and his family a hundred and fifty years earlier.

Who or what was Old Jeffrey? It is evident that Mrs Wesley thought at first that it might be the spirit of one of her three sons, Samuel, John or Charles, who were all away at school in London. Later she believed the noises to be due to the presence of rats and finally she came to feel that the disturbances might herald the death of her brother Samuel Annesley, at that time in India. In fact the three Wesley boys lived on for many years; it is simply absurd to attribute all the noises, tricks and reported happenings to rats; and Samuel Annesley survived for another eight years.

Samuel Wesley, the eldest child, seems to have subscribed to the belief that it was all caused by a spirit but he was unable to suggest any reason or cause. It is worth recognizing that he only came to this decision after making strict and exhaustive inquiries.

There were hints at the time of the disturbances and it has been suggested since that either the servants or some of the young members of the Wesley family were responsible — but on many occasions noises were heard by the whole family when all the servants were present. Dr Priestley (who first published the story) subscribed to the belief that the servants were responsible, assisted by neighbours, for the purpose of puzzling the family and amusing themselves. There is no shred of evidence to support such a theory and it is at complete variance with some of the evidence.

Twenty-one-year-old Susannah and her sisters Emilia (twenty-four), Mary (twenty) and Anne (fourteen) seem to have had no doubt that the whole affair was supernatural and it might be thought that they were closer to the matter than anyone. Alternatively one could suppose that they were acting in collusion. Emilia said at one point, 'About a year since there was a disturbance at a town near us that was undoubtedly occasioned by witches-, and, if so near, why may they not reach us? ' She added that for several Sundays before Old Jeffrey came, her father had preached against consultation with 'cunning men' and therefore it may have had a particular spite for her father. The visiting clergyman Mr Hoole also appears to have come to the same conclusion. John Wesley (thirteen when the disturbances began) and away from home at the time, always believed that the thing was evil and that it came from Satan as a punishment on the head of the family for parting from his wife for such a long period and for a rash vow he made at that time. In the narrative published by John Wesley in the Arminian Magazine during 1784 (he had founded the periodical, the earliest religious journal in Britain, in 1778) he states: 'The year before King William died my father observed my mother did not say "Amen" to the prayer for the king. She said she could not, for she did not believe the Prince of Orange was king. He vowed he would never cohabit with her till she did. He then took his horse and rode away, nor did she hear anything of him for a twelvemonth. He came back and lived with her as before. But I fear his vow was not forgotten before God.' The Revd Samuel Wesley deserted his pregnant wife and five children in 1701. Wesley had obtained the living of Epworth from Queen Mary to whom he had dedicated a poem on the life of Christ. It is interesting to speculate on the environment and atmosphere that could have made possible the Epworth phenomena. Such happenings are often associated with puberty, a time when the psyche seems to slumber before awakening into full flower; there are comparisons to be drawn between this state and that of pregnancy, and at Epworth there was hardly a year when Susanna Wesley was not pregnant and hardly a year when there was no adolescent child in the house; in 1719, the year of the disturbances (according to some authorities), it may be significant that Martha (Patty), her mother's favourite, was twelve years old.

The author of a history of the Isle of Axholme, the Revd W.B. Stonehouse, postulated the somewhat preposterous theory that in the large garret that extended over the ceilings of all the upper rooms, 'some piece of machinery was fixed ... by which all the noises were effected'. He does not pursue such matters as who might have been able to devise and construct such an apparatus in the neighbourhood of Epworth, how it was introduced into the house and by whom, nor what eventually happened to the mysterious machinery.

Furthermore, is it likely that Samuel Wesley should have thoroughly examined every part of the house and omitted the enormous garret?

Other people referred to a legendary tale of murder in the parsonage. It was said that a maid-servant was startled one night, after all the family had retired to bed, by being confronted by a man who was in the act of making his way into the house by crawling through a trough which ran between the sinkstone and a cistern. Terrified but aware that she must do something, the servant is supposed to have seized a meat cleaver which lay nearby and struck a mighty blow at the man's head and then, with a shriek, fallen to the floor unconscious with fright. Her loud cry is said to have awakened Mr Wesley who, supposing that the house was being attacked by robbers, took up a heavy pair of fire-irons and began to shout and make a loud noise in an effort to scare the thieves away. The man was said to have been rescued by his fellow robbers and a trail of blood showed where he had been taken but soon the trail stopped and the culprits were never located. Dr Adam Clark was among those who subscribed to the belief that this undated and uncorroborated story was the cause of all the later disturbances.

L. Tyerman, the author of The Life and Times of the Revd Samuel Wesley [(Simpkin, Marshall, 1866)], after thoroughly sifting the whole history of the Wesleys and having begun his researches with 'the strongest prejudice against the theory that the noises were supernatural', came, 'by force of evidence ... to the conclusion that the noises and other circumstances were occasioned by the direct and immediate agency of some unseen, and bad, spirit' [ibid., p. 359].

Robert Smith (1774-1843), Poet Laureate and historian, said he was 'as deeply and fully persuaded as John Wesley was, that the spirits of the departed are sometimes permitted to manifest themselves'; he professed a firm belief in the preternatural origin of the 'strange accounts' of the disturbances in Epworth Parsonage.

In recent years Guy Lambert, a former president of the Society for Psychical Research, has postulated a physical theory for poltergeist disturbances and hauntings, highlighting the many effects that might be caused by underground water. In the case of the Epworth phenomena he points to the fact that the village stands on a low hill which, from early times, had been much quarried for gypsum. The disused quarries had been filled in but some of the filling might have been washed out, without visible signs on the surface. He suggests it may well be significant that the tide comes up the Trent as far as Epworth and while there is no convincing evidence of tidal influence on the phenomena as researched 'their long-continued and noisy character is consistent with such influence'. One incident, he feels, is particularly suspect: Mrs Wesley was in the habit of reserving a quiet hour between five and six each day and when 'Old Jeffrey' manifested at this time, Mrs Wesley begged 'it' to desist, which it did, and from the next afternoon onwards all was quiet during her rest hour. Lambert says [Society for Psychical Research Journal, Volume 38, number 684 (June 1955), have started about fifty-five minutes later each day, until a month had elapsed and Mrs Wesley's request would have seemed to her to have been substantially complied with.' This is not altogether so. It is specifically stated that Mrs Wesley was never afterwards disturbed from five until six — not even once a month; nor was she ever, after her appeal, disturbed at any other time when she was employed in devotion. It is hard to see that there is much evidence to support Guy Lambert's theory with regard to the Epworth case although it would be interesting to discover whether, as Lambert suggests, there is a disused well under the house, with a shaft reaching down to tide level.

Harry Price [Poltergeist Over England (Country Life, 1945), p. 109] makes the interesting suggestion that Mehetabel (Hetty), nineteen at the time the disturbances began, seemed to be the centre of the phenomena; certainly it is reported that she trembled rather violently in her sleep, before and during a visitation. Furthermore Old Jeffrey appeared, on occasions, to follow her about the house, exactly as poltergeist phenomena follow the nexus of the disturbances in present-day cases. The predilection for bedsteads, bedrooms and young girls was very evident at Epworth as in so many authenticated poltergeist hauntings.

Can it be that the Epworth case was a genuine example of a mixed haunting, with poltergeist and haunting phenomena being overlaid and combined in an unusual but not unique manner? The poltergeist element might easily be explained as a spontaneous but limited exhibition of adolescent energy (in common with any genuine poltergeist activity) and the haunting element may also comprise the ingredients of many true hauntings.

A curious but common combination is often to be found in cases of haunting: an unhappy or frustrated woman is usually closely connected with the case and a tragic or violent happening has taken place in the house or on the site. I have noticed that these two features are present time and time again in disturbances that we call hauntings. At Epworth we have the presence of Mrs Wesley, in many respects a remarkable woman but also, perhaps, an unhappy and frustrated one. 'A poetess, accomplished scholar, learned student, correct philosopher and a profound divine' [L. Tyerman, The Life and Times of the Revd Samuel Wesley (Simpkin, Marshall, 1866), p. 125], Susanna Wesley was also graceful and beautiful; yet that she had an exceedingly difficult, frustrating and even unhappy life with Samuel Wesley can hardly be denied. Certainly they appear to have been affectionate and deeply attached to each other but the fact remains that Mrs Wesley struggled all her life in one direction after another and she was never able to exploit and use to the full her many undoubted gifts; her husband pulled her in a quite different direction. She knew the humiliation of being 'cooped up in the miserable little parsonage at South Ormsby' [ibid., p. 126] where for five long years she presented her husband with an additional child each year and did her best to live on £50 a year. She knew the darkness and the despair of deep disagreement with her husband; of long separation from him (a man who was supposed to set an example to his flock); of bearing him sixteen children of whom eight died in infancy; very soon after moving to Epworth her sister Dunton died and her father had died just before she moved: it was a double tragedy that has been described as 'a most painful trial'; most of her daughters had unhappy marriages — yes, Mrs Susanna Wesley may well have been frustrated and she must often have been unhappy.

As for a tragic or violent happening taking place at Epworth, it could be that there is a modicum of truth in the story of an intruder hacked to death with a kitchen chopper. Then there was the baby, born in 1705, smothered by its nurse and the body thrown into the mother's arms: there is a tragic and violent happening that must have been frustrating and unhappy all at the same time. That such occurrences can leave something behind them seems more than likely on the evidence that extends to every part of the world and to every age since the beginning of civilization; why certain violent happenings trigger off hauntings and others do not we do not know, but it seems probable that it has something to do with the people most closely concerned or occupying the site. There may be something in the idea that certain places are able to retain sound, like music imprisoned on a record, and the personality of certain people can release that sound. The household of the Wesley family was an ideal locale for some kind of psychic disturbance and, judging from the available correspondence, disturbances did take place for which we have at present no logical explanation.

THE HAUNTING AT HINTON AMPNER

Aerial view of the present Hinton Ampner House, showing the site of the former 'haunted' manor. The kitchen garden and some of the outbuildings date from the time of the earlier house

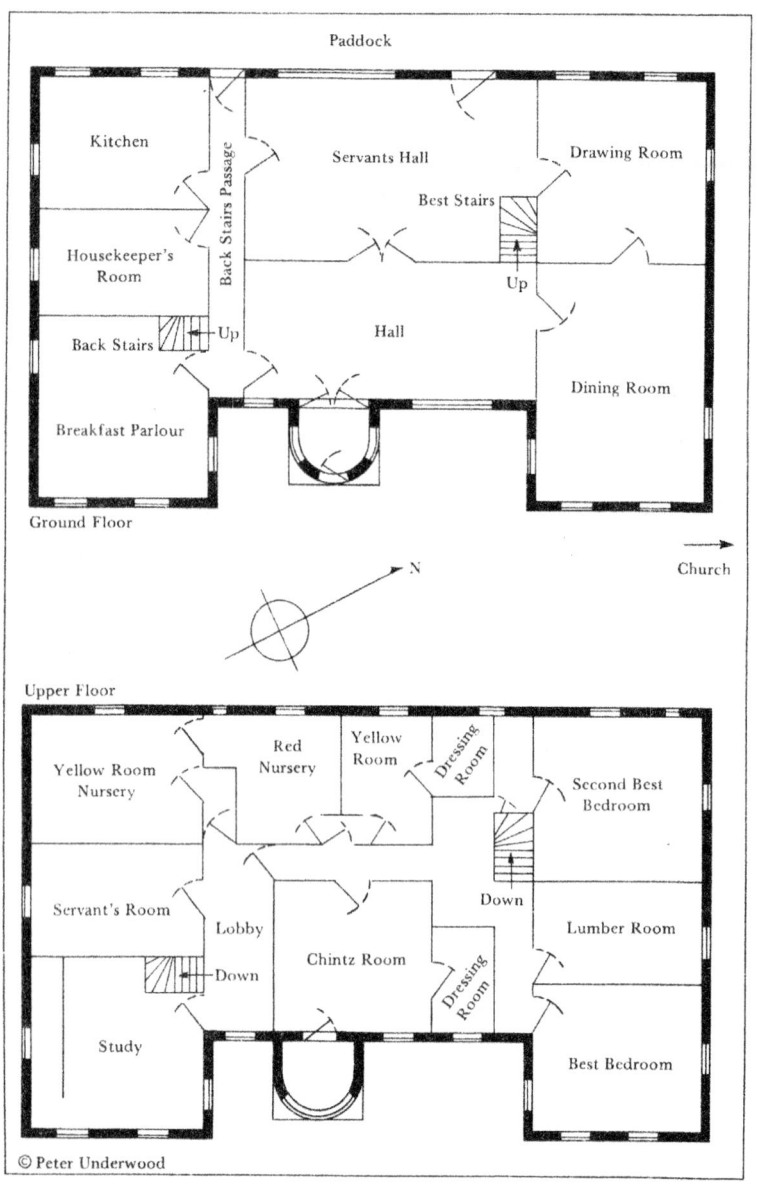

Speculative plan of the sixteenth-century Hinton Ampner Manor House, demolished in 1793, based on copies of crude plans drawn by Mrs Mary Ricketts, now in the possession of Ralph Stawell Dutton, owner of the present Hinton Ampner House, and on information contained in Mrs Ricketts' narrative of ghostly happenings

The strange and well-authenticated case of haunting and poltergeist phenomena associated with the old Manor House at Hinton Ampner, near Alresford in Hampshire, is vouched for by Earl St Vincent, a famous and respected sea captain, 'a character of known veracity, to whose word full confidence should be attached' [Sacheverell Sitwell, Poltergeists (Faber and Faber, 1940), p. 126]. It has been described as 'one of the most detailed, convincing, and best-documented stories of poltergeist haunting' [Harry Price in his Poltergeist Over England (Country Life, 1945), p. 129] and the quite remarkable story is supported by numerous affidavits and contemporary correspondence. It is generally regarded as originating in the publication of some of the original letters in the Gentleman's Magazine for November and December 1872; in fact we are indebted to the Revd Richard Barham, of Ingoldsby Legends fame, for the story.

Richard Harris Barham (1788-1845) was a minor canon of St Paul's whose original rhymes and inexhaustible humour found expression in amazing tales in verse which he published as The Ingoldsby Legends (written under the pseudonym 'Thomas Ingoldsby'), the first series being published in 1840, the second in 1842 and the third in 1847. After his death, Barham's son, the Revd R.H. Dalton Barham decided to write his father's biography which he did in 1870 under the title Life and Letters of Richard H. Barham. During the course of research Dalton Barham discovered, while searching through some old notebooks, a verbatim report of a very strange tale. It had been written by his father in 1836, the details having apparently been obtained from a Mrs Hughes who, in turn, had heard the story from a Mrs Gwynn, a personal witness to the remarkable events. The story had been confirmed by a number of people, including a titled lady resident in the neighbourhood, and Dalton Barham included the story in the biography of his father in all good faith although it contained some errors in names and dates. Later, at the request of the family concerned, the whole story was rewritten and then appeared, supported by affidavits, in the Gentleman's Magazine, under the title 'A Hampshire Ghost Story'.

Although the fact that some names in this version have been found to be inaccurate must detract from the value of the narrative, many of the characters were subsequently identified and certainly one of the chief witnesses, Mrs Mary Ricketts, seems to have been someone whose personal integrity was beyond question. She was a woman, it is said, who, like George Washington, could not tell a lie and her truthfulness was proverbial in her family; she was in 'vigorous middle age' when she took up residence at Hinton Ampner Manor House with her three infant children and eight servants. She lived to be ninety-one years of age and was said to have retained her great physical and mental powers to the end of her days. A woman of aristocratic connections, her favourite brother and constant companion being Admiral Jervis, afterwards Earl St Vincent, while other members of her family also held high positions in the church and the state; her husband was a Senior Member of Grey's Inn of Court and a West Indian landowner.

Earl St Vincent (1735-1823) entered the Navy as an AB seaman, became a lieutenant after six years, a commander four years later and post captain eleven years after joining the service. Created a Knight of the Bath in 1782 after seizing the French ship Pegase, in the same year he took part in the relief of Gibraltar by Lord Howe. He was Member of Parliament for Launceston in 1782 and for Yarmouth in the following year; in 1784 he was promoted rear-admiral and vice-admiral in 1793. In 1797 he manoeuvred in masterly fashion to engage with the Spanish fleet off Cape St Vincent in spite of tremendous odds and the result, in which Nelson participated, was a brilliant victory. Jervis was awarded an earldom and a pension of £3000, and he went on to serve as First Lord of the Admiralty. Always a strict disciplinarian, his strong measures once averted a mutiny in the fleet. Such was the man whose sister is the chief witness for the strange affair at Hinton Ampner and, indeed, Jervis himself witnessed some of the singular manifestations.

Mary Jervis, three years younger than her brother John, married in 1757 William Henry Ricketts of Canaan, Jamaica, whose grandfather had been a captain in Penn and Venable's army at the conquest of Jamaica. In 1769 Mary had to choose between accompanying her husband on his frequent and often long-lasting visits to the West Indies or remaining with her three young children in England. She chose the latter course and found herself in the middle of a series of strange disturbances.

An artist's impression of the old sixteenth-century Hinton Ampner Manor House, 'rendered uninhabitable by ghostly manifestations' and demolished in 1793.

The old Manor House at Hinton Ampner was probably built by Sir Thomas Stewkeley some time before 1623 and he seems to have been the first occupant. The property passed from father to son in the Stewkeley family and was at one time occupied by a Mary Stewkeley who, in 1719, married Edward Stawell. Mary's younger sister, Honoria, lived with them and when Mary died, in 1740, Honoria continued to live at Hinton Ampner with her brother-in-law and whispers of a love affair between the two grew into a credible scandal with stories of a child being born as a result of the liaison and of the babe dying in suspicious circumstances. Honoria died in 1754 and Edward, who had become Lord Stawell in 1742, died less than six months later. Very soon afterwards ghostly happenings were reported at lovely Hinton Ampner, and the property then passed to another branch of the family and after some years was reduced to being inhabited only by servants. Thus it came about that the Ricketts obtained a lease on the property.

As we have seen there were already reports of unexplained disturbances, and these included strange sounds and the figure of a gentleman in a drab-coloured coat that had been seen standing in the moonlight with his hands behind his back, in the manner of the last of the Stewkeleys. Sensible and practical Mrs Ricketts dismissed such reports as 'the effect of fear and superstition, to which the lower class of people are so prone'. She took occupation of the Manor House in January 1765 with an entirely new set of servants, brought from London, strangers to the locality of Hinton Ampner and its stories. Hardly had they settled in before unexplained noises were heard and in particular the almost continual sound of slamming doors, with no doors ever being found open. New locks on the doors had no effect and within six months the 'gentleman in drab-coloured clothing' was seen again, this time in the great hall. Subsequent incidents, for which no explanation was ever found, included the apparition of a woman dressed in dark clothes, rustling and groaning noises, footsteps, music, a 'murmuring wind', a fluttering sound, heavy knocks, the sounds of a man and a woman talking, crashes, shrieks and other distressing noises.

By the middle of 1771 Mary Ricketts had had enough, and the final straw was an experience that terrified this sane and sensible woman. She says, 'I was assailed by a noise I never heard before, very near me, and the terror I felt not to be described.' She gave no further details of this event although towards the end of her tenancy rewards of £50, then £60 and finally £100 were offered for the detection of anyone or any thing that caused the disturbances. The Bishop of Winchester loaned Mrs Ricketts premises at Winchester and she and the children left Hinton Ampner. Later the Bishop of St Asaph offered her his house in London which she occupied for a time, and then she rented a house of her own in Curzon Street.

Hinton Manor House was let to a family named Lawrence who apparently endeavoured by threats to stop the servants talking about the odd happenings at the house; then an apparition of a woman was seen. The Lawrences left suddenly in 1773 and the house was never again inhabited. Eventually it was pulled down, the present Hinton Ampner House being built, about

1793, some fifty yards from the site of the old building [Peter Underwood, A Gazetteer of British Ghosts (Souvenir Press, 1971),

p. 100]. It was not built on the same site as the 'haunted' house, as Guy Lambert assumed in propounding his physical theory for the disturbances such as a heavy flow of subterranean water making its way along old underground channels which normally carry a small quantity of water. The resultant noises, says Lambert, [Society for Psychical Research Journal, June 1955, Volume 38, number 684, pp. 59—69] 'might have been very alarming, especially if they were carried up into the house by the shaft of an old well'. He established, interestingly enough, that rainfall in the area was unusually high during August 1771 when Mrs Ricketts eventually left Hinton Ampner.

During the demolition of the old Manor House a small skull, 'said to be that of a monkey' was found in a small box under some floorboards in the lobby. It was of course whispered that the skull was that of the murdered babe but the matter was 'never brought forward by any regular inquiry or professional opinion resorted to as to the real nature of the skull'.

It has to be admitted that there are unsatisfactory aspects of the Hinton Ampner mystery, not least the alteration and disappearance of names in Mrs Ricketts' narrative account of the happenings. In 1893 John, third Marquess of Bute, obtained a copy of a pamphlet based on the Gentleman's Magazine article, which he proceeded to edit for the Society for Psychical Research and that society published the resulting article in their Journal for 1893-4 (Volume VI, pp. 52-74). But

Lord Bute not only edited the account, he also altered the names of some of the people mentioned therein, and although the names of all people and places are given in full in the Gentleman's Magazine — albeit inaccurately in some instances — most of them have disappeared in the SPR version, published twenty-one years later. It is all very curious. Mr Sacheverell Sitwell told me some years ago that he went to considerable trouble to discover and fill in some of the names, and Harry Price, in his Poltergeist Over England, verified and filled in some more. It seems likely that the following account, based on the first-hand narrative that Mary Ricketts wrote, dated and signed for her children to read when they were old enough to appreciate such things, is complete as regards the real names of people and places and utterly true, if we accept, as we surely must, that Mary Ricketts was a truthful and honourable person. Incidentally, examination of the relevant dates makes the reputedly illicit liaison somewhat unlikely. Mary Stewkeley was born in 1685, married in 1719 (aged thirty-four) and died in 1740 aged fifty-five. Honoria Stewkeley was born in 1688 and died in 1754, aged sixty-six. Edward Stawell was born in 1698, married in 1719 (aged twenty-one) and died in 1755, aged fifty-seven. Is it likely, one must surely ask oneself, that he married a woman thirteen years older than himself and had a liaison with her sister, ten years older than himself and fifty-two when his wife died? Yet such are the facts if the above dates are accurate.

In the course of research for this chapter during the summer of 1976 I spent many hours at the British Museum, reading through some fourteen volumes of correspondence pertaining to the case. I also spent some time with Mr Ralph Stawell Dutton, former High Sheriff of Hampshire and owner of the present Hinton Ampner House, who has himself written about the 'Hinton Ghost' [Hinton Ampner, A Hampshire Manor (Batsford, 1968), pp. 50—3] and I am particularly grateful to him for allowing me to borrow Mrs Ricketts' hand-drawn plan of the old manor house and for permission to reproduce for the first time recollections of the ghost story compiled for Lady Mary Long in 1862. But first Mary Ricketts' 'Legacy to her Children'. It is headed 'Hinton Ampner Parsonage' and dated 7 July 1772.

'To my dear children I address the following relation, anxious that the truths which I have so faithfully delivered shall be as faithfully transmitted to posterity, to my own in particular. I determined to commit them to writing, which I recommend to their care and attentive consideration, entreating them to bear in mind the peculiar mercy of Providence in preserving them from all affright and terror during the series of wonderful disturbances that surrounded them, wishing them to be assured the veracity of their mother was pure and undoubted, that even in her infancy it was in the family a proverb, and according to the testimony of that excellent person Chancellor Hoadley she was truth itself; she writes, not to gratify vanity, but to add weight to her relation. To the Almighty and Unerring Judgment of Heaven and Earth I dare appeal for the truth, to the best of my memory and comprehension, of what I here relate.

(Signed) Mary Ricketts, Hinton Ampner, near Alresford, in Hampshire.

'The Mansion House and estate of Hinton Ampner, near Alresford, Hampshire, devolved in 1755 to the Right Honourable Henry Bilson Legge in right of his lady, daughter and sole heiress of Lord Stawell, who married the eldest daughter and co-heiress of Sir Hugh Stewkeley, Bart, by whose ancestors the estate at Hinton had been possessed many generations and by this marriage passed to Mr Legge on the death of the said Sir Hugh.

'Mr (who on the death of his elder brother became Lord) Stawell made Hinton his constant residence. Honoria, the youngest sister of his lady, lived with them during the life of her sister, and so continued with Lord Stawell till her death in 1754.

'On the evening of April 2nd, 1755, Lord Stawell, sitting alone in the little parlour at Hinton, was seized with a fit of apoplexy; he articulated one sentence only to be understood, and continued speechless and insensible till the next morning when he expired.

'His lordship's family at the time consisted of the following domestics: Isaac Mackrel, house steward and bailiff. Sarah Parfait, housekeeper, who had lived in the family nearly forty years. Thomas Parfait, coachman, husband to said Sarah, who had lived there upwards of forty years. Elizabeth Banks, housemaid, an old servant. Jane Davis, dairymaid. Mary Barras, cook. Joseph Sibley, Butler, Joseph, groom. Richard Turner, gardener, and so continued by Mr Ricketts. Lord Stawell had one son, who died at Westminster School, aged sixteen.

'Thomas Parfait, his wife, and Elizabeth Banks continued to have the care of the house during the lifetime of Mr Legge, who usually came there for one month every year in the shooting season. On his death in August, 1764, Lady Stawell, so created in her own right, since married to the Earl of Hillsborough, determined to let Hinton Ampner Mansion, and Mr Ricketts took it in the December following. Thomas Parfait was at that time lying dead in the house. His widow and Elizabeth Banks quitted it on our taking possession in January, 1765. We removed thither from town, and had the same domestics that lived with us there and till some time afterwards we had not any house-servant belonging to the neighbourhood. Soon after we were settled at Hinton I frequently heard noises in the night, as of people shutting, or rather slapping doors with vehemence. Mr Ricketts went often round the house on supposition there were either housebreakers or irregularity among his servants. In these searches he never could trace any person; the servants were in their proper apartments, and no appearance of disorder. The noises continued to be heard, and I could conceive no other cause than that some of the villagers had false keys to let themselves in and out at pleasure; the only preventive to this evil was changing the locks, which was accordingly done, yet without the effect we had reasonably expected.

'About six months after we came thither, Elizabeth Brelsford, nurse to our eldest son, Henry, then about eight months old, was sitting by him when asleep, in the room over the pantry, appropriated for the nursery, and, being a hot summer's evening, the door was open that faces the entrance into the yellow bedchamber, which, with the adjoining dressing-room, was the apartment usually occupied by the lady of the house. She was sitting directly opposite to this door, and plainly saw (as she afterwards related) a gentleman in a drab-coloured suit of clothes go into the yellow room. She was in no way surprised at the time, but on the housemaid, Molly Newman, coming up with her supper, she asked what strange gentleman was come. Upon the other answering there was no one, she related what is already described and desired her fellow-servant to accompany her to search the room; this they did immediately without any appearance of what she had seen. She was much concerned and disturbed, and she was thoroughly assured she could no ways be deceived, the light being sufficient to distinguish any object clearly. In some time after it was mentioned to me. I treated it as the effect of fear or superstition, to which the lower class of people are so prone, and it was entirely obliterated from my mind till the late astonishing disturbances brought to my recollection this and other previous circumstances.

'In the autumn of the same year George Turner, son of the gardener of that name, who was then groom, crossing the great hall to go to bed, saw at the other end a man in drab-coloured coat, whom he concluded to be the butler, who wore such coloured clothes, he being lately come and his livery not made. As he passed immediately upstairs to the room where all the menservants lay, he was in great astonishment to find the butler and other men servants in bed. Thus the person he had seen in the hall remained unaccounted for, like the same person before described by the nurse; and George Turner, now living, avers these particulars in the same manner he first related them.

'In the month of July, 1767, about seven in the evening, there were sitting in the kitchen, Thomas Wheeler, postilion; Ann Hall, my own woman; Sarah, waiting woman to Mrs Mary Poyntz; and Dame Lacy; the other servants were out excepting the cook, then employed in washing up her things in the scullery.

'The persons in the kitchen heard a woman come downstairs and along the passage leading towards them, whose clothes rustled as of the stiffest silk; and on their looking that way, the door standing open, a female figure rushed past, and out of the house door, as they conceived. Their view of her was imperfect; but they plainly distinguished a tall figure in dark-coloured clothes. Dame Brown, the cook, instantly coming in, this figure passed close by her, and instantly disappeared. She described the person and drapery as before mentioned, and they all united in astonishment who or what this appearance could be; and their surprise was heightened when a man, coming directly into the yard and into the house the way she went out, on being asked who the woman was he met, declared he had seen no one.

'Ann Hall, since married to John Sparks, now living at Rogate, near Petersfield, will testify to the truth of this relation, as will Dame Brown, now living at Bramdean. The postilion is since dead.

'Meanwhile, the noises continued to be heard occasionally. Miss Parker's woman, Susan Maidstone, was terrified with the most dismal groans and rustling round her bed. At different times most of the servants were alarmed with noises that could no way be accounted for. In the latter end of the year 1769, Mr Ricketts went to Jamaica; I continued at Hinton with my three infant children and eight servants, whose names and connections were as follows: Ann Sparks, late Ann Hall, my own woman, the daughter of very industrious parents. Sarah Horner, nurse, sister to a substantial farmer of that name, and of a family of integrity and property. Hannah Streeter, nursemaid, of reputable parents and virtuous principles. Lucy Webb, housemaid, of honest principles. Dame Brown, cook, quiet and regular. John Sparks, coachman. John Horner, postilion, aged sixteen years, eldest son to the farmer above mentioned. Lewis Chanson, butler, a Swiss of strict integrity. Richard Turner, gardener, but did not live in the house.

'I have been thus particular in the description of those persons of whom my family was composed, to prove the improbability that a set of ignorant country people, excepting the Swiss alone, should league to carry on a diabolical scheme imputed to them so injuriously, and which in truth was far beyond the art and reach of man to compass.

'Some time after Mr Ricketts left me, I — then lying in the bedroom over the kitchen — heard frequently the noise of someone walking in the room within, and the rustling as of silk clothes against the door that opened into my room, sometimes so loud and of such continuance as to break my rest. Instant search being often made, we never could discover any appearance of human or brute being.

'Repeatedly disturbed in the same manner, I made it my constant practice to search the room and closets within, and to secure the only door that led from that room on the inside in such a manner as to be certain no one could gain entrance without passing through my own apartment, which was always made fast by a draw-bolt on the door. Yet this precaution did not preclude the disturbance, which continued with little interruption.

'About this time an old man, living in the poor house at West Meon, came and desired to speak to me. When admitted, he told me he could not rest in his mind without acquainting me that his wife had often related to him that in her younger days a carpenter whom she had well known, had told her he was once sent for by Sir Hugh Stewkeley and directed by him to take up some boards in the dining-room, known in our time by the name of lobby, and that Sir Hugh had concealed something underneath which he, the carpenter, conceived was treasure, and then he was ordered to put down the boards in the same manner as they lay before. This account I repeated to Mr Sainsbury, attorney to Lady Hillsborough, that if he thought it were a probability he might have the floor taken up and examined.

'In February, 1770, John Sparks and Ann, his wife, quitted my service, and went to live upon their farm at Rogate. In the place of John Sparks I hired Robert Camis, one of the six sons of Roger and Mary Camis, of the parish of Hinton, and whose ancestors have been in possession of a little estate there upwards of four hundred years — a family noted for their moral and religious lives. In the room of Ann Sparks I hired Ruth Turpin, but she being disordered in mind continued with me but few months. I then took Elizabeth Godin, of Alresford, sister to an eminent grocer of that place. Lewis Chanson quitted me in August, 1770, and I hired Edward Russel, now living with Mr Harris, of Alresford, to succeed him.

'I mention these changes among my domestics, though in themselves unimportant, to evince the impossibility of a confederacy, for the course of nearly seven years, and with a succession of different persons, so that at the time of my leaving Hinton, I had not one servant that lived with me at my first going thither, nor for some time afterwards.

'In the summer of 1770, one night that I was lying in the yellow bedchamber (the same I have mentioned that the person in drab-coloured clothes was seen to enter), I had been in bed half an hour, thoroughly awake, and without the least terror or apprehension on my spirits. I plainly heard the footsteps of a man, with plodding step, walking towards the foot of my bed. I thought the danger too near to ring my bell for assistance, but sprang out of bed and in an instant was in the nursery opposite; and with Hannah Streeter and a light I returned to search for what I had heard, but all in vain. There was a light burning in the dressing-room within, as usual, and there was no door or means of escape save at the one that opened to the nursery. This alarm perplexed me more than any preceding, being within my own room, the footsteps as distinct as ever I heard, myself perfectly awake and collected.

'I had, nevertheless, resolution to go to bed alone in the same room, and did not form any conclusions as to the cause of this very extraordinary disturbance. For some months afterwards I did not hear any noise that particularly struck my attention, till, in November of the same year, I then being removed to the chintz bedroom over the hall, as a warmer apartment, I once or twice heard sounds of harmony, and one night in particular I heard three distinct and violent knocks as given with a club, or something very ponderous, against a door below stairs; it occurred to me that housebreakers must be forcing into some apartment, and I immediately rang my bell. No one hearing the summons and the noise ceasing, I though no further of it at that time. After this, and in the beginning of the year 1771, I was frequently sensible of a hollow murmuring that seemed to possess the whole house; it was independent of wind, being equally heard on the calmest nights, and it was a sound I had never been accustomed to hear.

'On the morning of the 27th of February, when Elizabeth Godin came into my room, I inquired what weather. She replying in a very faint tone, I asked if she were ill. She said she was well, but had never in her life been so terrified as during the preceding night; that she had heard the most dismal groans and fluttering round her bed most part of the night, that she had got up to search the room and up the chimney, and though it was a bright moonlight she could not discover anything. I did not pay much attention to her account, but it occurred to me that should anyone tell her it was the room formerly occupied by Mrs Parfait, the old housekeeper, she would be afraid to lie there again. Mrs Parfait dying a few days before at Kilmston, was brought and interred at Hinton churchyard the evening of the night this disturbance happened.

'That very day five weeks, being the 2nd of April, I waked between one and two o'clock, as I found by my watch, which, with a rushlight, was on a table close to my bedside. I lay thoroughly awake for some time, and then heard one or more persons walking to and fro in the lobby adjoining. I got out of bed and listened at the door for the space of twenty minutes, in which time I distinctly heard the walking with the addition of a loud noise like pushing strongly against a door. Being thus assured my senses were not deceived I determined to ring my bell, to which I had before much reluctance on account of disturbing the nursery maid, who was very ill of a fever.

'Elizabeth Godin during her illness lay in the room with my sons, and came immediately on hearing my bell. Thoroughly convinced there were persons in the lobby, before I opened my door, I asked her if she saw no one there. On her replying in the negative, I went out to her, examined the window, which was shut, looked under the couch, the only furniture of concealment there; the chimney board was fastened and when removed, all was clear behind it. She found the door into the lobby shut, as it was every night. After this examination I stood in the middle of the room, pondering with much astonishment, when suddenly the door that opens into the little recess leading to the yellow apartment sounded as if played to and fro by a person standing behind it. This was more than I could bear unmoved. I ran into the nursery and rang the bell there that goes into the men's apartments. Robert Camis came to the door at the landing place, which door was every night secured, so that no person could get to that floor unless through the windows. Upon opening the door to Robert I told him the reason I had to suppose that someone was intrenched behind the door I before mentioned, and giving him a light and arming him with a billet of wood, myself and Elizabeth Godin waited the event. Upon opening the door there was not any being whatever, and the yellow apartment was locked, the key, hanging up, and a great bolt drawn across the outside door, as usual when not in use. There was then no further retreat or hiding place. After dismissing Robert and securing the door, I went to bed in my son's room, and about half an hour afterwards heard three distinct knocks as described before; they seemed below, but I could not then or ever after ascertain the place. The next night I lay in my own room; I now and then heard noises and frequently the hollow murmur.

'On the 7th of May, exactly the day five weeks from the 2nd of April, this murmur was uncommonly loud. I could not sleep, apprehending it the prelude to some greater noise. I got up and went in to the nursery, stayed there till half an hour past three, and then, being daybreak, I thought I should get some sleep in my own apartment; I returned and lay till ten minutes before four, and then the great hall door directly under me was slapped to with the utmost violence, so as to shake my room perceivably. I jumped out of bed to the window that commands the porch. There was light to distinguish every object, but none to be seen that could account for what I had heard. Upon examining the door it was found fast locked and bolted as usual.

'From this time I determined to have my woman lie in a little bed in my room. The noises grew more frequent, and she was always sensible of the same sounds, and much in the same direction as they struck me. Harassed and perplexed, I was yet very unwilling to divulge my embarrassment. I had taken every method to investigate the cause, and could not discover the least appearance of a trick; on the contrary, I became convinced it was beyond the power of any mortal agent to perform, but knowing how exploded such opinions were, I kept them in my own bosom, and hoped my resolution would enable me to support whatever might befall.

'After Midsummer the noises became every night more intolerable. They began before I went to bed, and with intermissions were heard till after broad day in the morning. I could frequently distinguish articulate sounds, and usually a shrill female voice would begin, and then two others with deeper and manlike tone seemed to join in the discourse, yet, though this conversation sounded as if close to me, I never could distinguish words.

'I have often asked Elizabeth Godin if she heard any noise, and of what sort. She as often described the seeming conversation in the manner I have related, and other noises. One night in particular my bed curtains rustled, and sounded as if dragged by a person walking against them. I then asked her if she heard any noise and of what kind. She spoke of it exactly in the manner I have done. Several times I heard sounds of harmony within the room — no distinct or regular notes, but a vibration of harmonious tones; walking, talking, knocking, opening and slapping of doors were repeated every night. My brother, who had not long before returned from the Mediterranean, had been to stay with me, yet so great was my reluctance to relate anything beyond the bounds of probability, that I could not bring myself to disclose my embarrassed situation to the friend and brother who could most essentially serve and comfort me. The noises continuing in the same manner when he was with me, I wished to learn if he heard them, and one morning I carelessly said: "I was afraid last night the servants would disturb you, and rang my bell to order them to bed." He replied he had not heard them. The morning after he left me to return to Portsmouth, about three o'clock and daylight, Elizabeth Godin and myself both awoke — she had been sitting up in bed looking round her, expecting as she always did to see something terrible — I heard with infinite astonishment the most loud, deep, tremendous noise which seemed to rise and fall with infinite velocity and force on the lobby floor adjoining to my room. I started up, and called to Godin, "Good God! did you hear that noise?" She made no reply; on repeating the question she answered with a faltering voice, she was so frightened she scarce durst speak. Just at that instant we heard a shrill and dreadful shriek, seeming to proceed from under the spot where the rushing noise fell, and repeated three or four times, growing fainter as it seemed to descend, till it sank into earth. Hannah Streeter, who lay in the room with my children, heard the same noises, and was so appalled she lay for two hours almost deprived of sense and motion.

'Having heard little of the noises preceding and that little she did not regard, she had rashly expressed a wish to hear more of them, and from that night till she quitted the house there was scarce a night passed that she did not hear the sound as if some person walked towards her door, and pushed against it, as though attempting to force it open. This alarm, so more than commonly horrible, determined me to impart the whole series to my brother on his return to Hinton Ampner, expected in a week. The frequency of the noises, harassing to my rest, and getting up often at unreasonable hours, fixed a slow fever and deep cough, my health was much impaired, but my resolution firm. I remained in anxious expectation of my brother, and he being detained a week longer at Portsmouth than he had foreseen, it occurred to me to endeavour, by changing my apartment, to obtain a little rest; I removed to that formerly occupied by Elizabeth Godin; I did not mention my intention till ten at night, when the room was prepared, and I went to bed soon after. I had scarce lain down when the same noises surrounded me that I before related, and I mention the circumstances of changing my room without previous notice, to prove the impossibility of a plan of operations being so suddenly conveyed to another part of the house were they such as human agents could achieve. The week following I was comforted by the arrival of my brother. However desirous to impart the narrative, yet I forebore till the next morning; I wished him to enjoy a night's rest, and therefore contented myself with preparing him to hear on the morrow the most astonishing tale that ever assailed his ears, and that he must summon all his trust of my veracity to meet my relation. He replied it was scarce possible for me to relate any matter he could not believe, little divining the nature of what I had to offer to his faith.

'The next morning I began my narrative, to which he attended with mixed surprise and wonder. Just as I had finished, Captain Luttrell, our neighbour at Kilmston, chancing to call, induced my brother to impart the whole to him, who in a very friendly manner offered to unite his endeavours to investigate the cause. It was then agreed that he should come late in the evening, and divide the night watch between them, keeping profoundly secret there was any such intention. My brother took the precaution, accompanied by his own servant, John Bolton, to go into every apartment, particularly those in the first and attic storey, examined every place of concealment, and saw each door fastened, save those to chambers occupied by the family; this done, he went to bed in the room over the servants' hall.

'Captain Luttrell and my brother's man with arms sat up in the chintz room adjoining, and my brother was to be called on any alarm. I lay that night in Elizabeth Godin's room, and the children in the nurseries; thus every chamber on that floor was occupied. I bolted and locked the door that opened to that floor from the back stairs, so that there was no entrance unless through the room where Captain Luttrell kept watch.

'As soon as I lay down, I heard a rustling as of a person close to the door. I ordered Elizabeth Godin to sit up a while, and if the noise continued, to go and acquaint Mr Luttrell. She heard it, and instantly Mr Luttrell's room door was thrown open, and we heard him speak. I must now give his account as related to my brother and myself the next morning.

'He said he heard the footsteps of a person walking across the lobby, and that he instantly threw the door open, and called, "Who goes there?" That something flitted past him, when my brother directly called out "Look against my door." He was awake, and heard what Mr Luttrell had said, and also the continuance of the same noise till it reached his door. He arose and joined Mr Luttrell. Both astonished, they heard various other noises, examined everywhere, found the staircase door fast secured as I had left it. I lay so near, and had never closed my eyes, no one could go to that door unheard. My brother and his man proceeded upstairs, and found the servants in their own rooms, and all the doors closed as they had seen just before. They sat up together, my brother and Mr Luttrell, till break of day, when my brother returned to his own chamber. About that time, as I imagined, I heard the chintz room door opened and slammed to with the utmost violence, and immediately that of the hall chamber opened and shut in the same manner. I mentioned to Godin my surprise that my brother, who was ever attentive not to alarm or disturb the children, should hazard both by such vehement noise. An hour after I heard the house door open and slam in the same way, so as to shake the house. No one person was then up, for as I had never slept, I heard the servants rise and go down about half an hour afterwards. When we were assembled at breakfast, I observed the noise my brother had made with the doors.

'Mr Luttrell replied, "I assure you Jervis made not the least noise; it was your door and the next I heard opened and slapped in the way you describe." My brother did not hear either. He afterwards acknowledged to me that when gone to bed and Mr Luttrell and I were sitting below, he heard dreadful groans and various noises that he was then and after unable to account for. His servant was at that time with mine below.

'Captain Luttrell declared the disturbances of the preceding night were of such a nature that the house was an unfit residence for any human being. My brother, though more guarded in his expressions, concurred in that opinion, and the result of our deliberations was to send an express to Mr Sainsbury, Lady Hillborough's steward, to request he would come over immediately on a very particular occasion, with which he would be made acquainted on his arrival.

'Unluckily, Mr Sainsbury was confined with the gout, and sent over his clerk, a youth of fifteen, to whom we judged it useless and improper to divulge the circumstances.

'My brother sat up every night of the week he then passed at Hinton Ampner. In the middle of one of these nights, I was surprised with the sound of a gun or pistol let off near me, immediately followed by groans as of a person in agonies, or expiring, that seemed to proceed between my chambers and the next, the nursery. I sent Godin to Nurse Horner, to ask if she had heard any noise; she had not. Upon my inquiry the next morning of my brother, he hadn't heard it, though the report and groans were loud and deep.

'Several instances occurred where very loud noises were heard by one or two persons, when those equally near and in the same direction were not sensible of the least impression.

'As the watching every night made it necessary for my brother to gain rest in the day, he usually lay down after dinner. During one of these times he was gone to rest, I had sent the children and their attendants out to walk, the dairymaid had gone to milk, the cook in the scullery, my own woman with my brother's man sitting together in the servants' hall; I, reading in the parlour, heard my brother's bell ring with great quickness. I ran to his room, and he asked me if I had heard any noise, "because," he said, "as I was lying wide awake an immense weight seemed to fall through the ceiling to the floor just by that mahogany press, and it is impossible I should be deceived." His man was by this time come up, and said he was sitting underneath the room as I before mentioned, and heard not the least noise. The inquiry and attention my brother devoted to investigate this affair was such as from the reach of his capacity and ardent spirit might be expected; the result was his earnest request that I would quit the place, and when obliged to return to Portsmouth, that I would permit him to send Mr Nichols, his Lieutenant of Marines, and an old friend of the family, to continue till my removal with me.

'One circumstance is of a nature so singularly striking that I cannot omit to relate it. In one of our evening's conversations on this wonderful train of disturbances I mentioned a very extraordinary effect I had frequently observed in a favourite cat that was usually in the parlour with me, and when sitting on table or chair with accustomed unconcern she would suddenly slink down as if struck with the greatest terror, conceal herself under my chair, and put her head close to my feet. In a short space of time she would come forth quite unconcerned. I had not long given him this account before it was verified to him in a striking manner. We neither then, nor I at other times, perceived the least noise that could give alarm to the animal, nor did I ever perceive the like effect before these disturbances, nor afterwards when she was removed with me to another habitation. The servants have the same account of a spaniel that lived in the house, but to that, as I did not witness it, I cannot testify.'

(Signed) Mary Ricketts.

The previously unpublished narrative that follows was recollected and written by A.S. Lowth for Lady Mary Long of Windsor and is dated 12 April 1862. I reproduce the manuscript since it includes several aspects and incidents not recorded elsewhere. It is headed 'The Hinton Ghost'.

> 'Mrs Ricketts, Colonel Kingscote, Mr Almius, afterwards Mr Luttrell, Lord Corhampton's son and Captain Jervis, afterwards Lord St Vincent were, I believe, the persons who could best relate what occurred. Mr Ricketts, the then Master of Hinton House, was in India.
>
> 'One night, late in the year, the Rector of Hinton was astonished by the arrival of Mrs Ricketts declaring that she could not go back to Hinton House, which was close by, to sleep, and entreating permission to remain as his guest; that she could not, dared not, tell him why her fears were aroused, because she was under a most solemn promise not to reveal, during her life, what had passed. She said that her life was in danger if she did so, but that she might leave in her account of all at her death. To her family it seemed very extraordinary that although Mrs Ricketts was decided by all to be a very sensible, strong-minded and courageous person, she seemed fully persuaded, from the little she did say, that whatever the agency which had driven her at length from

her home, she thought it supernatural. Not so her own woman, who attended upon her at the Rectory, continuing without fear to sleep at the house, as well as the other servants, and as they are generally the persons most apt to be alarmed by a "Haunted House", the family thought differently and that they were concerned in a trick to turn their mistress out, aided by some person or persons outside, and they felt highly indignant at a course of cruelty which had evidently hurt Mrs Ricketts' bodily health, and turned her out of her house. Some of the family resolved upon coming to a decision on the matter. Accordingly, Captain Jervis, Mr Almius and Colonel Kingscote agreed to visit Hinton and came in the afternoon riding, some from Rosehill, others from Westbury, putting up their horses at Hinton House and loitered about there. They went to the Rectory to see Mrs Ricketts, were asked to dine, and from thence went up the hill to the House, but instead of remounting their horses, they said they were so late that they must now sleep there. They said that they needed little preparation as they rather liked a scramble, and that they would have their candles and begged everyone to go to bed.

'When all the house was quiet, Colonel Kingscote who had laid his plans with the other two, lit a stable lantern and sallied forth outside and went round the house, ascertaining that there were no lights in any window above or below, — none. Then each of them took off his boots, put on felted socks, took each a bag of sawdust and went upstairs, candles in hands, with noiseless tread, went into all the principal rooms, particularly those with Tapestry or Arras on each panel, and made a minute examination with the swordpoints, which were worn in those days on the side. They especially went into Mrs Ricketts' own bedroom and sitting room, and a dressing closet and sanctum containing the books and papers belonging to Mr Ricketts which was adjoining in case there were any concealed closets or trap-doors, similar to those in Old Woodcote House [Two hiding places at Woodcote Manor, Hampshire, are mentioned briefly by

Granville Squiers in his Secret Hiding Places (Stanley Paul, 1934), p. 250] which were discovered in Mr Lowth's days. They advanced to the window, closets and fireplace and then retreating backwards to the centres of the rooms, littering sawdust in front of them, and then went from the centres of the rooms to the doors and exits, leaving a small slip of paper on the floor turned up to catch the bottom of the door, so that it would be moved if the door were moved unseen. This was to discover any collusion on the part of the domestics with any persons outside. All being arranged to their satisfaction above, and having gone through the cellars below, not without many a joke at the expense of Mr Almius, who boasted of his great valour but entreated not to be left alone for a minute, they returned to the sitting room next to the drawing room [This conflicts with Mrs Ricketts' sketch plan *(Author)*], and with greatcoats, lights and pistols on the table, their swords by their sides, made themselves comfortable till at least morning should break ere they would conclude their ghostly watch.

'It struck twelve. No sooner had the last stroke sounded than, violently to all of them, in the next room through a folding door, came the undeniable sound of a person, a woman they thought, dry-rubbing the oak floor as they do in France, up and down with great force, from the window to the door. The three looked at each other, rose, pistol in hand. Mr Almius whispered: "By Heaven! We have her the next time she comes this way. I'll shoot her in the back." As he spoke he knelt down opposite the centre or closing of the two doors with pistol cocked and pointed there. On she came to the doors as before, shaking them. Bang! He fired and simultaneously the other two opened the doors at the report. Lo! no woman, no noise, all smoke! and nothing but smoke from the pistol to be seen. What could it be? How managed? Mr Almius turned white because there was no one to kill but the rest laughed at his fears and Colonel Kingscote said, "Lose no time here. Let's be off . . . you two remain inside while I go outside." And the Colonel lighted his lanthorn [lantern] but returned having seen nothing strange.

'They felt sure that nothing more would occur that night, and they had to destroy all trace of their work above. "Catch me here another night, my good fellows, if you can," exclaimed Mr Almius as he returned to the sitting room once more. Then they gathered together their belongings to go to bed for much more sound would ere long rouse all Hinton. A good rest did not alter Mr Almius' previous resolution, never again to visit Hinton House, while people dry-rubbed floors at midnight, unseen, though heard. But the other two, like Brown's "Twa Dogs", resolved to "meet some other day", and not to consider the affairs of the Lords and the Commons, but for the good of Hinton.

'After some little time had elapsed, so as not to create suspicion, they suddenly arrived at Hinton after a long day's sport, craving beds, arranged themselves as before. Not for long were they left in peace. They were roused by the most tremendous noise, above, below, everywhere, as of thunder. They both started up and agreed to meet in the Long Gallery in the centre of the House, each ascending to it by a different staircase. It ran from end to end in the centre [Not according to Mrs Ricketts' plans *(Author)*]; also in the cellars was a passage under and at the top of the house was one over it, therefore the main or party walls composed it. Upstairs they rushed, swords and lights in hands. The sound caused them to meet exactly and met them with a crash which seemed to shake them to the ground in the middle of the Long Gallery. Their swords crossed each other. They called out each other's names and stared each other in the face, but Jervis, intent on discovery, stirred not but exclaimed, "You go the other way and meet me in the cellar". He bolted below and through all the cellars, which were as still as death and there was no sound in them but their echo.

'When the house was pulled down and the present one built, a subterranean passage parallel with that in the cellars was discovered. In this were found a great number of barrels full of great stones, and it was thought they they were rolled with great force along the passage from one end to the other so as to meet in the centre. This would cause a great concussion which would echo to the gallery and passages above. This passage led again to the hills towards Portsmouth, and a gang of smugglers in league with the servants, finding Hinton a good hiding place for goods, were deemed to be the ghosts. How did they manage the sound as of a woman dry-rubbing the floors at so short a notice?

'The foregoing I heard from my mother and from an old-fashioned lady at Hinton, a Miss Jemima Brereton, who also told me she occasionally received an old friend after a visit to Mrs Ricketts at Hinton House, as she was scared out of it. This lady I will call Bennett for I forget her name and that of the servants. As usual she had been at Hinton and related to Miss Jemima Brereton that one morning while there she observed that Mrs Ricketts appeared very pale when she came to breakfast, and that her hands trembled when she had it. This was very unlike her friend but she made no remark. When breakfast was over she said, "I have something to tell you. I am uneasy and am resolved to sift the matter.

Last night, there again occurred a circumstance which convinces me that my people are resolved to eject me from the house during their master's absence; for what reason I cannot divine, but I am resolved that I will not be dealt with in such a manner. You must know that months ago, one night I had gone to rest at the usual time and as well as I generally am. Some time after my maid had left me in bed with a light, I heard footsteps stealing, as it were, around my room on the oak floor near the wall; not on the carpet which covers the centre of the room only. "How very odd of Adams it is", I thought, "to come here in this stupid kind of way to place something which she has forgotten. However I will pretend not to know" and I went to sleep. A few nights afterwards the same thing occurred again. I called out. No answer. I sat up and rubbed my eyes and made sure that I was not dreaming. Hearing nothing more, I went to sleep thinking that it must be my fancy. Some nights elapsed and I thought no more about it. Then again the same thing occurred but the only difference was that the tread seemed heavier and I instantly thought that it was Adams, the stupid delinquent, and called out but received no reply. I rang the bell and she came. "Adams", I said, "what do you mean by coming about my room at this time of night? If you have forgotten anything, why not say so?" She looked quite amazed and said, "I assure you, mum, that I have just got out of my bed when you rang and have not been here since I left you for the night." "Oh! then I thought it, I suppose," I replied. "Good night! I am sorry!" I heard no more now for some time. Then precisely the same thing happened and being certain that I was awake, I rang the bell. Down came Adams and as before, stoutly denied she had been there, and thought that I could not be right and that I must be ill to be dreaming so, and so I spent the night on the sofa, and sent her to bed and had peace for many nights, assured that tricks had been played upon me in some way and for some purpose unknown, and I felt accordingly very indignant. Last night again occurred what I have had to bear before, until I cannot and will not gently endure it any longer. I had been asleep, — I am sure I had, and I was awakened by the close, tight pressure of the curtains of my bed against my left elbow and shoulder as if a person or a heavy body was sitting against it on the side of my bed. I felt that the person was large and heavy and the breathing hard and full like that of a man, I feel certain. I did not wait to parley but seized the bell which was close to my hand and rang loudly. Then as footsteps neared the door the pressure gave way, the person rose, and I caught hold of the curtains and looked out, to see only Adams with a light in her hand, looking very scared. "Adams", I said, "do you walk in your sleep or not, that you come here? Do you deny it and torment me out of my night's rest so often?"; for I did not choose to tell her that I was certain that there had been a man in my room, and I was obliged to account for bringing her down. As before she clearly denied coming to my room till I rang for her, or of walking in her sleep to her knowledge, and that she certainly had not left her bed when I rang. "Adams, I am resolved to ascertain this perplexing matter and therefore I shall assemble all my servants and give them small space to arrange their matters first." She rose from the breakfast table and rang the bell. "Watson, I wish to see everyone belonging to me in the housekeeper's room. Tell Hunter in ten minutes time. There is my watch, see? Be punctual, do you hear?" "Yes, madam."

'Her watch in hand as the minutes expired, Mrs Ricketts walked arm in arm with Miss Bennett and appeared at the door of the housekeeper's room. The fireplace faced her, three windows on her left hand faced two large presses, one for linen and one for china and glass. These stood on trestle legs and were full and heavy. Anyone would think that they were fixtures and part of the old white panelled walls, extending the whole side of the room. The servants ranged under the windows opposite. Mrs Ricketts advanced to the left and stood still. She said, "I beg you will all stand opposite to me in the light there, and I will stand here." They passed over with their backs to the closets. "I have assembled you all here that I may tell you all at once that I am sorely convinced that in Mr Ricketts', your master's absence, someone or all of you are resolved to alarm me out of my residence here by collusion with some person or persons outside; for what purpose I cannot conceive, but I am equally resolved that it shall not be accomplished, and I have thus called all of you before me that I may see in the countenance of some who are the guilty persons in my household."

'As she pronounced the last word, the two great presses behind the servants, bowed backwards and forwards slowly on their pedestals! Mrs Ricketts, harassed and worn, changed colour and saying, "I exonerate you all", gave her arm to her friend and left the room and was much exhausted on returning to the breakfast room.

'On Mr Ricketts' return from abroad, he ridiculed her fears, she being still at the Rectory, and he used to go up to the house to his sanctum and look over papers in an old escritoire there. One bright summer morning, being intent on his work, he for some time took no heed of a noise in his wife's old sitting room adjoining until he was roused to thinking "Why! I ordered every soul in the place into the hayfield. What on earth is that woman about, dry-rubbing that floor today?" and he rose and opened the door. No woman! No broom! He rushed downstairs hoping to catch the culprit. Lower and lower he went but there was no one anywhere until he reached the scullery and there was an old woman from the village. "What are you doing upstairs, having the floors rubbed, Dame?" he asked. "Everyone but me is in the hayfield, sir," she replied. Out he rushed into the grounds but not a creature belonging to him was missing, to his amazement.

'How did the smugglers manage that? And how did they manage to frighten poor Mrs Ricketts actually out of her home, where her maid continued to sleep and married the gardener? What were the sights and sounds that led to the extortion of a promise that she was not to reveal until her death? And what drove her at length to the safety of the Rectory?

'Mrs Garnier asked me to ascertain from the family if I could her solution of the mysteries of Hinton. The reply was that it was thought so very unlike the strong, good sense evinced by Mrs Ricketts during a long life, to suppose any supernatural appearance had annoyed her peace, and that the family would not make known her account. Those of them who had it to read were not allowed to make any copy of it and thus it remains a mystery how Mrs Ricketts was driven from her home at Hinton House, near Alresford in Hampshire.'

Fortunately we have Mrs Mary Ricketts' original letters and 'Legacy' so today we are in some position to judge exactly what happened at Hinton Ampner and we do not have to rely on what may be a somewhat inaccurate account of some of the disturbances; certainly to judge by some of the statements, the odd and conflicting positioning of certain rooms and passages and the mention of Mr Ricketts being in India (instead of the

West Indies) for example; this particular narrative cannot be regarded with any great degree of confidence but it is nevertheless interesting to look at the case from a different viewpoint and catch a glimpse of some of the leading actors in this curious drama, without their masks, as it were.

I think we can discount the somewhat unlikely theory involving smugglers. It is interesting to note that Lord Bute was convinced that Lucy Camis told Mary Ricketts a great deal about the Legges and the Stawells and that on the basis of this information Mrs Ricketts could only account for the phenomena experienced as being due to an undiscovered murder. At the same time she felt that she must not make such a terrible accusation against the memories of the father and aunt of the then living titled lady who, as she has acknowledged, always treated her with the utmost courtesy and consideration; this reticence would also account for her reluctance to broadcast the story of the haunting. She made only two copies of her long statement, one being in the possession of a grand-daughter, Mrs Edmund Palmer, and the other in the possession of a great granddaughter, Mrs William Henley Jervis, who gave the world the 'true facts' in her article 'A Hampshire Ghost Story' in the Gentleman's Magazine.

The fourth Baron Stawell's only daughter, who was created Baroness Stawell, married the Right Honourable Henry Bilson Legge and their grand-daughter, an only surviving child, married, in 1803, John Dutton, second Baron Sherborne. The present owner of the present manor is Ralph Stawell Dutton, their great-grandson. As we have seen a new Hinton Ampner House was built about 1793 and this Georgian house forms the centre part of the present building. Mr Ralph Dutton told me, when I was there a few years ago, that there were some reports of unexplained noises being heard in the new house, usually just before dawn, but between 1936 and 1939 the house was much altered and in 1960 the main part was gutted by fire. Since then there have been no more strange noises (which would appear rather to shatter Mr Guy Lambert's theories) and the present beautiful structure enjoys a peace that it richly deserves. But, unless we discount the evidence of Mrs Mary Ricketts, and other equally good witnesses, the old Hinton Ampner Manor House would appear to have been the scene of strange and possibly paranormal happenings for a certain limited period, possibly induced or promoted by the presence of children, and conceivably triggered by a combination of frustration, unhappiness and violent death years earlier.

GLAMIS AND ITS GHOSTS

The tree-lined approach to Glamis Castle, long known as Scotland's house of mysteries

Glamis Castle: inside the main entrance showing the stairway to the clock tower

Glamis Castle: the chapel where a 'Grey Lady' has been seen on many occasions in recent years.

Glamis Castle: the large and hollow stone newel on the right contains cords and weights of the clock, high up in the tower, and the movement of these weights within a confined space may result in some of the strange noises repeatedly heard at Glamis

Glamis Castle: plan of first floor and Great Hall

Glamis Castle is probably the best known 'haunted' building in existence. Indeed, the centuries-old, romantic-looking castle, solid and silent at the end of a tree-lined drive, is famous throughout the world for possessing a wide variety of phantom forms. Its dark, uncertain history adds to the charm and the mystery that is Glamis yet, as recently as February 1976, the factor James Kemp, told me 'The ghostly associations are a feature that is not stressed at the castle...'

This fairy tale building with its thick stone walls and its rounded towers with witch-hat pinnacles has an air of detachment, aloofness and withdrawal from the everyday world, almost as though its history, its secrets and its reputation lie heavily upon this massive, brooding pile. The castle may have enjoyed the distinction of being haunted at the time when Shakespeare wrote Macbeth; indeed, there is a tradition that Glamis Castle was the scene of the murder of Duncan by Macbeth, Thane of Glamis. For many years the stone-floored King Malcolm's Room, where the murder may have taken place, was shown to the public together with an 'everlasting bloodstain' that would never wash out; finally the whole floor was boarded over but the sword and shirt of chain-mail that are said to have belonged to Macbeth can still be seen [Charles G. Harper, Haunted Houses (Chapman & Hall, 1907), p. 169].

At all events King Malcolm II of Scotland was assassinated hereabouts and James Wentworth Day maintains that his ghost (one of nine, 'more or less') 'may open your bedroom door' [James Wentworth Day, The Queen Mother's Family Story (Robert Hale, 1967), p. 17]. There are references to this splendid seat of the Earls of Strathmore in thirteenth-century records, and in the sixteenth century the widow of the lord of the castle was condemned as a witch and burned alive. The combination of such half-historic and half-legendary events and the ethereal unreality of the isolated, pinky-grey, majestic castle set against a background of the distant snow-capped Grampians all help to provide a perfect setting for ghosts and legends, confused history and mysteries galore.

A typical example is the noise 'of far-off hammering' and creaking timbers that some people think are psychic echoes of the carpenters hammering as they built the scaffold at Glamis for Janet the witch. In 1880 a contributor to All the Year Round, while declaring himself to be an utter sceptic on the subject of 'supernatural manifestations' recounts 'on good authority' the experience of 'a lady, well known in London society' who said she had spent a disturbed night at Glamis on account of carpenters who began work at four o'clock in the morning. When she made this observation in the morning, at breakfast, she was asked by the family not to speak to them on that subject again for there had been no human carpenters.

Princess Margaret was born at Glamis and the castle has been in the Lyons family for over six hundred years. In 1371 (or 1372) Sir John Lyon (dubbed 'The White Lyon' from his appearance: he was tall, fair and strong) married Princess Joanna, daughter of King Robert II of Scotland (grandson of Robert the Bruce) and so the lordship of Glamis passed into the Lyons family. Sir John — who was killed in a duel in 1383 — took more than his bride to Glamis, however, for he took also a kind of family curse, a hereditary possession, the 'lion cup', a golden goblet that is reputed to have been responsible for many tragedies in the family. This Lion Cup is only the first of many elusive and mysterious secrets that we shall encounter at Glamis.

It was the young and beautiful Janet, widow of the sixth Lord Glamis, who, together with her sixteen-year-old son and other relatives, was indicted for the practice of witchcraft and found guilty of attempting to end the life of James V by arts of magic and sorcery. Her own servants were among those who gave perjured evidence and Janet Douglas was burned on Castle Hill, Edinburgh, in 1537. Her son was more fortunate. Under torture he falsely accused his mother of the crime of which they were both charged; he was also found guilty but was granted postponement of suffering the penalty until he became of age. At length he was, in fact, released, restored to his ancestral home and became the seventh Lord Glamis. His son, the eighth earl, was killed in a chance meeting with the Lindsays, a cherished feud existing between the Lyons and the Lindsays since time immemorial.

But it is with Charles, the sixth Earl Strathmore, that one of the chief ghost stories is concerned and, although there are several versions, the main story — which has the ring of some sort of truth — is centred around a fatal game of chance. It would seem that the protracted feud between the Lyons and the Lindsays had healed to the extent that the two families occasionally dined together, drank together and played dice together, with each side cautious of the other, the consequence of centuries of suspicion and open aggression. The story goes that the stakes grew higher and higher and the Earl of Glamis was trying to cope with a long run of bad luck. Having lost most of his money, he resolved to risk some of his estates on the chance of winning everything back, but success still eluded him. One property after another passed from Lyon to Lindsay ownership across the gaming table until, at last, Glamis itself stood at hazard and, by the turn of a card, was lost. Lord Strathmore could not believe that luck alone could have cost him so much and, dazed and desperate, he accused his opponents of cheating.

Tempers rose, blows were exchanged, swords were drawn and at the end of it all, the sixth Earl Strathmore lay dying with a sword through his body, a sword wielded not by a Lindsay but by James Carnegie, we learn from the trial that followed the death. On to the framework of this story has been built a body of myth and legend, of wishful thinking and sensational exaggeration, until it is difficult to divide fact from fiction. Even the circumstances surrounding the death of the sixth Earl are conflicting. One story even places the brawl outside the castle and in the streets of nearby Forfar.

Into these fabrications have been woven the allegedly evil characteristics of earlier owners of Glamis and in particular 'Earl Beardie' or 'Earl Patie', thought by some to be an ancient Lord Crawford who quarrelled with the Lord Glamis of the day, and by others to be the first Lord Glamis himself, who died in 1454 and whose real or imaginary cruelty earned him the dubious honour of becoming the family bogyman and the terror of the nurseries of Glamis and the surrounding countryside.

These stories portray Earl Beardie as a dedicated and degenerate gambler whose whole life revolved around the addiction and whose gambling — with anyone who would play with him — often lasted days and nights at a time. One Sunday in November (naturally a 'dark and stormy night') Earl Beardie is supposed to have been desperate for a game of cards but he had no partner and he could persuade no one to play with him on the Sabbath day. At length he stormed off to his room, high up in one of the towers, and there he laid out the cards and called on the Devil himself to come and play with him, since no one else would ... a moment later a single knock sounded on the door and a deep voice asked if he was still looking for a partner. 'Yes,' replied the Earl. 'Enter, whoever you are ...'

The door opened to reveal a tall, dark man, wearing a long cloak. He nodded to the Earl, who wondered who the stranger might be. Without another word his guest sat down, picked up his hand of cards and play began. The stranger proposed high stakes which the Earl accepted, adding that if he were the loser and found himself unable to honour his debts, he would sign a bond for whatever the stranger required. The games followed one after the other, each more boisterous than its predecessor, and the loud oaths, curses and swearing attracted the attention of the servants who, terrified yet fascinated, crept up the stairs, the better to hear what was going on.

An old butler, braver than the rest, applied his eye to the keyhole, only to recoil and fall back among the servants with a scream of agony. The next moment the door of the Earl's chamber was flung open and there stood the Earl, his face dark and full of fury. He upbraided the servants in no uncertain manner and sent them about their business while he returned to settle with his guest. But the stranger had disappeared and with him the bond that the Earl had signed. While the final game had been in progress it is said that the stranger had suddenly turned his eyes towards the keyhole in the door of the chamber and, throwing down his cards had exclaimed, with an oath, 'Smite that eye!' whereupon the butler's eye received a blast of flame.

After the death of Earl Beardie, five years later, the sounds of boisterous card-playing, of oaths and curses, of tumult and disagreement, resounded from the Earl's old room on Sunday evenings for the Devil had redeemed his bond — the soul of Earl Beardie — and now the Devil and the Earl returned to play their games for ever. Be that as it may there is considerable evidence for strange sounds issuing from 'Earl Beardie's' Room late at night, and not a few visitors to Glamis Castle claim to have heard these curiously echoing sounds or to have encountered the frightening spectacle of Earl Beardie himself. Sir Shane Leslie told me that his Aunt Mary had seen this formidable ghost at Glamis and other witnesses include the daughter of a former Lord Castletown; Dr Nicholson, a former Dean of Brechin; Dr Forbes, a Bishop of Brechin; Mr and Mrs Hunter, who lived and worked at the castle, and other servants; but few will talk about the matter. A typical undated and unauthenticated account tells of the visit by a lady and her child to the castle and of the child being asleep in an adjoining room when the mother, in bed but not yet asleep, felt a cold blast of air sweep into the room. She saw a tall, mailed figure pass through her bedroom and disappear into the room where her child lay, and it was immediately followed by a shriek from the child. When she reached the frightened child, the mother learned that 'a giant' had leaned over the little one's bed. Interestingly enough, a strikingly similar story is recounted by Lord Halifax- (who had Lyon blood in his veins) that apparently dates from November 1869 [Lord Halifax's Ghost Book (Geoffrey Bles, 1936), p. 27f].

It seems that three sets of rooms on the Clock Landing were allotted to Lady Strathmore's sister, Mrs John Streatfield and her husband; the Trevanions, Lord Strathmore's sister; and Mr and Mrs Munro from Lindertis, who occupied the Red Room with their young son sleeping in an adjoining room. During the night Mrs Munro was awakened by someone or something bending over her — and a beard brushed her face; she awakened her husband and both plainly saw a figure pass into the room occupied by their son. He immediately shrieked with terror and, when comforted, declared that he had seen a giant in the room. All three had heard a fearful crash that seemed to originate in the child's bedroom, followed by the big clock striking four o'clock. Next morning they learned that Mrs Trevanion's dog had howled for no apparent reason during the night, awakening her, and she had been startled to hear a tremendous crash, followed by the clock striking four. Next night the three couples sat up to watch and although on that occasion they saw nothing of an inexplicable nature, they all heard a loud crashing noise from the direction of the landing, just before the hour of four o'clock. The Clock Tower, according to Antony D. Hippisley Coxe [Haunted Britain (Hutchinson, 1973), p. 180], is haunted by the ghost of the alleged witch, Janet, wife of the sixth Lord Glamis.

A variation on this story suggests that 'Earl Beardie', who may well have been the Earl of Crawford whose portrait hangs at Abbotsford, Sir Walter Scott's haunted home [See Peter Underwood, A Gazetteer of Scottish and Irish Ghosts (Souvenir Press, 1973), pp. 138-9], and the Lord Glamis of the day, played and gambled and eventually quarrelled with the result that Earl Beardie, a huge man by all accounts, was thrown down the stone staircase of the tower. He returned, roaring with rage and swearing to play cards with the Devil if Glamis would not play with him; instantly a tall, dark man in a cloak strode into the room and play began again. No one knows what happened during the course of that long night but the mysterious stranger was never seen again and after 'Earl Beardie' died, a few years after that strange encounter, the ghost of the Earl was reported to be heard and seen in the room where he had gambled with the Devil. This uninhabited room at the top of the tower is empty but for two doors and an ominous trapdoor, and some intangible presence is always perceptible to certain people.

Yet another version tells of Earl Beardie being heard to swear that he would play until the Day of Judgment and, especially on stormy November nights, the sounds of gambling, accompanied by oaths and curses, have been heard to this day.

There does seem little doubt that inexplicable noises are a feature of the hauntings at Glamis. Dr Frederick George Lee in his Glimpses of the Supernatural [London, 1875] quotes a correspondent who says, 'There is no doubt about the reality of the noises at Glamis Castle. On one occasion, some years ago, the head of the family, with several companions, was determined to investigate the cause. One night, when the disturbance was greater and more violent and alarming than usual — and, it should be premised, strange, weird, and unearthly sounds had often been heard, and by many persons, some quite unacquainted with the ill-repute of the castle — his lordship went to the Haunted Room, opened the door with a key, and dropped back in a dead swoon into the arms of his companions; nor could he ever be induced to open his lips on the subject afterwards.' [Fortuitously relocking the door, presumably, before becoming quite unconscious! *(Author)*] In explanation it has been suggested [John H. Ingram, The Haunted Homes and Family Traditions of Great Britain (Reeves and Turner, 1912), p. 99] that during the days of the bitter and constant feud between the Lyons and the Lindsays, a band of Ogilvies, fleeing from some Lindsays, arrived at Glamis Castle and begged for refuge. The owner admitted them and, on the excuse of hiding them, led them to the Haunted Room, locked them in and left them to die. Their bones, according to tradition, lie there to this day for their bodies were never removed and it is that sight that so startled the former Lord Strathmore and caused him to have the room walled up.

Some of these unfortunate captives are said to have died in the act of gnawing the flesh from their own arms. Today the white-walled and bare chamber does seem to exude a sense of brooding unease. On the other hand Sidney Toy, FSA, FRIBA, in his monumental work, The Castles of Great Britain [William Heinemann, 1953, p. 225] puts forward an interesting and plausible explanation for some of the 'mysterious' noises reported at the castle. Speaking of the earliest part of the present castle, the rectangular tower with the short wing attached to it at the south-east corner, around which the later buildings are grouped, he says, 'The central stairway, rising from ground floor to roof... is wide and of easy gradient, winding round a large hollow stone newel, down the centre of which pass unseen the long cords and weights of the large clock seen outside at the head of the stair turret. The rumbling of the weights in their confined space especially at the striking of the clock in the dead of night, may account for some of the "ghostly" manifestations associated with the castle.'

Yet it is difficult to dismiss all the nocturnal noises at Glamis in such prosaic terms. Florence Foster, an Australian-born cook at the castle, said she was prepared to swear that she had heard the noise of rattling dice, heavy stamping of feet and the sound of voices raised in anger, and knocks and other loud and distinct sounds that had no rational explanation and they had caused her to lie in bed and shake with fright.

There is a story of the fairly recent visitor to Glamis who was awakened in the middle of the night by the sound of knocking at his bedroom door. Thinking that fire or some other emergency must be the cause for the urgent sounding knocks, he hurriedly rose from his bed and opened the door; but outside all was quiet and no one was anywhere in sight. As he prepared to return to bed it sounded again and now appeared to originate from the spot where he stood, the doorway itself, although no human being was producing the persistent knocking which gradually grew fainter and finally ceased. A frightful shriek then sounded at his elbow whereupon the visitor rushed back to his bed and left the castle early next morning.

It is equally difficult to discount entirely the many stories of secret rooms at Glamis. Even the well-known search by a party of young people probably had its foundation in fact. The story goes that during a house party someone mentioned the mystery of the secret room and it was decided to try and locate such a room by hanging a towel from the window of every room in the castle. It took a long time to do this but eventually a towel fluttered from every window except one, which was small, dark and high up on the face of the old square tower, part of the ancient fortress of Glamis. The puzzled young people moved round the corner — and saw another window at the same height without a towel, and another: the whole floor had not been investigated and none of them could discover any entry to that part of the tower. In fact there is little doubt that there are several bricked-up rooms at Glamis and probably several bodies-, the last Lord Strathmore once told me that he was convinced that there were undiscovered human remains within the massive walls and 'probably half a dozen rooms bricked up . . .' Even if unlocated, sealed rooms and human remains do not constitute a haunting, they do provide substantial material for travellers' tales that lose nothing in the telling.

The legend of a secret room at Glamis is often coupled with the strange story of a monster, a story that has been investigated by James Wentworth Day who was given the freedom of the Charter Room, a secret cell within the walls of the castle, and permission to make full perusal of family papers dating back five hundred years. The first Earl of Strathmore had a secret room, with an entrance from the Charter Room, built in 1684, as we know from the Earl's Book of Record that was discovered and published by the Scottish Historical Society in 1890. It does seem likely that a deformed heir was born into the family but kept a secret from everyone except the existing earl, the family lawyer and the factor of the estate — a child that grew to manhood confined in a secret room built especially for the purpose.

I have talked with Paul Bloomfield about his article in the magazine Queen [Christmas number, 1964], and there is little doubt that he has uncovered the answer to the mystery of the monster of Glamis. After much patient research he discovered that in October 1821 a male heir was born to the then Earl of Strathmore and is recorded as having died within a month. It is likely that the child was hideously deformed, probably mongoloid, could never inherit the title and estates and would in all probability die within a short period of time. Bloomfield reasons that the family would have decided to look after and care for him as long as he lived but they must have hoped another heir would be born before the title was passed on and the unfortunate and deformed creature would be dead long before then. But it seems that he lived on and on, possibly shaped like an enormous egg with tiny arms and legs, a grotesque and bloated figure, physically and mentally deformed but immensely strong.

George, Lord Glamis, who was not possessed of the estate, married Charlotte Grinstead on 21 December 1820. An early edition of Cockayne's Complete Peerage records the birth and death of a son on 18 October 1821; Douglas' Scots Peerage states that a son was born and died on 21 October 1821. At all events there was a son born and recorded as having died in October 1821 and a second son, Thomas George (who was quite normal) was born on 22 September

1822. Bloomfield suggests that when he became the twelfth Earl of Strathmore, on the death of his grandfather, he was told that he had an elder brother living whose physical and mental deformities caused him to be kept out of sight. The secret was passed from heir to heir as long as the true heir lived and there is evidence to suggest that he lived to a very great age: James Wentworth Day quotes 'an admiral, who knows the story and an outstanding hero of the last war' who believes the 'monster' lived until 'about 1921'! [The Queen Mother's Family Story (Robert Hale, 1967), p. 134] Even the staid Notes and Queries, not a publication that interests itself in gossip, idle speculation or sensationalism, contained a letter in 1908 from a writer who stated, categorically, 'In the castle of Glamis there is a secret chamber, in which is confined a monster who is the rightful heir to the titles and property, but is so unpresentable that it is necessary to keep him perpetually out of sight'.

Certainly no Lord Strathmore, for the past century and a half, has been a very happy man. Augustus Hare, a guest at Glamis in 1877, was struck by the 'ever-sad' look of the then Earl and a fellow-guest at the time, the Bishop of Brechin, quietly offered the Earl any help he could give as an ecclesiastic. 'Lord Strathmore was deeply moved. He said that he thanked him but that in his most unfortunate position, no one could ever help him.' The Dowager Lady Granville, sister of the Queen Mother, has revealed that the subject was always taboo: 'We were never allowed to talk about it when we were children. Our parents forbade us ever to discuss the matter or ask any questions about it. My father and grandfather refused absolutely to discuss it,' The last Lord Strathmore maintained that he knew nothing of the subject and suggested that the 'secret' may have died with his father or with his brother who was killed in the last war.

One Earl of Strathmore, more than a century ago, said to his wife on being 'initiated' into the secret: 'I have been into the secret chamber and I have learned what the secret is — and if you wish to please me, never mention the matter to me again. I can only say that if you could guess the nature of the secret, you would go down on your knees and thank God it was not yours.'

There is no doubt that several — perhaps most — of the heirs of Glamis were changed men after they came of age or inherited the title, and more than one joked and laughed with his friends on the eve of learning the secret, saying that he would tell his friends all about it the following evening.

Invariably it was a sombre man who met his friends twenty-four hours later, a man who said it was quite impossible for him to reveal what had taken place and he would regard it as a favour if the matter was never mentioned again.

If Bloomfield is right there are three factors or stewards of the Glamis estates who, in a position to know all the family secrets, would have each been one of the three men alive at any one time who knew the truth about the monster. Peter Procter, who held the post from 1765 to 1815, died before the birth in 1821 but his son, David Procter, appointed in 1815, could well have been the first factor to see the monster and to know the secret. He was followed by Andrew Ralston in 1860 who served for fifty-two years, to be succeeded by his son Gavin Ralston who was probably the last factor to share the secret. None of them would ever divulge what they knew — not even to the Ladies Strathmore.

The Queen Mother's mother, the late Lady Strathmore, once asked Gavin Ralston to tell her the truth of the story but he shook his head and replied: 'Lady Strathmore, it is fortunate you do not know it and will never know it, for if you did you would never be happy.' Ralston, incidentally, a hard-headed, down-to-earth and practical man, would never sleep at Glamis Castle and one winter's night he made gardeners and stablemen dig a path for him through the snow so that he could go home rather than accept the hospitality of the existing Lord Strathmore.

It seems likely that the family tended to encourage stories of ghosts, hauntings and strange nocturnal noises as long as the monster was alive and needed feeding and exercise, but once the poor creature was dead there was no need to 'bolster-up' the legends. In recent years the family have progressively tended to 'play down' the stories of ghosts. In as much as smuggling and wrecking contributed to the perpetuation of ghostly legends about our coasts, the monster of Glamis helped to reinforce and sustain the ghosts of Glamis. Indeed there is little doubt that the monster was the explanation for the walk, high up on the roof, known to this day as the 'Mad Earl's Walk', where the lawful heir would be exercised and from where, perhaps, he escaped one night and raced across the wide parkland, giving rise to the persistent story of a strange, elusive, running figure nicknamed 'Jack the Runner' who has, reportedly, been occasionally glimpsed on moonlit nights.

A similar escape might even be the explanation for the 'Tongueless Woman' apparition. This arresting spectacle has been claimed to have been seen by many people over the years — a pale figure racing across the park, pointing to her bleeding mouth or, more startling perhaps, a white face with staring eyes, pleading, imploring help without making a sound. Such a face, usually seen staring from an iron-barred window high up in one of the turrets, strikes terror into those who see it. While still a boy Sir David Bowes-Lyon learned the story associated with this ghost. It involved a guest who was taking an evening stroll close to the castle when he saw a pale and frightened face pressed close to the windowpane, seemingly imploring his help. He was about to speak when the face disappeared abruptly and a high-pitched scream, stifled at its height, was followed by utter silence. A few moments later, as the visitor was preparing to move on, he heard a series of soft thuds from the direction of the tower, as though something limp was descending the stone steps. Next the startled guest heard the sound of heavy breathing and, cautiously and surreptitiously, the door of the tower opened and an old woman staggered out bent almost double by a heavy and bulky bundle on her back. When she saw the wide-eyed visitor she quietly turned and hurried away across the lawns, out of sight among some trees. The guest was too frightened to follow and it was many years before the sequel to the story came when the same man was holidaying in Italy.

Caught in a blizzard in the mountains, he was rescued by some monks and given food and shelter at their monastery. Later, to pass the time, they all talked of odd happenings and the monks mentioned that a mysterious British woman was living in a nearby nunnery. It seemed that she had discovered some terrible secret about a prominent British family and had been barbarously silenced by having her tongue cut out and hands cut off. She was then smuggled to the lonely nunnery. The man succeeded in arranging for the monks to take him to see the woman and it was the tongueless woman whom he had seen at Glamis. Sir David Bowes-Lyon was among those who regarded this story as typical of the utter nonsense that was written about Glamis in Victorian days.

That some people have been silenced about what they have seen at Glamis seems likely but hardly in such a barbaric fashion. In 1860 a London periodical carried an account of a workman who had been employed to make some structural alterations at Glamis and while driving his crowbar into what he thought was solid stonework, had inadvertently broken into a large cavity. Puzzled by his discovery he had enlarged the hole until he could clamber through and had then found himself in a kind of corridor which he had followed until he had reached a very solid, locked door. Somewhat overawed by his own boldness, he had then returned the way he had come and reported the matter to his foreman. The existing earl was in London at the time but as soon as the factor heard about the matter, he hurriedly informed the earl who immediately returned to Glamis. The workman, if the account is to be believed, was presented with a large sum of money, induced to emigrate to Australia with his family, and was never heard of again.

Other, less credible, stories associated with Glamis include the theory that the Lyon family are cursed with a vampire, born hundreds of years ago, who is kept hidden for ever in a secret room but who has escaped once or twice during the passing centuries and is responsible for some of the more sensational and lurid stories associated with the castle. Another version of the vampire story tells of a distant female relative who was discovered in the act of attacking a guest, sucking his blood as he lay sleeping. She was eventually captured and imprisoned in a secret room that became her tomb, where she lies to this day ...

Other reported ghosts and ghostly happenings at Glamis include a bedroom door that opened of its own accord every night. Lock it, bolt it, bar it in all manner of ways but in the morning the door would stand open, defiant and inexplicable, even with heavy furniture pushed against it; not until the wall was taken down and the door used elsewhere in the castle would it stay closed.

Then there is the Queen Mother's bathroom, a cheerless little room that was once a small bedroom. The people who occupied it then reported various strange happenings, odd noises, the movement of objects and the sensation of being watched; often the bed-clothes would be pulled off the bed during the night. After the room was turned into a bathroom there were no more reports of inexplicable happenings.

The occupants of Glamis always seem to be prepared to make alterations to placate their ghosts and Virginia Gabriel, a composer, has revealed that in several of the bedroom cupboards there are stones with iron rings in them. The Lord Strathmore at the time had all the cupboards converted into coal stores 'with strongly-boarded fronts' and he ordered the servants to see that these stores were always full so that no inquisitive visitor would be tempted to make any kind of exploration.

The lure of Glamis has endured for several hundred years and it is as strong today as ever it was, a fact that can be verified any summer day when hoards of visitors from all over the world descend on the impressive castle, wander about the gardens and explore those rooms that are open to the public. Sir Walter Scott visited Glamis for he wanted to experience the atmosphere for himself and although during the night he spent there he saw no ghost he wrote afterwards, 'I must own that when the door was shut I began to consider myself as too far from the living and somewhat too near the dead.'

The wife of a former Archbishop of York, on a visit to Glamis, walked into her room and saw a huge bearded man dozing in a chair by the fire; before she had time to say or do anything, the figure began to fade and a few seconds later had completely disappeared. A Provost of Perth saw the same figure and also a lady in white who glided about the corridors at dead of night. Augustus Hare neither saw nor heard anything he could not explain during his stay at Glamis but he reports that at the time of his visit a whole extra wing of the castle was given over for children and servants to sleep in because there had been so many reports of frightening happenings in the older parts of the castle at night time.

Certainly some of the reported ghosts can be dismissed as stories put about by the family and factors for their own reasons. Figments of the imagination, misinterpretation of actual events, distortion and exaggeration of other than first-hand experiences, and deliberate fabrication can account for some stories but there do appear to be 'real ghosts' at Glamis and certain rooms are never slept in, such as Earl Patie's Room and the Hangman's Chamber — where a butler once hanged himself.

Another ghostly white lady (or possibly the same one taking the air) has been seen outside the castle, perambulating the lawn beside the castle walls, and there are reports of various people seeing the figure from various viewpoints. Indeed the Lady Strathmore, two of her nieces and Lady Glasgow have all said they saw the figure from different windows at the same time, although their descriptions are admittedly vague.

Far more substantial (if that adjective can be applied to a ghost) are the reports of a Grey Lady who haunts the tiny chapel. The last Lord Strathmore told me that he had seen the figure several times and the Dowager Countess Granville is among those who have also seen the silent, almost pathetic little figure. Lady Granville was inside the chapel one sunny afternoon, playing some music, when she suddenly had the feeling that there was someone behind her. She looked round and saw a little lady in grey, kneeling in one of the pews, praying. The figure seemed to be completely solid and natural and Lady Granville particularly noticed the detail of the dress, the large buttons and the overall neat appearance; but she also noticed that the sun shining in through the window behind the Grey Lady actually shone through the figure and made a pattern on the floor. Lady Granville didn't feel at all frightened or even perturbed and she turned back to her music and continued playing quietly; when she had finished the Grey Lady had vanished. The Queen Mother is among other witnesses for this apparition.

Timothy, the sixteenth Earl, went into the chapel one afternoon to check some detail in one of the de Wint pictures that hang there. After looking at the picture he turned round to walk out and saw the Grey Lady, kneeling, apparently praying, just as his aunt had seen her. Lord Strathmore felt no sense of fear or even surprise but he had no wish to disturb the lady at her devotions so he quietly tiptoed out of the chapel and left the Grey Lady to her own devices. He told James Wentworth Day that other people have also seen this ghost at different times of the day but no one has any idea who she is or why she haunts the chapel at Glamis; there are those who say she is Janet, Lady Glamis, wife of the sixth Lord Glamis, who was burned alive at Edinburgh more than four hundred years ago.

In any re-examination of the ghost stories of Glamis — as far as this is possible — it seems crystal clear that a lot of nonsense has been talked and written about Glamis Castle, its secrets, its mysteries and its ghosts. An unbiased analysis of the many and varied reports would suggest that the only remaining mysteries are in the actual location of the secret rooms; the possible whereabouts of human remains; and the identity and validity of the Grey Lady — but then it would really be a shame to strip all the mystery from Glamis.

THE MYSTERY OF AMHERST

The haunted house at Amherst, Nova Scotia, scene of the 'Great Amherst Mystery'

Walter Hubbell, actor and author of *The Great Amherst Mystery*, the only contemporary account of one of the most remarkable and interesting cases of haunting on record

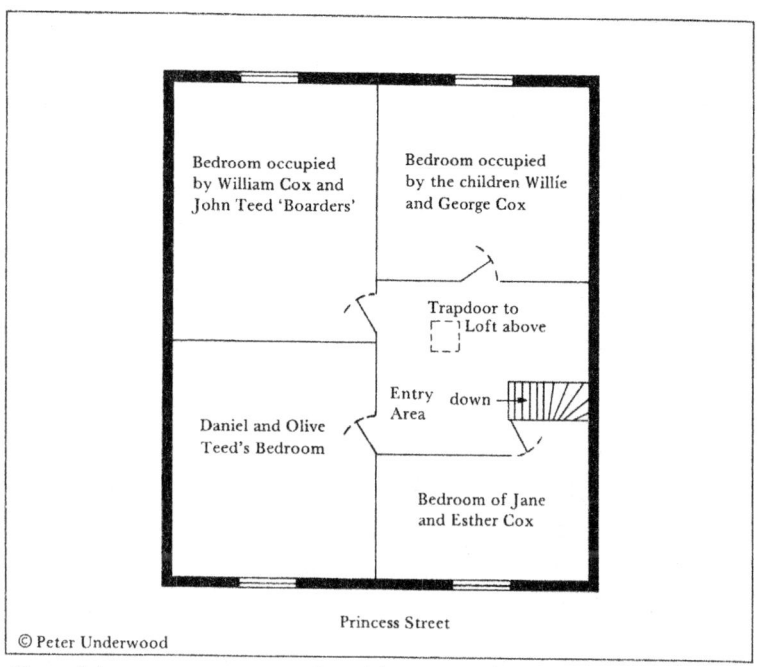

Plans of the two storey cottage of Daniel Teed and his family, Amherst, Nova Scotia, compiled from information in Walter Hubbell's *Great Amherst Mystery*, 1879

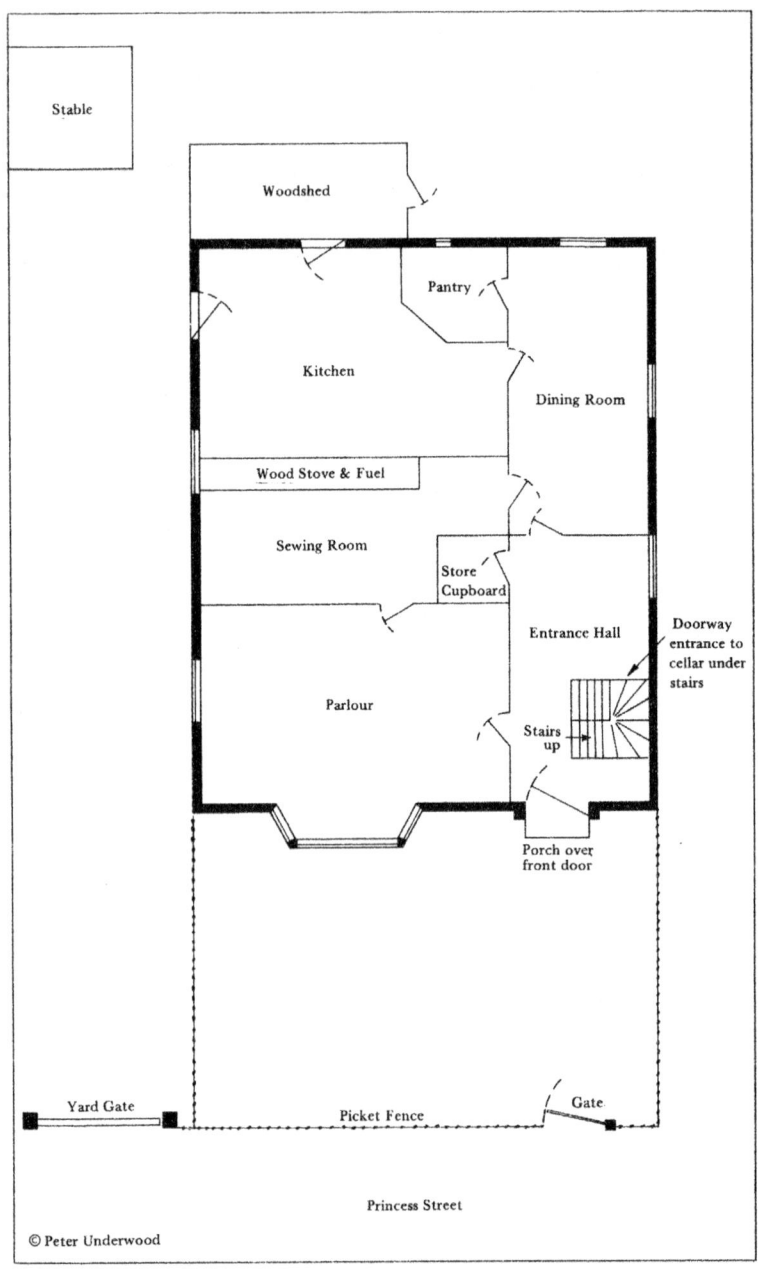

Plans of the two storey cottage of Daniel Teed and his family, Amherst, Nova Scotia, compiled from information in Walter Hubbell's *Great Amherst Mystery*, 1879

Described as 'one of the most famous poltergeist cases in history' [Hereward Carrington and Nandor Fodor, The Story of the Poltergeist Down the Centuries (Rider, 1953), p. 42] and 'one of the most interesting cases of its kind on record' [Professor William James during the course of his Presidential Address at the Society for Psychical Research, 1894], a critical reappraisal or even an unbiased reexamination of the so-called Great Amherst Mystery produces grounds for treating with considerable reserve the only contemporary record of the eleven months of strange happenings that took place at Amherst, Nova Scotia, and enhances the likelihood of a psychological explanation for some of the occurrences.

Walter Hubbell was a nineteenth-century strolling player, an actor and aspiring impresario, a man whose life was the unreal world of the theatre, the fairground and the music hall. He visited Amherst, heard about the strange happenings, went to see for himself and became involved with the story to such an extent that he presented the 'mystery' to the public by introducing the central figure on stage (with poor results) and in printed form [The Haunted House: A True Ghost Story. Being an Account of the Mysterious Manifestations that have taken place in the Presence of Esther Cox ... The Great Amherst Mystery (Saint John, NB, 1879)] with sensational results. The book ran into ten editions, many with additional material by the indefatigable Mr Hubbell, and sold some 60,000 copies. It is, to put it mildly, unfortunate that we have little more than Walter Hubbell's account of the Amherst mystery for consultation and reference, a case to which he gave the appellation 'Great', a typical gesture of the man and hardly inspiring confidence in his presentation of an exceedingly interesting haunting. According to Sacheverell Sitwell [Poltergeists (Faber and Faber, 1940)] it is 'a mystery, and one which becomes more, and not less, interesting the more that we examine it'.

Amherst, Nova Scotia, was (and still is) an attractive little township on the Bay of Fundy; it is a friendly place with an area of 3,500 acres, 128 miles from Halifax, and it likes to be known as the gateway to Nova Scotia. It is the chief town of Cumberland County and is now largely industrial with fine farmland all round and, in the distance, across the rolling marshes of Tantramar, the mountains of New Brunswick. In 1878, the date of the event that triggered off the disturbances, Amherst had a population of about 3,500; since then its population has roughly quadrupled. Amherst boasted at that time four churches, an academy, a music hall, an iron foundry, a shoe factory and a number of stores, shops and inns. There were some picturesque and sizeable private residences and many smaller houses; one of the latter, a neat, two-storey cottage on the corner of Princess Street in the middle of Amherst, was to become the focal point of Canada's best known ghost story.

Number 6, Princess Street, was a bright and clean-looking, yellow-painted wooden house with usually a bowl of flowers, often bright geraniums, in its front windows; it had a small yard at the front and a stable at the rear. Let us explore the interior of the cottage under the direction of Walter Hubbell:

'Upon entering the house everything was found to be so tastefully arranged, was so scrupulously dean and comfortable, that a visitor felt at home immediately, being confident that everything was under the personal direction of a thrifty housewife. The first floor [i.e. the ground floor] of the cottage consisted of four room. A parlour, lighted by a large bay window filled with beautiful geraniums of every imaginable colour and variety [!] was the first room to attract attention; then the dining room, with its old-fashioned clock, its numerous home-made rugs, easy chairs, and commodious table, made a visitor feel like dining, especially if the hour was near twelve, for, at about that time of day, savoury odours were sure to issue from the adjoining kitchen. The kitchen was all that a room of that kind in a village cottage should be; was not very large, and contained an ordinary wood-stove, a large pine table, and a small washstand; there was a door opening into the side yard near the stable, and another into the woodshed, besides the one connecting it with the dining room, making three doors in all and one window from which you could look into a narrow side yard. The fourth room on this floor was very small and was used as a sewing-room; it adjoined the dining room and parlour and had a door opening into each. Besides these four room, there was a large pantry having a small window about four feet from the floor, the door of this pantry opening into the dining room. Such was the arrangement of the rooms of the first floor. The doors of the dining room and parlour opened into a hallway leading from the front door. Upon entering the front door, at your right, you saw the stairway in the hall leading to the floor above, and upon ascending this stairway and turning to your left you found yourself on the second storey [i.e. upper storey] of the cottage, which consisted of an entry running at right angles with the hallway of the floor below.

'In about the centre of this entry was a trapdoor *without a ladder*, to the loft above, and opening into the entry, where the trapdoor was, were four small bedrooms, each one of which had one small window, and one door, there being no doors between the rooms. Two of these bedrooms faced Princess Street and the other two towards the back of the yard overlooking the stable. Like the rest of the house, all these bedrooms were conspicuous for their neat, cosy appearance, being all papered (except the one at the head of the stairs), and all painted, and furnished with ordinary cottage furniture. Everything about this little house would have impressed the most casual observer with the fact that its inmates were evidently happy and contented, if not rich. Such was the humble home of honest Daniel Teed, a shoemaker whom everybody knew and respected. He never owed a dollar to anyone if he could pay it, and never allowed his family to want for any comfort that could be provided with his hard-earned salary as foreman of the Amherst Shoe Factory.'

In 1878, the God-fearing, temperate and hard-working Daniel Teed was thirty-five years of age and the other occupants of his 'haunted house' consisted of his wife, Olive, their two small boys, Willie aged five years and George, coming up for two. In addition there were two of Mrs Teed's unmarried sisters, Jean and Esther Cox, aged twenty-one and eighteen respectively, their brother William, and John Teed, a brother of Daniel. The last two were 'boarders' who were also employed at the Amherst Shoe Factory, and the whole family were active members of the Wesleyan Methodist Church.

Jean (or Jennie as she was often called) seems to have been the 'village belle', an attractive — even beautiful — and self-possessed young lady with light brown hair, grey-blue eyes, a clear complexion and fine teeth. Understandably she had many admirers but she seems to have been a modest and religious girl; certainly she was a regular and presumably devout attendant at the local meeting hall. Esther, on the other hand, is described as 'low in stature and rather inclined to be short'; her dark brown, curly hair was cut short, her eyes were large and grey, and she had dark and very distinct eyebrows and long eyelashes. Her face was round with well-shaped features, she had handsome teeth, a pale complexion, small and well-shaped hands and feet and an 'earnest expression'. Esther was fond of housework and she was a great help in the house to her married sister. There was, it is said, an 'indescribable appearance of rugged honesty about her' that made this simple-hearted village maiden very attractive and appealing. She had lots of friends of her own age and was very popular with the younger children of the neighbourhood who were always ready for a romp and a game with Esther. She was a mild and gentle girl as a rule but with a determination and will of her own: when thwarted she would become moody or sulk for a while, becoming dark and sullen with 'a nervous temperament' — and it is with Esther that this case is primarily concerned.

On the night of 27th August Esther had a nightmare and it is obvious from the content that she was already worrying about her boy friend, Bob McNeal, and his desires and demands. It seemed, in her dream (which she related next morning to her sister Olive), that the colour of the cottage had changed from yellow to .green and all its occupants had changed into growling bears that glared at her with bloodshot eyes. Then she heard a noise in the street and on going to the door she saw hundreds of black bulls with blue eyes — very bright blue eyes — advancing on the house. Blood dripped from their mouths and their feet made sparks on the ground . . . roaring loudly they came straight for the cottage and broke down the picket fence . . . Esther, in her dream, hurriedly shut and fastened the front door and ran to the back one and shut that and locked it. Then the bulls began to butt the house so violently that it nearly fell over; it shook so that Esther woke up and found that she had fallen out of bed.

Next evening, 28 August 1878, Esther went out with Bob McNeal, who is an indistinct and vague figure in this drama of which he was, perhaps, a prime cause. Bob McNeal also worked at the Amherst Shoe Factory; he was tall and handsome, with jet-black hair, dark eyes and sported a fashionable small moustache. Although he was considered to be a good workman, there was something about the fellow that made people distrust him and he was regarded as an unsteady character. Neither Daniel nor Olive Teed were particularly pleased to see innocent Esther keeping company with such a lad — but what could they do?

It seems that for a while Esther and Bob had a happy time, Bob driving the starry-eyed girl through Amherst in the two-seater buggy that he had borrowed and then out into the surrounding woods. It was a merry and light-hearted evening with the carefree girl and the handsome boy holding hands and talking, making plans and exchanging promises — but as the shadows lengthened in the quiet woods so Bob's ardour increased. He was rebuffed three times for going too far, and calmed down, but soon he tried again to take advantage of the young girl in his arms with never a soul anywhere near . . . why couldn't she get down from the buggy and go with him into the woods? Again he was repulsed but this time he took offence and turned nasty. Jumping to the ground he suddenly produced a pistol, pointed it at Esther and told her to get out and walk ahead of him into the now darkening woods. Esther's determination at once showed itself: she liked Bob well enough and she had dreams of their future together but he wasn't going to force her to do anything she didn't want to do. She sat tight and told him not to be a silly fool, to put the gun away, get back into the buggy and put the cover up to keep off the rain that had just started.

Bob McNeal was used to having his own way with girls, if not by persuasion then by force, and with a stream of profanity that wiped the smile from Esther's lips, he jerked the pistol at her and repeated that she get down and do as he said, quickly — or it would be the worse for her. Esther turned her suddenly tear-stained face from him, sat tight and prepared herself for whatever might happen, for this was a different Bob from the boy she thought she knew and loved. He really looked as though he would use that pistol; yet surely he wouldn't, not after all those promises they had exchanged...?

As Esther braced herself and Bob's finger tightened on the trigger, they both heard the rumble of wheels approaching from the direction of Amherst. Bob hesitated, thought better of what he had almost done, suddenly put away the pistol, climbed back into the buggy, snatched up the reins and set the horse's head back towards the village, frightening Esther by the pace at which he drove, by his glowering face and by not saying a single word all the way back. He hadn't even bothered to raise the cover so Esther got more and more wet as the rain increased, but she wasn't going to ask him to do anything — anyway she had to concentrate on holding on and twice they were nearly upset. At the door of the Teed cottage Bob pulled the horse to a stop, Esther got down and turned to look up at 'her' Bob but, without a word, he drove off into the darkness. That night he left Amherst, evidently ashamed of his behaviour and alarmed at the possible consequences of attempting to rape Esther. As far as we know he never returned to Amherst and one wonders what he thought of the subsequent fame or notoriety of Esther Cox and the Amherst mystery — or did he do away with himself?

As for poor Esther, she ran indoors, drenched to the skin and without a word to anyone, packed herself off to bed and cried herself to sleep; and she cried herself to sleep for the next seven nights, until 3rd September. The following night saw the commencement of strange happenings. It was in fact a month before Esther found herself able to relate the events of that traumatic last evening with Bob McNeal.

A month, seven nights, a week; already something like a pattern was beginning to emerge, a pattern that was to run through the whole of the Amherst Mystery but before looking in detail at the peculiar happenings it might be of interest to consider some of the psychological implications of Esther's experience.

Esther was overshadowed by her more self-confident and beautiful sister; she had become very fond of Bob McNeal and was at an impressionable age; she was sexually mature and, from Hubbell's physical description, probably highly sexed; undoubtedly her shattering experience in the wood and Bob's subsequent action and disappearance must have come as a very severe shock and could well have sparked off a psychosomatic disorder — an ailment concerned with the interaction of body and mind. Psychologists tell us [A.J. Hadfield, Psychology and Mental Health (Allen & Unwin, 1950), p. 149] that there are few physical diseases which have no mental effects and few mental disorders that have no effect on the physiological organism. When a person is faced with a critical situation, such as imminent danger, organic changes take place first in the autonomic nervous system and visceral organs to prepare the organism for action, after which the energy liberated is normally discharged in voluntary action, either aggression or escape. But if the energy that is released cannot be discharged in voluntary action (when escape, for example, is impossible or impracticable for whatever reason), sobbing intermittently as sleep began to overtake her and the other drifting peacefully towards sleep.

Suddenly Esther sprang clean out of bed with a scream, exclaiming that there was a mouse under the bedclothes. Nearly startled out of her wits by the unexpected movement of her sister, just as she was about to drop off to sleep, Jean too jumped out of bed. Together the sisters stripped the bed but were unable to find a mouse or anything to explain Esther's alarm. Then Jean pointed out a movement within the mattress and, apparently satisfied that the mouse, if mouse it was, was inside the mattress and could not get out, the plucky country girls went back to sleep without further disturbance that night; and although no mouse was ever found (or rather there is no report of a mouse being found) it seems reasonable to suggest that this 'disturbance' was occasioned by a real live mouse or some other small rodent. We would probably never have heard of the event had it not been for subsequent happenings inside the neat yellow-painted cottage home of Mr and Mrs Teed and their family, but it is only fair to point out that in many genuine poltergeist infestations the initial disturbances are the easiest to explain.

The following night the sisters had not long been in bed before they both heard something moving about; but this time it seemed to be under the bed. The girls quietly got up, determined to find the mouse and kill it once and for all. They lit the lamp and, making a careful examination, they soon located a rustling noise emanating from a green cardboard box filled with pieces of patchwork that stood under the bed. Pulling the box into the centre of the little bedroom, the girls took up strategic positions for catching the mouse that they were convinced was inside the box when suddenly the box sprang into the air, a foot or more above the floor; then it dropped to the floor and turned on its side. Jean picked up the box. It seemed perfectly normal in weight but she could not see whether there was anything hiding among the patchwork. She stood the box upright again, in its old position — and started back in surprise when the box jumped again!

By now both girls were thoroughly frightened and they started screaming for help. Daniel Teed, in the adjoining room, quickly rose from his bed and went to see what was troubling the girls. They told him their story, pointing to the box, now stationary in the middle of the room, but Daniel, rudely awakened from his well-earned slumber, was in no mood to listen to such silly tales and he told the girls they must have been dreaming. He kicked the box back under the bed, telling the two sisters, still apparently frightened by their experience, to go back to bed and get to sleep and he was going to do the same.

Next morning, the girls still insisted that the box had jumped into the air by itself and turned on its side without either of them touching it but the rest of the family laughed at them for their silliness and treated the matter as a joke. It seems likely that a mouse had in fact got into the box and caused it to move about and fall on its side; perhaps the story of it jumping a foot into the air was something of an exaggeration, but that is understandable in the circumstances.

That day passed much like any other in the little cottage: Jean went to her work as a tailoress at Mr Dunlop's establishment; three of the household went to their work at the shoe factory; and Mrs Olive Teed, Esther and the two little boys busied themselves with their usual household chores and activities. The afternoon was pleasant, sunny and warm with a light breeze coming off the bay and Esther went for a walk, calling at the Post Office and at a bookshop before returning home in time for the evening meal. After supper Esther, seemingly relaxed and recovering from her shock and unhappiness of the past week, took up her accustomed place, sitting on the front doorstep, looking out into the peace of Princess Street. She remained there, alone with her thoughts, until the new moon rose high above the cottage; she even joked with Jean, saying she was sure that the next four weeks were going to be lucky ones for her because she had first glimpsed the new moon over her shoulder. Then, at eight-thirty, she said she felt feverish and both Mrs Teed and Jean suggested that she go to bed and have a good night's rest; little did they know what lay in store for poor Esther.

About an hour and a half later, around ten o'clock, Jean went to bed and she was relieved to see Esther in bed and soundly asleep. Slipping in beside her sister, carefully and quietly to cause as little disturbance as possible, Jean nestled down and prepared to go to sleep. She had been in bed perhaps fifteen minutes when suddenly and without any warning Esther sprang clean out of bed, dragging most of the bedclothes with her. The startled Jean turned to see her sister standing in the middle of the room, the bedclothes clutched around her, sobbing and calling pitifully, 'Jennie — Jennie — wake up — what is the matter with me? — Jennie — Jennie — Oh God! I'm dying!'

Jean quickly got out of bed herself, lighted the lamp and then turned towards Esther, still standing in the middle of the little bedroom and she was very startled at the sight that met her gaze. Esther's face was blood-red, her eyes were starting from their sockets, her short hair was almost standing on end and her hands grasped the back of a chair so tightly that her fingernails were denting the wood. She was trembling with fear, a pathetic figure in her dishevelled nightdress. Jean screamed for her sister, Olive, who came rushing into the bedroom followed by Daniel and the two boarders, all having been awakened by Esther's shouts. They stopped short when they saw poor Esther, obviously very much disturbed, physically and mentally — in fact the men all thought she had become mad. Not knowing what best to do they hurriedly covered her with one of the blankets that had dropped to the floor and sought to comfort her. After a little while they were relieved to see the awful high colour begin to ebb from the girl's face and she soon became very pale; but then she seemed to grow terribly weak and they had to help her back to her bed where she sat for a moment and then suddenly started to her feet, gazed about the room 'with a vacant stare' and exclaimed in an almost unrecognizable voice that she felt as though she was going to burst. Her family again helped her back to bed, persuaded her to lie down and covered her with a blanket; all the time she complained that her whole body was swelling up.

Daniel, quite convinced by now that he had a mad woman in the house, looked closely at the fluttering hands and restless face, turning first one way and then another. 'Why! the girl is swelling,' he exclaimed. 'Look at her hands and feet.' He touched her cheek and found it burning hot. Now Esther alternately flushed red and blanched white; she began to scream with pain as her whole body seemed to swell, the bedclothes rising up and up, her head, neck, hands and arms all visibly swelling. The family gazed at her, not knowing what to do for the girl who was grinding her teeth one moment, screaming the next, and all the time getting bigger and bigger — and then there was a loud report, like a clap of thunder but without any characteristic rumble. Mrs Olive Teed, thinking the cottage had been struck by a thunderbolt, feared for the safety of her two little ones and rushed to their bedroom, only to find the children sleeping peacefully — which suggests that the noise was confined to the bedroom containing Esther.

Back in Esther's room Olive pulled back the window

curtain and looked out. It was a quiet and peaceful night, lit by bright starlight. As she replaced the curtains three more terrific reports sounded in the room, and this time they seemed to originate from underneath the bed where Esther lay. The whole room shook and vibrated with the frightening noise but, after the three 'explosions', the watchers realized that Esther had stopped screaming. Hurrying to her bedside they were relieved to find that she had resumed her normal size and colouring and now seemed to be sleeping peacefully. For a while the family talked quietly about the strange occurrence (more like an epileptic fit than anything) and then, satisfied that Esther was indeed soundly slumbering in a natural sleep, they all went back to their beds, leaving Jean to watch over her sister. She too decided that all was now well with Esther and, quietly resuming her place beside her in the bed, the rest of the night passed uneventfully.

Next day Esther remained in her bed until about nine o'clock in the morning but when she did eventually get up she seemed to be her old self again, quite fit and strong, and she prepared a good breakfast for herself and ate it. Later she helped Olive with the housework, as usual, and went for a walk in the afternoon. At supper that evening the conversation turned to the unexplained sounds heard by all the adults in the house, but no one was able to offer any explanation; they all agreed that it was something 'too deep for them to explain' and it was agreed that the subject should be regarded as a family secret and that no one, friend or neighbour, should be told of the affair.

Four nights later, on 19th September, Esther suffered a

similar attack. It came on about ten o'clock, just as she was about to go to bed, and this time she had the presence of mind to get into bed and cover herself just as the swelling began. Jean, who was already in bed, advised Esther to remain perfectly quiet, saying that she was sure the attack would pass more quickly and then she would be able to go to sleep without any further disturbance. But it was not to be.

Esther, who had not stopped to put out the lamp, did her best to remain perfectly still in bed but after about five minutes all the bedclothes, except for the bottom sheet on which the girls lay, flew off the bed and settled in a confused heap in a corner of the bedroom. Both girls saw the sheet and blankets pass through the air by the light of the lamp which stood by their bed; by now they were thoroughly frightened and they both screamed at the top of their voices. Their cries brought all the adults in the house rushing into the little front bedroom and there they all saw the bedclothes piled into a heap in a corner, Esther visibly swollen again but quite conscious and Jean lying as though dead, for she had fainted.

Mrs Teed hurriedly covered the exposed forms of the two girls, picking up some of the bedclothes to do so but no sooner had she arranged them over the girls and stepped back than the coverings flew off the bed again and landed in the same corner. Furthermore the pillow, on which Esther's head had been resting, slid from under her and flew across the room into John Teed's face. This surprise attack on an innocent bystander was too much for John Teed, Daniel's brother, and he said he had had enough of it and was going back to his room, nor could he be persuaded to assist the others who were contriving to cover the girls, having to sit on both sides of the bed to prevent the covers flying off.

By this time Jean had recovered. William Cox was sent to the kitchen to fetch a bucket of water to bathe Esther's aching head but, just as he arrived back at the bedroom door, a rapid succession of reports sounded from the direction of the bed where the two frightened girls lay. So loud were these reports that, according to Walter Hubbell, the whole room trembled and vibrated. Esther, who only a moment earlier had been lying there painfully swollen, instantly resumed her natural and normal appearance, all signs of swelling disappeared and within a very few moments she had fallen into a deep and healthy sleep. Once again the cottage seemed peaceful and after a few moments' discussion all the members of the family returned to their rooms. But there was little sleep for anyone that night and each person in the house tossed and turned in their beds asking themselves what had come to plague this happy little family and especially poor, unhappy Esther.

In the morning both Jean and Esther complained of feeling very weak (as though strength had somehow been drained from them during the night or by the events preceding the night) and this applied especially to Esther who, although she rose with her sister, found that she had to lie down in the parlour while breakfast was being prepared. During the course of this meal the noises, the movement of objects and the sufferings of everyone, particularly Esther, were naturally the main topics of conversation and it was unanimously agreed that the local doctor should be consulted.

Accordingly that afternoon Daniel Teed left his work early and went to see Dr Carritte. As soberly and sensibly as he could in the circumstances Daniel related to the doctor the story of the curious happenings that appeared to be centred around Esther; Dr Carritte laughed at the story and scorned Daniel's concern until, at long last, the hard-working little man whom the doctor had known for many years succeeded by his earnest demeanour and honest behaviour in convincing the doctor that something was amiss at the cottage. At length Dr Carritte said he would call at the cottage that evening — and remain all night if he felt that it was necessary. He added, however, that he was quite certain that what Daniel Teed had told him was a lot of nonsense and he was convinced that nothing of the kind would happen while he was at the house.

At ten o'clock that night, just as all the occupants had given up any hope of his coming, the doctor arrived at the Teed cottage. He learned (nodding his head wisely as though to say it was no more than he had expected) that Esther had not been subjected to any strange fit so far that night, nor had any odd noises been heard. In fact Esther had been in bed a full hour and all seemed to be well. Dr Carritte said, since he was there, he would see Esther and sit with her for a while. The doctor felt Esther's pulse, looked at her tongue and her eyes, tested her reflexes and then confirmed to the waiting family that Esther seemed to be suffering from nervous excitement (she could have been sexually excited) and that she had evidently received a tremendous shock of some kind. He had just given this opinion and was still seated beside Esther's bed when the pillow beneath her head started to move. As the doctor — open-mouthed in amazement — and the rest of the family watched, the pillow came out as though it might have been pulled by some invisible power; out it came, the whole pillow with the exception of one corner; then the pillow straightened itself out as if filled with air, remained so for a moment and then went back into place beneath Esther's head!

The doctor looked at the watching family. There could be no doubt about it — that pillow had moved by itself and everyone in the room had seen it. John Teed nodded as he caught the doctor's eye. 'Yes, it moved; and if it moves again I'll grab hold of it — even if it did bang me over the head last night...' No sooner were the words spoken than the pillow again moved out from underneath Esther's head, exactly as before. As good as his word John Teed stepped forward and, waiting until the pillow began to return back under Esther's head, John took hold of it with both hands and held on with his whole strength. All his efforts were as nothing — the pillow was pulled from his strong young hands by some far stronger but invisible force or power — and the pillow resumed its position beneath Esther's head.

Dr Carritte was suitably impressed and he rose from his chair — when suddenly loud reports began to sound, apparently emanating from beneath the bed upon which Esther lay. The doctor was quickly on his knees, searching for their origin or cause but he found nothing to explain the reports or loud raps; he left the bed and walked towards the door of the bedroom where the family were huddled, watching and waiting. As the doctor walked across the bedroom floor the sound of sharp raps seemed to follow him and to come from the floorboards of the little room.

A moment later all the bedclothes covering Esther lifted themselves from the bed and flew across the room, leaving the terrified girl exposed and trembling with fright. As Dr Carritte and Mrs Teed struggled to replace the bedclothes and to get them to remain on the bed, a new and frightening phenomenon demonstrated itself. A loud scratching noise attracted their attention; it seemed to come from the wall above Esther's head. There was a metallic quality about the sound, a disquieting and startling noise. They looked up at the wall and saw writing form there, huge characters being traced by an invisible hand wielding an invisible instrument, but the words were written plainly enough, in fact they were deeply indented into the wall as though caused by an iron spike or something of the kind. The words struck terror into the heart of Esther and chilled the blood of everyone in the room for in plain letters, uneven but clear, inelegant but deeply cut into the plaster, was the terrible message: 'Esther Cox, you are mine to kill.'

This writing was seen by everyone in the room at the time, that is, Mr and Mrs Teed, Jean and Esther Cox, John Teed, William Cox and Dr Carritte. According to Walter Hubbell, it remained visible for years afterwards and was seen by literally hundreds of people, local folk from Amherst and visitors who came to see something of the odd happenings at the cottage of Daniel Teed. But by the time the prominent American psychical researcher Hereward Carrington visited Amherst in 1907 [see his Personal Experiences of Spiritualism (T. Werner Laurie, 1913)] the cottage had been occupied for some years by a Mrs Cahill; it had been entirely renovated, repapered, painted and restored, and all traces of any markings on the wall of the bedroom once occupied by Jean and Esther Cox had been entirely removed or were no longer visible. We will return to Hereward Carrington's findings a little later. As Dr Carritte stood by the door talking to Mr and Mrs Teed and wondering what it all meant and what explanation he could offer, a large piece of plaster came flying through the air and fell at his feet. It somehow detached itself from a wall and, it was subsequently established, to reach the spot where it landed, it had to turn a corner! Dr Carritte, more than a little bewildered by all that had happened in such a short time, more or less mechanically picked up the piece of plaster and placed it carefully upon a chair nearby. No sooner had he done so than the loud pounding sounds began again, seemingly with redoubled power, so that the whole room and its contents shook, including Dr Carritte and the other persons present, while Esther still lay on her bed, frightened and trembling.

After about two hours the noises became less violent and finally ceased, enabling Esther to go to sleep and the doctor to leave the house with a promise that he would return in the morning. Although he was unable to suggest any explanation for the strange happenings he had witnessed, he had no doubt that what he had heard and seen were manifestations of some invisible power that seemed to possess intelligence 'of a very low order' and of a 'demonical type' — directly connected with Esther's nervous excitation. He said he would bring a sedative for her when he came again.

When he duly arrived at the cottage next morning (doubtless wondering whether the events of the previous night had perhaps been a dream) he was more than a little surprised to find Esther up and dressed and helping Mrs Teed with various household duties. In reply to his questions, she insisted that she felt quite well, except that she was so nervous that any sudden sound startled her and made her jump. Esther told Dr Carritte that she had just gone down to the cellar with a pan of milk and soon rushed back up again (very out of breath) because someone or something had 'thrown a plank at her' in the cellar. Dr Carritte said he would go down into the cellar himself and see what was down there. He did so, Esther remaining in the dining-room; and a moment later he returned to say that the cellar was devoid of any person or any thing that could throw a piece of plank or anything else. He asked Esther to accompany him and together they went down into the cellar but no sooner had their feet touched the cellar floor than several potatoes came flying across the cellar, apparently aimed at their heads, and they both beat a hasty retreat up the cellar stairs. Shortly afterwards the doctor left the house saying he would return later in the day.

Dr Carritte returned to the cottage in the evening, to prescribe and administer an injection of morphia since Esther was still complaining of her nerves and of what she called 'electric currents' passing through her body. As he left her bedside the doctor assured Esther that she would enjoy a good night's rest and feel all the better for it in the morning but he had not reached the door of the bedroom before a series of loud reports sounded from the direction of his patient's bed. As he stopped to listen and judge the sounds, which he decided were louder and more frequent than those he had heard the previous evening, the sounds seemed to move out into the centre of the room and then to leave the room entirely and ascend to the rafters or roof of the house. Thinking the noises might be the result of some external cause, Dr Carritte went out of the house and into the little yard in front of the cottage. It was a bright moonlit night and, although he was satisfied that there was nothing visible on the roof to account for the sounds, and that no person was anywhere about, yet he could still hear the noises, just like someone pounding the roof with a sledgehammer. The doctor remained at the cottage until after midnight when the mysterious reports were still sounding and he could hear them, as he walked away from the cottage, until he was out of earshot.

Such disturbances could not be kept secret and during the following week it became common knowledge that Daniel Teed's cottage was the centre of strange manifestations; passers-by heard the loud hammering noises which were now incessant and it is reported that Esther 'seemed to derive physical relief from their occurrence' [R.S. Lambert, Exploring the Supernatural (Arthur Barker, n.d.), p. 96]. Reports of the disturbances appeared in the local newspaper, the Amherst Gazette, and they were picked up by other papers. The story spread and grew, and lost nothing in the telling... the pounding noises, it was said, began soon after daybreak and went on all through the day and long into the night; this continued for three weeks with Dr Carritte calling three times a day. By now the puzzled doctor did not know what to do to help his patient and then one night the odd happenings took a fresh turn. As Dr Carritte sat at Esther's bedside, as he had so often done during the past weeks, Esther was suddenly seized by a spasm: she threw her arms high above her head, her whole body became rigid and she lapsed into a cataplectic trance. In this state she began to talk in a strange, flat voice and for the first time revealed the full story of what had taken place between her and Bob McNeal on the night of 28th August, more than a month earlier. It was the first time the family really knew what had happened and when Esther came out of the trance, they told her what she had said and, tearfully, Esther agreed that it was the whole truth.

At this point Mrs Olive Teed made a curious and somewhat puzzling pronouncement. Although, as far as is known, neither she nor anyone else knew where Bob McNeal was or what had happened to him since he brought Esther home a month earlier, Olive Teed remarked that 'it must be Bob who is responsible for Esther's trouble'. This statement seems to have met with an immediate response and three loud raps sounded on the bedroom wall, which prompted Jean to suggest that whatever was producing the noises seemed to have intelligence and to understand what was said. Three raps immediately greeted this statement. Dr Carritte then began to ask questions and by means of a simple code on the lines of one rap for 'yes', two for 'no' and three for 'doubtful' or 'unknown', sensible answers were obtained to simple leading questions — such as the number of people present in the bedroom — but all his efforts to obtain an explanation or solution to the mystery were unrewarded.

Soon various people began calling at the cottage, wishing to see and hear something of the wonders that were being reported. Among the early visitors were two ministers, Dr Edwin Clay, a Baptist and the Revd R.A. Temple, the Wesleyan pastor at Amherst. Dr Clay was fortunate enough to hear a number of loud reports and he saw the sinister writing on the wall; he said he was fully satisfied that neither Esther nor any of the family were in any way consciously responsible for what was happening and he agreed with Dr Carritte that the severe shock to Esther's nervous system might, in some unknown way, have caused the unfortunate girl to become a sort of electric battery: invisible flashes of lightning left her person, coinciding with periodic spasms of pain, and the sounds that everyone could hear were simply minute peals of thunder. Indeed Dr Clay was so convinced that he had hit on the solution to the Amherst Mystery that he produced and delivered lectures on the subject. Electricity was as yet little understood and something of a novelty, commercial electric lighting having been in use for about three years and electric trams and street cars only about a year. In fact these reverent gentlemen pestered the lives out of Esther Cox and the Teed family at all hours of the day and night for months, until Esther fell ill with diphtheria. But it should be emphasized that they always defended Esther and the family when anyone talked about fraud, and they sometimes mentioned the manifestations from their pulpits.

Another minister, however, Dr Nathan Tupper, repeatedly voiced his opinion that Esther was either a mesmerist or a fraud. He may have been nearer the answer than many people thought for it does appear that Esther may have exerted what amounted to an hypnotic influence, first on Jean, then on the rest of the family, and extending to Dr Carritte and many other visitors. It also seems very likely that fraud played a part, especially in the latter stages of the case, as we shall see. Dr Tupper thought the evil could be driven out of the girl by a strong raw-hide whip 'laid across Esther's bare shoulders by a powerful arm'.

The Revd R.A. Temple, their own minister, said he was witness to a particularly curious incident when a bucket of cold water, standing on the kitchen table, became agitated as though boiling, although the water remained cold. Esther was present but nowhere near the bucket at the time. It is an effect that could have been produced in a number of ways and it is perhaps the first incident in the house of mystery that smacks of conscious fraud.

More and more people made their way to the simple little cottage, sometimes as many as a hundred being squeezed into the house or inside the fenced yard. Many heard the strange sounds and would loiter about the cottage for hours until the local police were called to keep order. As well as the noises there were more 'messages', written on scraps of paper that 'came out of the air' and fell at the feet of inhabitant or visitor; and all the messages were threatening in character, mostly towards Esther. So things continued until December when Esther was ill with diphtheria and during the two weeks that she was confined to her bed with this illness, the disturbances completely ceased.

When she recovered Esther went to stay with another married sister, Mrs John Snowdon, at Sackville, about ten miles away, and for a further two weeks she was completely free from any of the troubles that had so disturbed the household of Mr and Mrs Daniel Teed at Amherst. As Walter Hubbell put it, 'The power did not follow her, and while there she was free from the torture it gave her, when moving about in her abdomen, which caused her to swell so fearfully and feel like bursting.' This revealing description strongly suggests a psychosomatic illness, perhaps a phantom pregnancy.

On return to the Teed cottage in January 1879, more 'startling and peculiar' manifestations were reported. Esther and Jean had been put in another bedroom in the hope that the 'power' would not follow them and, one night, as they lay side by side in bed, Esther told her sister that she could hear a voice telling her that the house would be set on fire by a ghost. The voice said it had once lived on earth but had been dead for some years and was now only a ghost: the threat was not treated with any seriousness but nevertheless the family were called in and Esther told them what the voice had said. Even as the matter was being discussed everyone present saw a lighted match fall from the ceiling on to the bed where it would almost certainly have started a fire had not Jean hurried forward and put it out. During the next ten minutes, eight more lighted matches fell on to the bed and about the room but they were all extinguished before they could do any damage. Walter Hubbell tells us they 'came out of the air'. Later that night the loud reports began again.

Having previously established to their satisfaction that the entity haunting the cottage could communicate by means of rapping, Daniel Teed now asked whether the house would really be set on fire and the reply was, 'yes'. In fact, no more than five minutes later one of Esther's dresses was found rolled up under the bed and alight! Fortunately Daniel acted quickly: he pulled the dress out from under the bed and stamped out the fire. Nevertheless the family spent a worried night and in the morning all the occupants were much concerned that fire would break out in some inaccessible part of the cottage where it could not be extinguished and nothing could then save the place from being burned down. They kept careful watch and for three days there were no inexplicable outbreaks of fire and then, just when the family were beginning to relax, Mrs Teed, busy churning butter in the kitchen, shouted that she could smell burning and that it appeared to be coming from the cellar.

Esther, in the dining room at the time, came running and together they filled buckets with water and hurried down into the cellar. There, in the far corner, they found a barrel of wood shavings well alight and blazing fiercely. Realizing that the fire was beyond their power to extinguish, they ran back upstairs and out into the street, half-choked with the smoke, shouting 'Fire' at the top of their voices. While they were so engaged a passer-by picked up their doormat, found his way down into the cellar and there put out the fire — and left without giving his name. When the firemen eventually arrived they listened to the story and seemed to think that Esther had been responsible. They were especially annoyed because, as they pointed out, had the

Teed cottage really been on fire and the wind blowing in a certain direction, half of Amherst could have been burned down.

During the following week the rappings, loud reports and occasional outbreaks of fire continued and Daniel was advised to send his sister-in-law away from the house. All the family were by this time convinced that the mysterious power was about to claim to be the ghost of some evil man who, in some unknown manner, had managed to torture poor Esther. Walter Hubbell states that Daniel Teed 'explained the true nature of the torture . . . but it must be nameless . . .'. It seems likely that the torture to Esther was of a sexual character. A neighbour, John W. White, offered to take Esther into his household in return for some housework and so Esther again moved out of the cottage and again the manifestations ceased completely; then during her third or fourth week at the White home, a scrubbing brush flew from Esther's hand as she worked. It went upwards, bounced off the ceiling and hit Esther on the head as it returned to the floor.

John White could see the beginning of trouble and he sought to keep Esther busy outside his home. He owned a restaurant in the main street of Amherst and he took Esther there each morning. He decided that there might be something in the idea that the disturbances were due to electrical discharges and he therefore arranged for Esther to insulate herself from contact with the ground by wearing thin glass soles inside her shoes! However Esther found that these insulations gave her headaches and caused her nose to bleed (or so she believed) so they were discarded — and then the White restaurant began to be plagued by various disturbances: doors refused to remain closed, furniture moved without visible contact, loud knocking noises were heard and on one occasion a little boy's penknife flew out of his hand and stabbed itself in Esther's back, drawing blood; and three large iron spikes, laid in Esther's lap by curious visitors, grew so hot that they could hardly be touched and then they jumped out of her lap and finished up twenty feet away. Understandably John White decided that Esther was more of a liability than an asset and he sent her back to the Teeds but she was there only a short time before Captain James Beck and his wife invited her to stay with them at their house in St John, New Brunswick, 135 miles from Amherst.

While a guest in the Beck household for three weeks during March 1879, Esther was the subject of some scrutiny by several medical men and scientists who sought to discover an explanation for the phenomena that had reportedly happened in her presence. Esther obligingly recounted her many experiences and related that a number of 'ghosts' were threatening her with mischief of one kind and another. The chief entities that were now troubling Esther were (she said) named 'Peter Cox', 'Maggie Fisher' and 'Bob Nickle' — all interesting names with sexual connotations, the last obviously based on the troublesome and elusive Bob McNeal. This ghost, said Esther, specialized in threatening her with fire and stabbings.

After leaving the Becks, Esther stayed for eight weeks with Mr and Mrs Van Ambergh on a farm three miles from Amherst where she found peace and freedom from the 'ghosts'. It was now almost midsummer and Esther prepared to return to the Teeds, seemingly cured, but she had hardly settled back with her sister Jean and everyone else before the affair reached yet another stage.

During the previous few weeks Daniel and Olive Teed had been corresponding with a man who had contrived to get himself accepted as a 'paying guest' by the Teeds, while he observed Esther and studied her phenomena at first hand. That man was Walter Hubbell, an out of work actor who saw in Esther and her manifestations the chance to pocket a few shillings, one way or another. No good reason has ever been advanced or discovered for Hubbell having anything to do with Esther Cox, her family or even Amherst and it would not seem to be unduly unfair to attribute his presence to a combination of curiosity and the possibility of making some money out of the strange and well-attested happenings; nor would it seem to be unfair to say that Hubbell 'dramatized' and 'embellished' the story here and there (indeed Olive Teed told Hereward Carrington as much in January 1907 [Personal Experiences in Spiritualism (T. Werner Laurie, 1913), p. 114]) but allowing for all that we are still left with some very peculiar occurrences taking place at Amherst in the presence of Esther Cox and other reliable witnesses in 1878 and 1879.

During the course of his first day at the Teed's cottage, Hubbell must have wondered what he had let himself in for — or been overjoyed at the wealth of apparently paranormal phenomena that was still manifesting itself; he had hardly had time to meet the family before his umbrella, which he had placed in a corner of the dining room, sailed over his head and landed fifteen feet from where he had left it. Almost at the same time a large carving knife apparently projected itself over the top of Esther's head and fell to the floor at his feet. Shortly afterwards the bag containing his papers and documents was propelled a distance of ten feet and a little later a chair slid across the floor without anyone touching it, knocking into the one on which Hubbell was sitting with enough force to almost knock him to the floor. Then, he reports, whatever chairs there might be in whatever room he entered began to move and slide about the various rooms: Esther informed him that she thought this must be a sign that he was unpopular with the 'ghosts' — perhaps in common with many 'ghosts' they disliked the presence of a sceptic. Unfortunately Hubbell does not relate these odd happenings in any kind of scientific manner; even the witnesses (other than Esther, presumably) are not named. At no time does he detail the exact positions of those present so that we are entirely dependent upon his somewhat colourful account of the happenings that day. Nor were the strange happenings by any means finished. During the midday meal raps were heard and Hubbell tells us that he carried on a conversation by means of the already established code.

After the meal Hubbell lay down on the sofa and pretended to take a nap. Soon he saw Esther come into the room and look for a newspaper and as he surreptitiously watched her, he saw a large glass paperweight at the opposite end of the room suddenly fly through the air for a distance of about fifteen feet. It struck the arm of the sofa where he lay, rebounded on to a chair, spun for a few seconds and then became stationary. Hubbell pretended to wake up and asked Esther to remain in the room; at this moment little George wandered in and sat down. No sooner had he done so than one of his shoes flew up and struck him on the head. Anyone who has ever had anything to do with young children might be forgiven for rejecting this little incident as having a paranormal origin and in fact it is generally considered that, after Walter Hubbell went to live with the Teeds, the case almost degenerated into farce. But for the sake of completeness it might be interesting to review briefly these latter incidents.

Walter Hubbell arrived at the Teed cottage on a Saturday and the following day, Sunday, no manifestations were reported. On the Monday, however, the disturbances included the disappearance of a china sugar bowl which reappeared ten minutes later, apparently falling from the ceiling. Several mats were moved. A flowerpot containing a plant in full bloom and a can full of water were moved, one from the bay windows in the parlour and the other from the kitchen and set down side by side on the parlour floor. A large inkstand and two bottles 'flew through the air' in the direction of Hubbell, a fire was started upstairs and all the chairs in the parlour were found piled in a heap that collapsed with a crash without anyone being near them.

Next day, a Tuesday, noises suggesting the sawing of wood and the drumming on a washboard were heard from underneath several tables; a number of knives were thrown at Hubbell; and Esther said she was being plagued by six 'ghosts' and that some of them were sticking pins into her! These pins apparently appeared from out of the air and Hubbell says he pulled thirty from different parts of Esther's body. A chair, says Hubbell, followed Esther downstairs from her bedroom when the only other person in the house at the time was Mrs Teed who was in the kitchen. It will have been noticed that phenomena of a new and hitherto unparalleled nature attended the appearance of Walter Hubbell at the cottage, and after the family had experienced such disturbances as — forty-five fires in one day (none of them serious); the sound of a trumpet that was heard all over the house and ceased when an actual silver German trumpet was found in one of the rooms, an article that no one claimed to have seen before; Esther had her head cut open and was stabbed in the face with a dinner fork after she had visited the Revd R.A. Temple and asked him to pray for her; and the disappearance and reappearance of various small objects, seemingly falling from the ceiling—then Walter Hubbell revealed an ulterior motive for his interest, study and prolonged stay with the Teeds.

Hubbell suggested that Esther's 'gifts' should be commercialized and he was the man to do it. At length it was agreed and Hubbell hired a public hall and sold tickets to the people of Amherst and the surrounding district, presenting them, as he put it, with the opportunity of seeing Esther actually produce some of the manifestations that had become the talk of the area. The experiment was a fiasco. So many people were there that the hall was crowded, and Esther was there, but of the 'ghosts' there was no sign. So great was the disappointment of the audience that many of them demanded the return of the money they had paid to see Esther 'perform'.

It was a setback for Hubbell and was probably instrumental in his decision to write a book about the curious happenings. For Daniel Teed it was the final straw. It was now July 1879 and he and his wife were weary of the whole affair; nor were they alone. The Teeds were only the tenants of the cottage; the owner, a Mr Bliss, did not like the way his property was being treated and he insisted that Esther leave the house. The Teeds' two paying boarders had already left. Much of the crockery and furniture in their home was broken, their food was continually being spoiled, the walls and doors of the cottage were damaged and their homely little cottage was beginning to become a place of disorder and turmoil instead of the neat and tidy home of a year earlier. Daniel and Olive Teed agreed that Esther should leave and also the 'paying guest', Hubbell, whose flagrant publicizing of the disturbances grew with each day. It was arranged that Esther would again go to stay with the Van Amberghs and Hubbell left the Teed household at the same time; the following month Hubbell visited Esther at her new home and found her completely free from any manifestations and far more serene and contented than he had ever known her. He returned to St John, where he had lodgings, and began to put into some order the notes he had about Esther and the disturbances at the Teed cottage and to prepare publication of the work that was to be the only comprehensive and contemporary record of the Great Amherst Mystery.

Three months later he wrote to Mr and Mrs Teed to inquire after Esther's health and to receive news of any recent manifestations. The reply came from Jean, who wrote on behalf of the family to tell him that Esther was in prison where she had been for a week and where she was to stay for four months. It seemed that after staying with the Van Amberghs, Esther had obtained a position as a servant at a neighbouring farm belonging to a family named Davison. Soon after she left, the Van Amberghs missed various articles of clothing and they were discovered hidden in a barn belonging to the Davisons. Esther was accused (by Davison) of taking the clothes but, before anything could be proved, the barn where the clothes were found was burned to the ground; Esther was the last person seen near the place and she was accused of arson and convicted. Local public opinion, however, was on Esther's side; many people had experienced happenings at the cottage that they were satisfied Esther could not have contrived or engineered and she was soon released from prison. Before long she was married, not too happily by all accounts, but there are no more reports of odd or inexplicable happenings and Esther Cox fades into oblivion. We know that she died in 1912.

In January 1907 Hereward Carrington, the noted American psychical researcher, went to Nova Scotia in order to inquire into an alleged poltergeist case and he took the opportunity of calling at Amherst to see what he could gather in the way of first-hand evidence pertaining to the 'Amherst Mystery'. Many of the witnesses were dead, including Dr Carritte, while others, including Jean Cox, John Teed and William Cox seemed to have disappeared without trace; but he was able to see and talk with Daniel and Olive Teed and Esther Cox herself.

Mr and Mrs Teed were no longer living at Number 6,

Princess Street (as we have seen) and Carrington seems to have been impressed by Mrs Teed's testimony. She remembered very well all that had happened and maintained that Walter Hubbell's book was substantially correct although he had 'dramatized and embellished' in places; she even recounted one or two incidents not included in Hubbell's book; these involved the jumping into the air of a 'dish-pan' in the kitchen and the movement of furniture in Esther's room when Esther was asleep and under observation and other apparently inexplicable movements of objects. Mrs Teed insisted that to her knowledge nothing in the nature of fraud had ever been discovered in connection with the case and certainly the 'independent voices in the air' and the writing on the wall were 'terrible realities'. The whole family had been terrified and had constantly sought for a normal explanation but without success. Carrington came away from Mr and Mrs Teed (having obtained Esther's address) convinced that, whatever the interpretation of the facts, Esther alone was responsible for them and all the other members of the family were entirely innocent of any participation.

Carrington then proceeded to interview Esther in Massachusetts where he found her living with her husband in a small cottage. In answer to his questions, she replied, with considerable reluctance, that the 'power' had not visited her since her marriage although Carrington gained the distinct impression that she still believed in the supernatural origin of the manifestations. When he questioned her further, however, she said she didn't want to talk about it as she was 'afraid they would come back'; she showed great reluctance to discuss the matter and seemed somewhat annoyed and irritated by Hubbell's book and by her sister having given Carrington her address. Carrington tried his best to get more information out of her but the more he questioned her, the more irritated she became and finally her husband intervened to say that she would give him all the necessary details for a hundred dollars! Carrington pointed out the worthlessness of any information obtained in such a manner and, deciding that it was pointless to prolong the interview, he left. Subsequent inquiries by Hereward Carrington revealed that Esther was regarded by her employers as a very hardworking woman, respectable, honest and reliable, 'not at all of an imaginative turn of mind' and not likely to make up stories. A second attempt to obtain testimony from Esther was no more successful than the first; she said she 'dared not talk about it' and it may be that she was by then acting under orders from her husband. Poor Esther, one feels she deserved better.

In June 1908 Walter Hubbell revisited Amherst (what a pity Hereward Carrington did not interview him) and, doubtless using his persuasive powers to the full, he obtained a testamentary document signed by sixteen inhabitants who stated that from their own personal knowledge 'manifestations and communications of an invisible intelligence and malicious power' demonstrated for the period described by Walter Hubbell and that his written account of the case was a 'true narrative of the supernatural'; he also seems to have obtained possession of a letter from Arthur Davison (the owner of the burned-down barn) to a Mr Fred E. Morgan, dated 24 April 1893, during the course of which Davison reveals that Esther worked for him for three months and 'a better girl we never had since', adding, revealingly 'I have often watched her to find out how she came downstairs, she seemed to fly'. He described her as 'not good-looking, very ignorant, only a common education, could read and write but not spell and very afraid of "it"'. Davison states that he tried several times to teach Esther to exert control by will-power but just as he gained a point she would become very afraid and nothing would induce her to go any further nor do anything more that he asked. On several occasions he and Dr Carritte found Esther in a semiconscious state and once the doctor thought she was going to die. Tappings were heard, Esther would swell up 'from her breasts down to her legs', articles were thrown and there were other curious happenings. He ends his letter: 'We put up with all these things, as it was hard at the time to get help, especially like her, until she set my barn on fire; we then had her put in jail, since then I don't know if she has had any of her turns. She got married, married poor, and has several children...'

Twelve years later Dr Walter F. Prince, another prominent psychical researcher, published a critical study of the Amherst case in the Proceedings of the American Society for Psychical Research [Volume XIII, 1919]. He complained of the dearth of witnesses, the lack of detail, the fact that incidents which occurred before Hubbell arrived at Amherst are described by him in greater detail than those at which he was present; he points out a number of inconsistencies and discrepancies and he theorized that Esther was a case of dual-personality; that she had a 'psycho-neurotic' constitution, liable to disintegrate under shock and strain and that her frustrated love affair and attempted rape by Bob McNeal was such a shock that it led to self-repulsion so severe that it exploded to expose a secondary personality. It was this personality which was responsible for the 'crafty performance of all the various antics' while Esther herself, in her normal personality, had no idea of what she did in her altered and abnormal personality.

Any detailed examination of the case reveals that Esther was an hysterical and abnormal individual and that she was capable of criminal and fraudulent acts. It seems within the bounds of possibility that, certainly during the later period of the 'haunting', she 'helped out' the phenomena. It is tempting to believe that Esther Cox consciously produced most of the remarkable manifestations and that the remainder were the result of malobservation, fraud and inaccurate description. However, Esther herself suffered more than anyone as a result of the disturbances. She was the one who swelled up until she thought she was going to burst; she was the one who lost her sleep and was so frightened that she became rigid with terror; she was the one who was stabbed; she was the one who was threatened and attacked and was the subject of hatred and ridicule. It was her home that was repeatedly set on fire and almost destroyed, forcing her to leave — and it does seem incredible that any girl would do such things when she stood to gain nothing. In fact, on the evidence presented, it is impossible for Esther to have been responsible for all the manifestations although it must be generally agreed that, while the earlier disturbances were probably paranormal in their origin, later happenings have the flavour of fraud.

It cannot but be interesting to recall that the onset of

the curious happenings followed a terrifying sexual assault upon a young adolescent girl, and that, according to Walter Hubbell, many of the subsequent manifestations took place at regular intervals with, the 'power' always at its greatest strength every twenty-eight days — a periodicity, as Harry Price points out [Poltergeist Over England (Country life, 1945), p. 377], corresponding with the menstrual flux.

A very different reason for this twenty-eight day cycle has been suggested by Guy Lambert (a former president of the Society for Psychical Research) during the course of his interesting theory that subterranean flood water accounts for many so-called poltergeist cases ['Poltergeists: A Physical Theory', Society for Psychical Research Journal, Volume 38, number 684, pp. 49—71] and he points out that 'Amherst is on the Bay of Fundy where the tides run higher than anywhere else in the world'. His researches have revealed another tide effect, in addition to the direct action of tidal water, and this is the idea that the great weight of a rising tide advancing towards the land depresses the shore. He quotes G.H. Darwin [The Tides (John Murray, 1898), p. 122]: 'As low tide changes to high tide the position of an enormous mass of water is varied with respect to the land; accordingly the whole coastline must rock to and fro with the varying tide.' The difficulty with such a theory is always much the same: why, if there is such a simple physical cause, are the disturbances confined to one small cottage in the centre of a community and often to one room in one house; why does the trouble suddenly flare up and as suddenly cease, and why does it appear to follow one of the occupants of the affected property, usually an adolescent, when that person, more often a girl than a boy, is removed to another place often miles away? On the other hand problems in the psychological make-up of certain individuals associated with 'hauntings' often well repays investigation and one is not then faced with such insuperable problems.

Remembered guilt or sense of shame or embarrassment can cause sensations of perspiration and heart palpitations, as when one is faced with an objective danger: an emotion has been aroused and it does not matter whether it is subjective or objective, it automatically produces the physiological effects. Subjective and emotional problems that remain unsolved can cause psychosomatic illness and as long as the cause remains, the psychosomatic result will also remain. Swelling of the body is not unknown in the history of psychosomatic medicine; nor are disorders of breathing, flushes, loss of appetite and other disturbances attributed to poltergeist activity; nor should it be forgotten that 'poltergeist mediums' may be able to influence other people around them to throw objects by unconscious automatism. On reflection it must seem probable that the 'Great Amherst Mystery' can be answered in terms of psychosomatic disturbance and inaccurate or exaggerated reporting of incidents that took place in the vicinity of the unfortunate and unhappy Esther Cox.

THE GHOSTS OF BERKELEY SQUARE

The haunted house in Berkeley Square where a 'nameless horror' is said to have resulted in several deaths

Height of Room 8' 8"
Window, 5' 6" high, from ceiling to 3' 2" panelling

Spiked iron railing 6 feet out from window some 30 feet below

N

4' 1"

Window

2' 0"

Partition wall — linking to No. 49

Fireplace

5' 0"

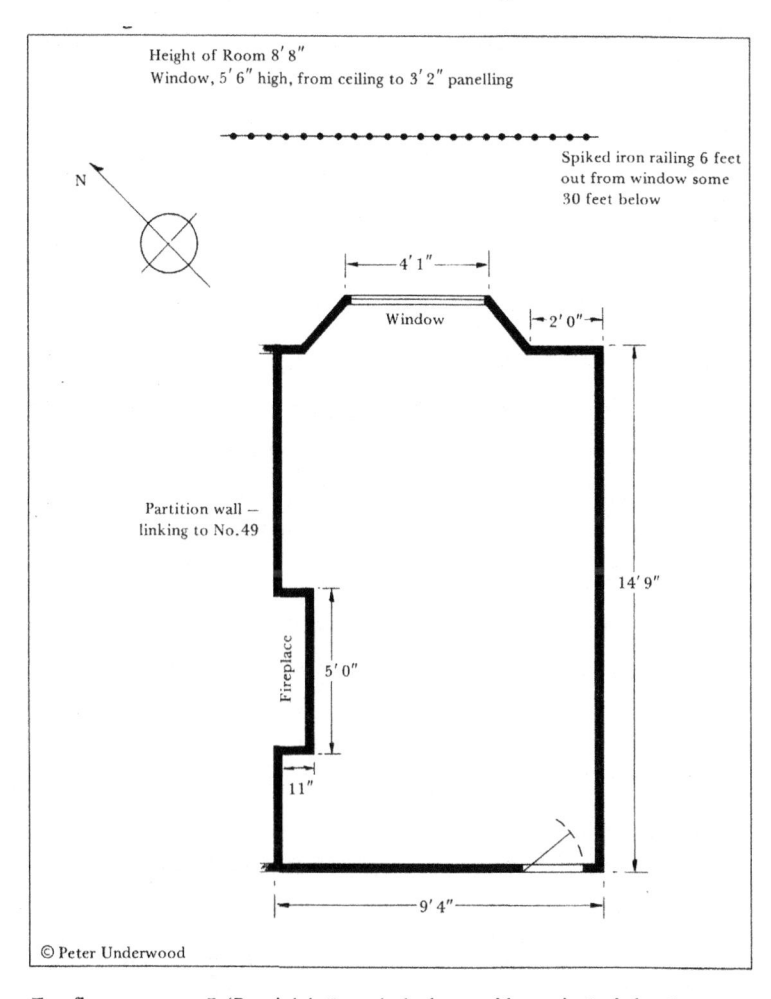

11"

14' 9"

9' 4"

© Peter Underwood

Top floor room no. 7, 'Dominic's Room', the haunted house in Berkeley Square

Haunted houses, one might be forgiven for supposing, are situated in lonely places. Borley Rectory, known as 'the most haunted house in England', stood at the top of a long hill a mile from the village; apart from the church across the road and the lonely village lane winding past, there were open fields nearly all round the great house almost hidden by tall trees. The Drummer of Tedworth plagued John Mompesson at his lonely old house set in miles of parkland; Hinton Ampner Manor House also stood in surrounding parkland; Glamis Castle stands remote and aloof in its grandeur; Epworth is the capital of the ancient Isle of Axholme in a remote part of England — but a real haunted house in the middle of London's Mayfair, in Berkeley Square itself? Perhaps this famous haunting is the exception that proves the rule although, in fact, London has many, many haunted houses.

The story of the ghosts and the reports of haunting associated with Number 50, Berkeley Square are nebulous, difficult to substantiate, unreliable and strangely elusive yet there is no doubt that for well over a hundred years the house has been considered to be haunted. Number 50, a plain, four storey building that has altered little since it was built, faces the centre of the Square from the west side. It was the last home of George Canning (1770-1827), an outstanding politician, statesman and prime minister who died suddenly at Chelsea; otherwise, unlike most of the other properties in the Square, the house has little background because, suggests Harry Price [Poltergeist Over England (Country Life, 1945), p. 193], the house was so often empty and deserted on account of its 'haunted' reputation.

It is extremely difficult to sort fact from fiction in this 'classic case of haunting', but perhaps a resume of the various stories associated with the house and the occasional verifiable fact will enable some kind of conclusion to be reached on the merits of the case as a genuine haunting. As long ago as 1907 Charles G. Harper [Haunted Houses (Chapman and Hall, 1907), p. 94] was saying, on the one hand, 'The famous haunted house in Berkeley Square was long one of those things that no country cousin came up from the provinces to London on sight-seeing bent, ever willingly missed' and on the other hand, 'There are those who declare it was never haunted and that the story was indeed invented by a more or less popular novelist of years ago.'

The first puzzle is what the haunting consisted of. It is often referred to as a 'nameless horror', a 'something' that haunts one particular room (variously described as a front room on the second floor and a similar room at the top of the house) that is, apparently, sufficiently awful as to cause the death of those who encounter it. Deaths there certainly have been at the house, and more than one might be described as taking place in suspicious circumstances; but all that was long, long ago and much of the haunted house reputation and some of the stories are traceable to the staid periodical Notes and Queries (founded in 1849) where questions on factual rather than speculative topics are asked and answered by readers.

November 1872 saw the beginning of what was to be a veritable spate of correspondence on the subject in this journal. It began by someone writing to ask whether the place was in fact haunted, to which Lord Lyttelton, no less, replied (16 November 1872): 'It is quite true that there is a house in Berkeley Square said to be haunted and long unoccupied on that account.' A few weeks later another correspondent wrote to say that he had taken the trouble to visit the house with the object of making some kind of personal investigation. His repeated knocking eventually brought an elderly woman housekeeper to the door but she refused to discuss the subject of the reputed haunting or reveal anything of the history of the house; she did say that the place was occupied but failed to qualify even this snippet of information so that the statement she did make could equally have applied to human beings or ghosts! The persistent Notes and Queries correspondent made a number of inquiries locally about Number 50 and learned that both the houses adjoining had been troubled by strange noises and that in one adjacent house a woman who spent a night alone had been found completely mad the morning . . . but there were no names, no dates, no verification and no other details of a haunting.

Seven years later the strange reputation of the house in Berkeley Square was still being explored by Notes and Queries and on 12 August 1879 correspondent W.E. Howlett brought to the attention of readers a reference that had appeared in another periodical, Mayfair, dated 10th May:

> 'The story of the haunted house in the heart of Mayfair is so far acquiesced in by the silence of those who alone know the whole truth, and whose interest it is that the whole truth should be known. That story can be recapitulated in a few words. The house in Berkeley Square contains at least one room of which the atmosphere is supernaturally fatal to body and mind. A girl saw, heard, or felt such horror in it that she went mad, and never recovered sanity enough to tell how or why. A gentleman, a disbeliever in ghosts, dared to sleep in it, and was found a corpse in the middle

of the floor after frantically ringing for help in vain. Rumour suggests other cases of the same kind, all ending in death, madness, or both, as the result of sleeping, or trying to sleep in that room. The very party-walls of the house, when touched, are found saturated with electric horror. It is uninhabited save by an elderly man and woman who act as caretakers; but even these have no access to the room. This is kept locked, the key being in the hands of a mysterious and seemingly namelesss person, who comes to the house once every six months, locks up the elderly couple in the basement, and then unlocks the room, and occupies himself in it for hours. Finally, and most wonderful of all, the house, though in Berkeley Square, is neither to be let nor sold. Its mere outside shows it to be given up to ghosts and decay.'

The following year, 1880, saw a Notes and Queries reader from Brussels (a Mr T. Westwood) suggesting something on the lines of a legal inquiry, an idea which drew a cynical reply from a writer who hid behind the initials 'J-CM.'. He wrote:

'This mystery vanishes the moment we use ordinary means of arriving at truth instead of indulging our imaginations. I pledge myself for the accuracy of the following facts: The house in question belonged to an eccentric gentleman. He was in good circumstances, but chose to spend no money on it. For many years soap, paint, and whitewash were never used. He was occasionally visited by a sister, the only person seen to enter the house except his two maidservants. Then by degrees began the stories — "insanity", "murder", "walls saturated with electric horror", etc. He died. The sister sent in an estate agent to see whether it would be worth while to put the house in order for the remainder of the lease. The agent, an intelligent and cultivated man, told me that he found the house in hideous disrepair. He asked the maids if they ever heard any strange noises. They said "No". "Do you ever see ghosts?"

Again the reply was in the negative.

A sceptical correspondent using the pseudonym 'Clarry' then drew readers' attention to the fact that an account of the Berkeley Square 'Mystery' had appeared in Twilight Stories and he states (Notes and Queries, 25 December 1880):

'The case, as related to me, was, that Mr Myers the then occupant being engaged to be married, he took the house, No. 50 Berkeley Square, which was furnished, and that every preparation was made for, as he supposed, his future happiness; but just before the time appointed for the wedding the lady jilted him. This disappointment is said to have "broken his heart and turned his brain". He became morose and solitary — would never allow a woman to come near him. A male servant only was allowed occasionally to see him, and he lived alone. Sometimes, but very rarely, could he be seen in the back yard. At night he would "keep his assignation with his woe", and flit about the house. At this time doubtless "strange noises would be heard by the neighbours". And thus, upon the melancholy wanderings of this poor lunatic, was founded that story of the ghost by which so much space in your columns has been from time to time occupied. Those whom so many persons persist in calling "mad doctors" could tell of hundreds of cases of mind diseased and conduct similar to that of poor Myers. His sister was, it was said, his only relative, and she was too old or too great an invalid to interfere. About two years ago I saw his hatchment [a frame bearing the escutcheon of a dead person] up at No. 50 and I then hoped that the poor unhappy man's story, together with his ghost, would have been interred with his bones. But fondness for, and craving after, the marvellous have, I am sorry to say, revived the present discussion. The house having now been treated to "soap, paint and whitewash", and all that can be gathered of the wretched and lonely eccentric being told, let no one seek further "to draw his frailties from their dread abode"; and let no one believe that there was ever the slightest foundation for the existence of a ghost.'

There is some evidence to suggest that a mixed-up version of this story has become associated with a nearby house in Berkeley Square. Here, a story dating back to the eighteenth century (some say the seventeenth century) tells of the house being occupied by a widower and his young daughter who ran away to marry a man of whom her father disapproved, with the promise that she would return from time to time to see her beloved father. Years passed, however, and (so runs the story) the daughter never went back to see her father who grew old and embittered; he died an unhappy man, alone with his memories. Soon after his death reports began to circulate that the figure of the old man was seen silently rambling about the house and in particular around the vicinity of the front door — a figure that was seen by neighbours, strangers and even passing police officers. More recently a similar figure is said to have been seen by nearby workers from their office windows, but names, dates, times and precise details are sadly and disastrously lacking.

Also in the 25 December 1880 issue of Notes and Queries (a significant date perhaps?), a correspondent, Mr J.F. Meehan, quoted from a letter dated 22 January 1871, addressed to 'the late Bishop Thirlwall':

> 'Ghosts remind me that I never told you a story Mrs X related to us when she was here last, about the haunted house in Berkeley Square; S. pointed it out to me last spring. One side of it looks towards the street which, crossing Mount Street, runs into the Square itself. The dilapidated, forsaken, dusty look of this house quite suits a reputation for ghosts. By the way, I am not sure whether it is the corner house or next door to the corner house, but Lady M declares that the real site is at the end of Charles Street, where the street opens into Berkeley Square. This house, she says, is watched strictly by police. None of its inhabitants ever cross its doorstep and false coining is supposed to be carried on there, but has never been detected. Miss H (who repeated the tale

to Mrs X) was told by some R.C. friends of hers that a family they knew hired the haunted house — wherever it is — in Berkeley Square for a London season, as there were daughters to be brought out, one of whom was already engaged. They spent a short time in the house without finding anything amiss; then they invited the young lady's lover to join them, and the next bedroom, which they had not occupied, was made ready for him, and the nursemaid was either sleeping there, or else still busy with her preparations at twelve o'clock the night before his arrival. The hour had no sooner struck than piercing shrieks were heard, loud enough to rouse the whole household. They rushed upstairs, flung open the door of the haunted room, and found the unfortunate housemaid lying at the foot of the bed in strong convulsions. Her eyes were fixed, with a stare of expressive terror, upon a remote corner of the chamber, and an agony of fear seemed to possess her, yet the bystanders saw nothing. They took her to St George's Hospital, where she died in the morning, refusing to the last to give any account of what she had seen; she could not speak of it, she said; it was far too horrible. The expected guest arrived that day. He was told the story, and it was arranged that he should not occupy the haunted room. He voted it all nonsense, and insisted upon sleeping there. He, however, agreed to sit up until past twelve, and to ring if anything unusual occurred. "But", he added, "on no account come to me when I ring first; because I may be unnecessarily alarmed, and seize the bell on the impulse of the moment: wait until you hear a second ring." His betrothed expostulated in vain. He did not believe in apparitions, and he would solve the mystery. She listened, in a misery of suspense, when the time of trial drew near. At last the bell rang once, but faintly. Then there was an interval of a few dreadful minutes and a tremendous peal sounded through the house. Every one hurried breathless to the haunted room. They found the guest exactly in the same place where the dead housemaid had lain, convulsed as she was, his eyes fixed in horror upon the same spot where hers had been fixed the night before, and, like her, he never revealed his experiences. They were too awful, he said, even to mention. The family left the house at once.'

Investigations into this letter and its implications proved difficult and disappointing but at length it was found that the story in Twilight Stories (by Miss Rhoda Broughton) was practically identical with the story in Notes and Queries. When Miss Broughton was approached for details and further information, however, she replied (from 27 Holywell Street, Oxford, 2 February 1881):

> 'You are mistaken in supposing that my story has anything to do with the so-called Berkeley Square Mystery. Its incidents happened, as I was told by my informant, in the country, and I clothed it in fictitious characters and transposed it to London, which I have since regretted, as so many people have thence assumed that it must refer to the house in Berkeley Square. The slip you enclose is clearly my story mistakenly applied to a wrong house. I am sorry to be unable to assist you in your search, but I can at least divert you from a wrong track.'

The researcher concerned summed up his findings on the haunting as 'unproven' since

> 'the only distinct legend told of Berkeley Square has been shown not to belong to it, there remains only the general belief, to all appearance unfounded, that the house is "haunted", which it seems to me may be well accounted for by its neglected condition when empty and the habits of the melancholy and solitary hypochondriac, already mentioned in Notes and Queries, when it was occupied by him. With respect to the story, I undertook to inquire into it as connected with Berkeley Square; and as Miss Broughton, doubtless for that reason, has given me no evidence or authority for it, I have made no attempt to gain it from her or others.'

The late Harry Price, in his monumental Poltergeist Over England [Country Life, 1945] quotes most of these accounts and adds another story that he acquired from one of the residents in the Square. This refers to pandemonium sometimes breaking out in the house, Number 50, which was then empty, in or about the year 1840, and always at night.

> 'Although the house was not furnished in any way, the sounds of massive furniture, or heavy boxes, being dragged across bare floors were heard periodically — perhaps once in two months. Sometimes, bells were heard ringing. On more than one occasion, local investigators entered the house during these manifestations and invariably saw nothing, except the still swinging bells. Then a curious development occurred. During the height of some such disturbance a window would be flung open and small objects such as stones, old books, a pair of spurs, etc., would be hurled into the street...'

Price refers to this being typical poltergeist activity and then adds: 'One morning, after a particularly noisy night, the good people of Berkeley Square found that every window of Number 50 had been smashed — at least, every window that looked on to the Square.'

Most of the stories of ghosts at 50 Berkeley Square date from the days when it stood empty and had an uncared-for appearance, when years of grime and dirt clothed its brickwork and boarded-up windows, when rubbish trapped among the ornamental railings rattled in the wind and broken glass sprinkled the doorstep. There were occupants who lived in the house for years and never saw or heard anything of a strange nature, but they, it is said, kept the haunted room locked and barred and hardly ever went near it.

Typical of the stories told about the house (without names, dates or other details) is one that tells of an insane member of an aristocratic family, a man whose madness took the form of extreme violence so that he had to be restrained in an upper room and fed through a slot in the door. Such activities could well give rise to stories of strange happenings and who knows what atmosphere might be left behind after the death of such an unfortunate person? Even the 'nameless horror' has been described in several different guises. One report maintains that the ghost is that of a man with grotesque and horrible features, white and flaccid cheeks bordering a gaping red mouth; another describes a terrifying creature with numerous legs (or tentacles) that periodically emerged from the darkness of London's sewers; while yet another tells of a shapeless, pulsating mass of evil-smelling, panting matter that seemed to have dozens of little red eyes, an indescribable blob that oozed and spread throughout the haunted room.

There is another story (unauthenticated, undated and unsubstantiated) that is said to involve a baronet who, for a wager, spent a night in the haunted room at the Berkeley Square house against the advice of the owner. He only agreed to the scheme on condition that other friends should be on hand and would immediately investigate if the intrepid baronet gave two distinct pulls on the bell that could be rung from the haunted room. So it was arranged and the baronet duly installed himself in the haunted room, armed with a pistol and prepared for anything that might happen. There was a bed in the room and although he did not plan to sleep, he settled himself comfortably on the bed, propped up by pillows, the pistol in one hand, the bell-pull in the other, prepared to sit out the night.

For a long time all was quiet and the waiting friends were becoming drowsy as the clock chimed midnight.

Shortly afterwards the bell from the haunted room gave one light peal. The watchers sat up and half-wondered whether they should ensure that their ghost-hunter friend was safe and at ease, but the arrangement had been that they would only interfere when they heard two definite peals. Even as they hesitated a second peal sounded, this time so violent that it seemed the bell must be jerked off its spring. Without further ado the watchers raced out of the room, up the stairs and into the haunted room where they were brought to an abrupt halt by the sight that met their gaze. Their friend the baronet lay sprawled across the bed, his head nearly touching the floor, his legs apart as they might be following a paroxysm, his left hand still grasping the bell-pull that had been wrenched from its holder and, apparently having dropped from his right hand, lay the unfired pistol. But it was the look on his face that brought his friends to a sudden stop in their headlong rush to help their erstwhile friend, for there could be no doubt that he was dead. Wide open but unseeing eyes stared at them almost starting from their sockets; the lips were drawn back over clenched teeth in a travesty of a grin; the neck was twisted at a curious angle; but it was the impression of abject terror occasioned by the frightening posture of the still figure and by the terrifying look on the poor creature's face that was to be a memory that would haunt each one of those men for the rest of their lives.

Within a few months, it is said, the house was vacated and so began one of those long periods when it stood empty, becoming more and more derelict, inhospitable and overgrown.

Another story is told of this haunted house in Berkeley Square, a tragic story of two sailors. It was wintertime, perhaps just before Christmas, around the middle 1880s when two sailors were making their way through London to their homes. They had been celebrating the festive season and their shore leave with some of their shipmates but now they were on their own, it was getting late and they were looking for somewhere to sleep for a few hours.

It chanced they were walking through Berkeley Square when they passed Number 50. They both looked at the house, dilapidated, dirty, unkempt and obviously uninhabited, and they looked at each other. Here surely was shelter for the night. They climbed over the gate, made their way through the dead weeds, past the FOR SALE notice, and climbed into the house through a broken ground floor window. Once inside they explored the house from top to bottom and found it quite empty, apart from cobwebs, deep shadows and the occasional rat. They settled for a front room at the top (some versions of the story say a second storey room overlooking the Square); at all events they made themselves as comfortable as they could and lay down for the night.

Some time later one of the sailors was rudely awakened from his slumbers by his companion who said nothing but pointed across the room towards the door. In the deep silence of the winter night padding footsteps seemed to be approaching the room they were occupying; slowly and stealthily they came nearer and nearer, long pauses between each footfall. The sounds reached the door and all was silent for a moment. Then the door began to slowly open and, when it was half-open, 'something' glided through the opening and into the room. By the indistinct light of the dying fire the sailors had lit in the fireplace and the pale moonlight shining through the broken window, they saw that whatever had come in through the door was approaching them: with a loud cry they leapt up, one of them seized a broken curtain rail that stood propped against a wall and they turned to face the 'thing' that was between them and the door.

The room was full of shadows and neither could make out the exact form of the intruder but, as the sailor with the broken curtain rail raised it menacingly, 'it' began to edge its way forwards, making a weird scratching sound on the uncovered wooden floor. As it moved away from the door, the other sailor seized his opportunity and dashed across the room, through the half-open door, down the stairs and out into the street. He raced away from the house in Berkeley Square and, at the corner of a side-street, almost collided with a policeman on his beat. Breathlessly the sailor implored the help of the constable and, as they hurried back towards Number 50, they heard the sound of crashing glass, a few cries and then silence. At the front door the policeman began to remonstrate with the sailor, not only for breaking in but, it seemed, for going anywhere near 'that haunted house', when the constable's lantern lit up a dark shape on the railing at the front of the house. It was the other sailor. He had either been thrown or had jumped out of the window and he was impaled on the spiked railings. He was quite dead and on his face was such a look of terror that it was to stay with those who saw it as an irrepressible memory.

Lord Lyttelton, who had encouraged the correspondence that subsequently appeared in Notes and Queries, is also said to have had first-hand experience of the haunting. He, apparently, spent a night alone in the haunted room on the top floor and lived to tell the tale, although he was always reluctant to do so. Armed with two blunderbusses loaded with buckshot and silver (to ward off evil), he fired at 'something' that he saw leap towards him during the darkest hours of the night. He was aware that after firing at the vague and indistinct shape that materialized near the door, 'something' fell to the floor with a thud but he never found any physical thing that he had shot. Sir Edward Bulwer-Lytton (1803-73) produced at least one and possibly two classic ghost stories and his famous narrative, The Haunted and the Haunters, regarded by some as 'the most terrifying ghost story ever written' [Walter Frewen Lord, quoted by Harold Armitage in the Introduction (p. 13) to The Haunted and the Haunters by Lord Lytton (Simpkin, Marshall, Hamilton, Kent & Company, 1925)] is thought to have been founded on the haunted house in Berkeley Square, although Andrew Lang believed that it was based on the Willington Mill ghosts [ibid, p. 17].

In his collection of hereditary curses and family legends, published in 1907 [Haunted Houses (Chapman and Hall, 1907)], Charles G. Harper states that the secret of the house, according to Mr Stuart Wortley, lies in the fact that the property once belonged to Mr Du Pre of Wilton Park whose lunatic brother was confined to one of the attic rooms. His groans and cries frequently disturbed the neighbours. Harper also says that at one time the house was let on very curious terms, namely

£100 for the first year, £200 for the second and £300 for the third, with the tenant forfeiting £1000 if he left within that period!

In 1912 Jessie Adelaide Middleton, in her Grey Ghost Book, stated that the house in Berkeley Square was haunted by a little girl who wore a plaid frock. She was said to have died painfully in the top room, having either been frightened or tortured to death, and thereafter her ghost was seen periodically wringing her hands and weeping, the sound of weeping sometimes being reported when no figure was visible and the figure sometimes being seen when no sound was heard. Another story in this book concerns an older girl named Adeline or Adela. She is supposed to have lived at the house under the eye of a lecherous and wicked guardian or uncle who, one day, pursued the girl with evil intent, cornering her at the top of the house where, rather than be raped, she threw herself to her death from a top storey window. Yet another story tells of a man who lived in the upper storey of the house and who was obsessed with the idea that a certain message would come for him. Various messages, it is said, did indeed appear, written by a ghostly hand, but the right one never materialized and the old man went mad and after his death his ghost haunted the place. Jessie Middleton also quotes a letter from Mr Ralph Nevill, a relative of the mad eccentric, Mr Myers, wherein it is suggested that the Berkeley Square ghost dates from the eighteenth century, when the house was built.

The story of the two sailors is certainly one of the most persistent stories associated with the house. It is retold in the two books devoted to London's ghost population [Jack Hallam, Ghosts of London (Wolfe Publishing, 1975) and Peter Underwood, Haunted London (Harrap, 1973)], and in the volume edited by John Canning, Fifty Great Ghost Stories (Souvenir Press, 1971) and my own earlier volume A Gazetteer of British Ghosts (Souvenir Press, 1971). Soon after the latter book appeared in paperback (Pan, 1973) I received a letter from Miss H. Berenice McKague, a Canadian then teaching in Dar es Salaam, Tanzania, who said she was fascinated by the thought that the story might contain a clue to a family tragedy and mystery almost thirty years old. Miss McKague continues:

'In 1945, at the end of World War II, my young cousin, Carman McKague, who had been serving with the Canadian Navy, was taking her embarkation leave in London and was due to be back in Canada with her parents by Christmas. Unfortunately instead of seeing her, her parents were given the sad news that she had not survived her embarkation leave. So far as I know, all that the family was able to learn was that Carman had stayed in a big house (I think in Berkeley Square) with her buddy. A policeman on the beat had seen them enter at 10 pm. At 4 am the same policeman found Carman's lifeless body impaled on the spiked railings below a window from which she had either been pushed or had fallen. Somehow it appears that no clear information was obtainable from the close buddy who was with her, although she was apparently never held on suspicion, and the mystery was left unsolved as far as we were to know.

'The circumstances of my cousin's death accord so closely with the account of the death of the sailor to which you allude in your book that I cannot help but wonder if there has been some mistake or misunderstanding of the time period involved with this incident. I note that you were told by Maggs Bros, who acquired the property in 1939, that nothing untoward has happened there in recent years "though throughout the Second World War fire-watchers used the building night after night". It is just possible that this period at the close of the war was the "unoccupied" period when two Canadians unluckily stumbled into it. It should not be difficult to establish (either through Scotland Yard or the daily papers of the time — late 1945, probably December) whether my cousin's death was indeed associated with this house, and I might even be able to ascertain it by questioning another of my cousins at this time, though it is long past and the area would have no other association for them. At any rate, no one could be deeply hurt by the revelation now since the parents too are long dead. My own interest has been aroused and if you can obtain any further information to clarify this seeming discrepancy I would very much appreciate it.'

Perhaps this story is typical of the unintentional confusion that can surround so-called haunted houses. Although my initial inquiries were unsuccessful, subsequently the Metropolitan Police Record Office and the Greater London Council Record Keeper for the Director-General informed me that the death of Carman C. McKague, female, aged twenty, was reported to the Coroner on 10 December 1945, death being caused by a fractured spine following a fall from a window. 'Post Mortem and Inquest held. Verdict — Accidental Death.' Further research at the office of the Registrar General, General Register Office, brought the search to a close when I discovered the area in which this death had taken place: Chelsea.

When I examined the 'haunted room' at 50 Berkeley Square in July 1976 and ascertained its dimensions, I was told that sceptics of the haunting believe the story of the two sailors may have some foundation in fact, except that the two men, perhaps the worse for drink, quarrelled during the night and one of them ended up by being thrown, or falling, out of the window to land on the railings below — even though the window is more than three feet from floor level. I have found it quite impossible to sort fact from fiction, legend from reality, history from hypothesis in respect of the 'haunted house' in Berkeley Square. The building must remain a house of mystery, although it must surely be significant that not one single first-hand experience of this famous haunting is available.

THE CHELTENHAM GHOST

St Anne's, Pittville Circus Road, Cheltenham, where an apparently well-authenticated apparition of a former inhabitant was seen by several witnesses both inside and outside the house. But the figure may not have been what it seemed . . .

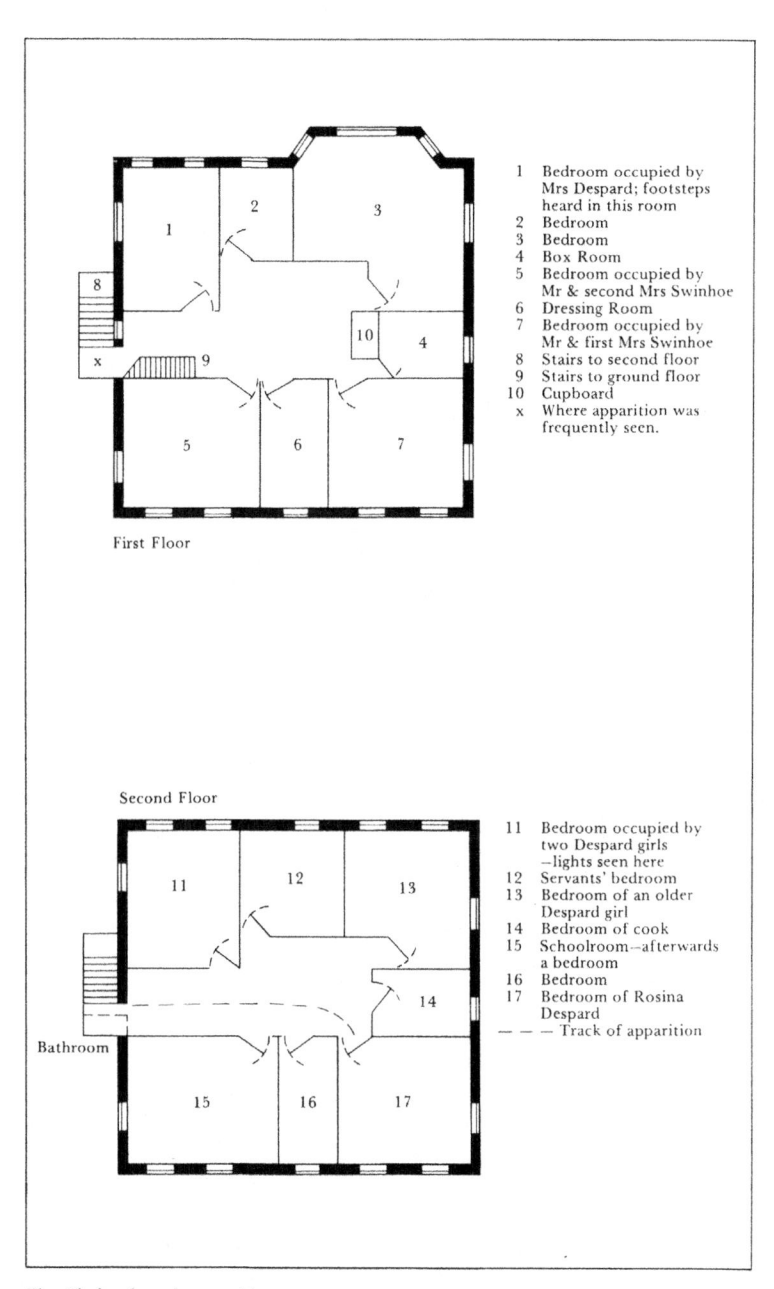

1 Bedroom occupied by Mrs Despard; footsteps heard in this room
2 Bedroom
3 Bedroom
4 Box Room
5 Bedroom occupied by Mr & second Mrs Swinhoe
6 Dressing Room
7 Bedroom occupied by Mr & first Mrs Swinhoe
8 Stairs to second floor
9 Stairs to ground floor
10 Cupboard
x Where apparition was frequently seen.

First Floor

11 Bedroom occupied by two Despard girls —lights seen here
12 Servants' bedroom
13 Bedroom of an older Despard girl
14 Bedroom of cook
15 Schoolroom—afterwards a bedroom
16 Bedroom
17 Bedroom of Rosina Despard
— — — Track of apparition

Second Floor

The Cheltenham haunted house

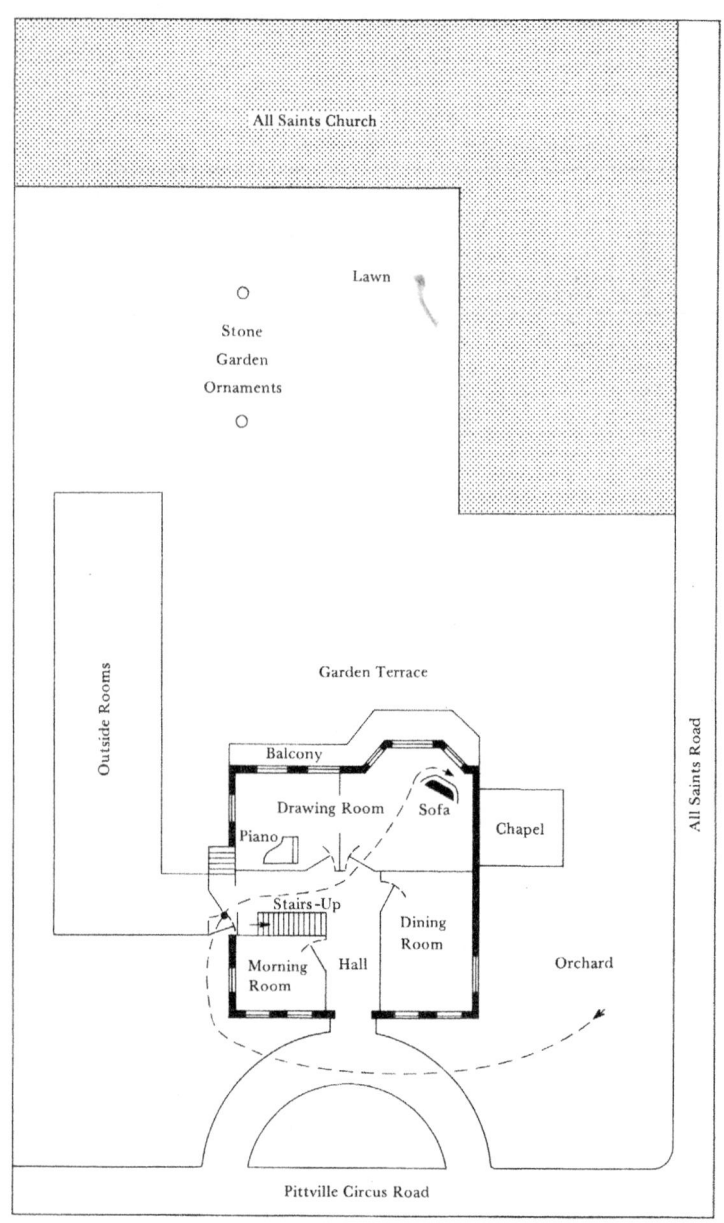

— — — Indicates routes most frequently taken by apparition
• Spot where apparition most frequently disappeared

Plans of the Cheltenham haunted house showing the routes most frequently taken by the mysterious figure of a woman in widow's weeds, usually holding a handkerchief to her face

Long regarded as one of the best authenticated cases of haunting ever investigated, the 'Morton Ghost' as it was known for many years, manifested from June 1882 until about 1886. The mysterious female figure that was seen so many times in and about the house then became gradually less distinct (according to available evidence) and, although there is some indication that such a form was seen by independent witnesses some years later, it is not strong or well-established evidence.

The case is often referred to as one of the most impressive on record, the chief witness being a 'lady of scientific training' who became a doctor in 1895. At least seven other people are said to have seen the apparition and upwards of twenty people heard noises that were attributed to the ghost. A wealth of contemporary evidence apparently existed in the form of letters, and the case was investigated by Frederick W.H. Myers, a poet, philosopher and experienced and careful psychical investigator, one of the founders of the Society for Psychical Research and for some years its honorary Secretary. The results of Myers' inquiries were published in the Society's Proceedings, Volume VIII, pp.311-32, under the title 'Record of a Haunted House'. Much of the value of the case lies in the fact that regular and frequent letters, comprising in effect a daily journal, were written by the chief witness to a friend in the north of England.

This main witness and authoress of the SPR paper, using

the pseudonym of 'Miss R.C. Morton' was in fact Miss Rosina Clara Despard, the eldest unmarried daughter of Captain F.W. Despard. Rosina was nineteen in 1882, when the Despards moved into the house, the family also including Edith, aged eighteen, two younger girls of fifteen and thirteen and two boys of sixteen and six. Mrs Pamela M. Huby, a member of the SPR has established beyond reasonable doubt that Rosina (the only Despard on the Medical Register) qualified in London in 1895 when she would be thirty-two, with examination results that were a distinguished achievement for a woman at the end of the nineteenth century. The London School of Medicine for Women, where she studied, had opened its doors in 1874 and women were only admitted to London medical degrees in 1878. To be accepted at the London School of Medicine was, in itself, a testimony of intelligence and enterprise, and it is certain that any evidence from Rosina Despard cannot lightly be dismissed.

The story of the haunting, as told by Rosina but incorporating new and recent evidence and material, relates to a large, detached, three storey house, with fourteen rooms on the first and second floors, and a short half-circle carriage drive. The house was and still is situated in Pittville Circus Road, Cheltenham. It was built in about 1860 and the house and grounds, including an orchard and large garden that extended to All Saints' Church, occupied the site of a former market garden.

The property was purchased before it was completed by the first occupants, Mr and Mrs Henry Swinhoe, a couple who were deeply devoted to each other. Mr

Swinhoe was an Anglo-Indian and he lived in the house for about twelve years, taking us up to 1872 when one day in August Mrs Swinhoe died suddenly. Afterwards Mr Swinhoe, inconsolable in his grief, took to drink. In 1874 Henry Swinhoe remarried, his second wife apparently hoping to cure him of excessive drinking, but instead she succumbed to the habit herself. It is evident, from the testimony of surviving relatives, that the married life of Henry and Imogen (his second wife) was a battleground of discord with constant quarrels, everlasting arguments and not infrequent violence. The chief subject of dispute, as so often happens in second marriages, was the management of the younger children of the first marriage and, in this case, the possession of the first Mrs Swinhoe's jewellery.

Some idea of the depth of feeling between Henry and Imogen can be judged by the fact that within months of the marriage and unbeknown to his wife, Henry had a local carpenter remove some floorboards in the small front sitting (or morning) room and there form a receptacle among the joists in which to hide the jewellery that had once belonged to Henry's beloved first wife. Some of the Swinhoe jewellery has never been located.

Henry Swinhoe died on 14 July 1876, some sixteen years after moving into the house, then known as 'Garden Reach'. Imogen had left him a few months earlier and gone to live in Clifton. As far as can be ascertained she was not at Cheltenham when Henry died, nor was she ever at the house afterwards. She died herself, mainly from alcoholism, at Clifton on 23 September 1878. Her body was brought back to Cheltenham and buried only a few hundred yards from the house in which she had lived in disharmony with Henry Swinhoe and his family.

Following the death of Henry Swinhoe 'Garden Reach' was bought by an elderly couple but, within six months of moving in, the man died suddenly in the small sitting room or morning room, the same room in which Henry Swinhoe had died, and where the jewellery had been concealed. Shortly afterwards his widow moved away and the house remained unoccupied for about four years.

This brings us to about 1880 when the property was purchased by a man who moved in but only stayed for a few months, although long enough to change the name of the house to 'Pittville Hall'. By this time the house and garden had acquired the reputation of being haunted and stories of a mysterious figure, a tall lady in black, began to circulate. These stories went back over the previous four or five years, covering the period when the property had stood empty and during the very brief occupancy of the last owner. He always maintained that he never saw anything unusual while he lived there, although Frederick Myers obtained a number of stories relating to this period that tell a different story.

One story concerned a gardener who worked opposite and was said to have frequently seen a tall lady in black in the garden of the empty house; but when Myers endeavoured to seek out the man in question, he found that he was dead and his wife could not be traced. Another story relating to this period told of a lady who had once resided in Cheltenham and, returning there after an absence of some years, met Rosina Despard (who later lived at the house). She expressed interest in reports of the apparition which she said seemed to be identical with one seen in the same house after the death of the second Mrs Swinhoe in 1878. What does seem to be factual is that the house, during the summer of 1879 or 1880, was offered at a rental of £60, a very low figure for such a property in the district in which it stands.

In 1882 Captain F.W. Despard took a lease on the property and promptly changed the name to 'Donore' as soon as he moved in, the Despards having Irish connections and Donore being the name of a village in County Meath. It was during the occupancy of Captain Despard and his family that most of the appearances and the majority of the apparently inexplicable noises were reported. It should be mentioned that the house was in thoroughly good repair when the Despards moved in; neither rats nor mice had ever been seen in the house and Rosina stated in her narrative supplied to Frederick Myers, 'there are no owls in the neighbourhood'; it would seem therefore that rodents and owls can be eliminated from the list of possible origins for the various sounds heard.

The complete Despard family consisted of Captain Despard and his invalid wife; a married daughter of twenty-six who was only a visitor from time to time, sometimes with her husband; four unmarried daughters and two sons, the older boy being away from the house at boarding school most of the time. It might be worth noting at this stage that if we allocate separate bedrooms to Captain and Mrs Despard, a bedroom to each of the children and a spare one for the visiting married daughter — a total of nine rooms — there are still five bedrooms to accommodate three servants. It will be recalled that the sixteen-year-old boy was mostly absent from the house and it is more than likely that he shared a room with his younger brother. It is also known that at one time the younger daughters shared a room: the significance of this observation will become apparent later.

Captain Despard took over the tenancy of the house in March 1882; the family, none of whom had heard anything unusual about the house, moved in towards the end of April and in the following June Rosina first saw the up to now unexplained figure. She had gone up to her room (Room 17 on the plan) but was not actually in bed when she thought she heard someone outside her bedroom door. Thinking that it might be her mother, she opened the door and at first saw no one, but on fetching a candle and proceeding a few steps along the passage, she saw the figure of a tall lady, dressed in black, standing at the head of the stairs. After a moment the figure descended the stairs and Rosina followed 'for a short distance' but then her candle went out and 'being unable to see more' she returned to her room.

Since this is the initial first-hand recorded instance of the Cheltenham ghost it is perhaps wise to explore the possibility of a normal explanation for this experience. Leaving on one side for the moment the completely new theory that will be explored later, the serious investigator will note that, hearing some sounds that suggested that someone was outside her bedroom door, the girl opened her door and found no one there. She then fetched a candle and we can picture the girl, in some apprehension surely, leaving her room for the darkness of the passage with seven doors opening into it but only a single window lighting the stairs at the far end of the passage and out of sight. We do not know the time of night or whether there was moonlight; we are only told that, once the candle went out, it was so dark that she was unable to see anything and that she therefore returned to her bedroom. A flickering candle is not the best light in which to observe anything and it must be considered possible that the 'figure' had a normal explanation — some odd formation of shadows, the natural fall of a curtain viewed in an unusual light, an uncommon reflection of clouds in moonlight through the window, a swaying branch silhouetted at the head of the stairs — something like any of these perfectly natural scenes could have been misconstrued into the 'figure' that Rosina saw. When she moved forward with her candle, the shadow or reflection might well have shrunk or seemed to her eyes in that uncertain light to have moved down the stairway.

If it was no more than a 'dark figure' that Rosina saw, no further explanation would be required. But she goes on to describe the figure in some detail, and it should be remembered that she was talking about a dark figure, seen in darkness, for a 'few moments', probably seconds in reality. She says the figure was 'that of a tall lady, dressed in black of a soft woollen material, judging from the slight sound of moving. The face was hidden in a handkerchief held in the right hand.' Subsequently Rosina says she was able to 'observe her more closely' and she saw the upper part of the left side of the forehead and a little of the hair above. The left hand was almost hidden by the sleeve and a fold of the dress. 'As she held it down a portion of a widow's cuff was visible on both wrists, so that the whole impression was that of a lady in widow's weeds. There was a cap on the head but a general effect of blackness suggesting a bonnet, with a long veil or a hood.'

During the next two years, that is through the rest of 1882, throughout 1883 and most of 1884, Rosina saw the same figure 'about half a dozen times; at first at long intervals and afterwards at shorter'; yet she mentioned these strange appearances to no one, apart from one friend 'who did not speak of them to anyone'. In the same period there were also three appearances to other people.

During 'the summer' of 1882 Rosina's married sister saw what she took to be a Sister of Mercy who had called at the house, and she did not pursue the matter any further. She saw the figure as she was descending the stairs rather hurriedly from her first-floor bedroom (Number 5) since she was a little late for dinner, at 6.30 pm. It was then quite light and she saw the figure cross the hall in front of her and pass into the drawing room as she made her way along the ground floor passage towards the dining room. There she asked the rest of the family, already seated for the evening meal, 'Who was that Sister of Mercy whom I have just seen going into the drawing room?'. On being told that there was no such person, a servant was sent to look, returning with the information that the dining room was deserted and no one answering such a description had come into the house. The witness apparently insisted that she had seen a tall figure in black, 'with some white about it', but nothing further was done about the matter.

In the autumn of 1883 the same figure was reported to have been seen by a housemaid at about ten o'clock at night. Thinking that someone had broken into the house, she made a search but no one was found and 'her story received no credit' although her description agreed fairly well with the figure previously seen by Rosina.

The third independent appearance was on or about 18 December 1883, when the figure was seen by Rosina's seven-year-old brother and another little boy. They were playing outside on the terrace at the back of the house when they said they saw the figure through the window in the drawing room. It appeared to be close to the window and crying and they ran in to see who it could be and why she was crying. Finding no one in the drawing room, they sought out the parlour maid who told them no one had come into the house.

Rosina, after that first glimpse in the darkness of the upstairs passage, says she several times followed the same figure downstairs and into the drawing room where it remained 'a variable time, generally standing to the right-hand side of the bow windows'. From the drawing room the figure sometimes went along the passage towards the garden at the side of the morning room at the front of the house, where it always disappeared. Rosina says she first spoke to the figure on 29 January 1884:

> 'I opened the drawing room door softly and went in, standing just by it. She came in past me and walked to the sofa and stood still there, so I went up to her and asked her if I could help her. She

moved, and I thought she was going to speak, but she only gave a slight gasp and moved towards the door. Just by the door I spoke to her again, but she seemed as if she were unable to speak. She walked into the hall, then by the side door she seemed to disappear as before.'

The above is quoted from a letter said to have been written on 31 January 1884.

During May and June 1884, the resourceful Rosina tried some experiments such as fastenings strings with marine glue across the stairs at different heights from the ground. She also tried to touch the figure but it always eluded her. 'It was not that there was nothing there to touch, but that she always seemed to be beyond me, and if followed into a corner, she simply disappeared.'

During the first two years that the Despards lived in the house, the only noises Rosina heard (that she could not explain) were those of slight pushes against her bedroom door, accompanied by footsteps, the commonest reported sounds in haunted houses, and whenever she opened her door on hearing these noises, she invariably saw the figure. Her letter (31 January 1884) also states: 'Her footstep is very light, you can hardly hear it, except on the linoleum, and then only like a person walking softly with thin boots on.' During the two months, July and August 1884, the appearances of the figure apparently became 'much more frequent' and indeed sightings were at their maximum during these two months 'from which time they seem gradually to have decreased'. It may or may not be relevant that the summer months saw the deaths of three people associated with the house: Henry Swinhoe on 14 July 1876; the first Mrs Swinhoe during the month of August 1872, and the second Mrs Swinhoe, Imogen, died on 23 September 1878, but not at Cheltenham, although she is buried in the churchyard adjoining the original land that was part of the old garden.

Rosina Despard, as we have seen, kept an almost daily record of the 'ghost's' activities in letters which she wrote to her friend, Catherine M. Campbell (then resident in the north of England). In producing the 'Record of a Haunted House' for Frederick Myers and the SPR, she was fortunate in being able to refer to these letters; it is the greatest misfortune that we are not able to do so today. The letters have never been in the possession of any independent investigator or society and they appear to have disappeared without trace.

On 21 July 1884, Rosina tells us she wrote:

'I went into the drawing room, where my father and sisters were sitting, about nine o'clock in the evening, and sat down on a couch close to the bow window. A few minutes after, as I sat reading, I saw the figure come in at the open door, cross the room and take up a position close behind the couch where I was. I was astonished that no one else in the room saw her, as she was so very distinct to me. My youngest brother, who had before seen her, was not in the room. She stood behind the couch for about half an hour, [?] and then as usual walked to the door. I went after her, on the excuse of getting a book, and saw her pass along the hall, until she came to the garden door, where she disappeared. I spoke to her as she passed the foot of the stairs, but she did not answer, although as before she stopped and seemed as though *about* to speak.'

On 31 July 1884, after she had been in bed for some time, Rosina's second sister, her junior by a year and then aged twenty, who had remained one floor down talking to her married sister in Room 5, came to Rosina's room to say that as she came up someone had passed her on the stairs. Rosina tried to persuade her sister that it must have been a servant (three of the servants slept on the second floor) but inquiries next morning seemed to rule out this idea since none of them claimed to be outside their rooms at the relevant time. Furthermore the detailed description of the figure tallied exactly with what Rosina had seen.

The very next night, 1 August 1884, Rosina saw the figure yet again. This time she was asleep in her room; she found herself awake at about two o'clock in the morning when she heard soft footsteps in the passage outside her bedroom door. She got up at once, opened the door and saw the figure standing in the passage, at the head of the stairs, side view on. The figure remained motionless for 'some minutes' and then walked down the stairs, stopping again when it reached the hall below. Rosina hurried ahead, opened the drawing room door and the figure went into the room, walked across to the couch in the bow window, stayed there for a little while and then walked out of the room, passing along the passage and disappearing, as usual, by the garden door. Again on this occasion, Rosina spoke to the figure, but received no answer.

The following night, 2 August 1884, apparently inexplicable footsteps were heard by three of Rosina's sisters and by the cook, all of whom slept on the top floor in Rooms 11, 13 and 14 and where Rosina slept in Room 17, and by her married sister, occupying Room 5 on the first floor; next morning they all said that they had plainly heard footsteps pass and re-pass their rooms.

The cook, explains Rosina in her report, was middle-aged and a very sensible sort of person. On Rosina asking her whether any of the servants had been out of their rooms during the night, after retiring to bed, the cook said she had heard the footsteps before and had seen the figure on the stairs one night when she had gone down to the kitchen to fetch some hot water after the rest of the servants had gone to bed. She described the figure as being that of a lady in widow's dress, tall and slight, with her face hidden in a handkerchief held in her right hand.

Unfortunately, adds Rosina, 'We have lost sight of this servant; she left about a year afterwards on her mother's death and subsequently could not be traced.' Unfortunate indeed, for the same servant is also credited with seeing the ghost figure outside the kitchen windows on the garden terrace, when she was herself in the kitchen at about eleven o'clock one morning. The kitchen was situated below the dining room at the rear of the house. It has to be recorded that this is the only occasion when the figure is said to have been seen on the garden terrace from the kitchen window.

On 5 August 1884, Rosina told her father about the mysterious figure and described what she and others had seen and heard. This was two years and two months after Rosina said she first saw the figure in June 1882, yet there is no word of explanation from Rosina as to why she had not discussed the subject with her father earlier or how he could not have heard of the matter: two years with the figure having been seen or heard by most of his family and servants. It really is quite remarkable — unless there was some very good reason for

Rosina remaining silent; this is a point we will return to a little later on. It was indeed no wonder that Rosina says she found her father was 'much astonished' for he declared that he had never seen or heard anything untoward himself; nor had Rosina's mother, although the latter point is dispensed with by Rosina who adds 'but she is slightly deaf and an invalid'.

Captain Despard, it seems, now made inquiries of the landlord, who lived close by, as to whether he knew of anything unusual about the house, since, as we know, he had himself lived there for a while. But the landlord, who said he had only lived in the house for three months, insisted that he had never seen anything unusual.

On 6 August 1884, a retired general, who lived opposite, sent his son over to inquire about Rosina's married sister for he thought he had seen a lady crying in the orchard, at the front of the house, where it occupied a position at the junction of Pittville Circus Road and All Saints' Road. The general described the figure to his son, as he did later to the Despards, as a tall lady in black, wearing a bonnet with a long veil, standing in the orchard, crying and holding a handkerchief up to her face. He did not know Rosina's married sister by sight although he knew she was staying with her father and that she had recently lost her baby son. Rosina points out, however, that the sister was not in the orchard at all on the day mentioned by the general, and in any case she was rather short and wore no veil. The general apparently commented upon the solid appearance of the figure with its distinct outlines and the fact that he had no doubt at the time that what he saw was a real person.

How unfortunate, again, for Rosina to have to add that the general 'who is a friend of the landlord, now tells us that he has no recollection of this incident'. At the time the general seemed to be anxious to see the figure again for the same evening that he had related his story, Rosina says that he went across the road to 'Donore' and he and some of the family and their servants took up various positions and spent some hours watching for the figure. It was not, however, seen by anyone that night, although Rosina's sister and brother-in-law said they distinctly heard footsteps going first up the stairs and then down, at two o'clock in the morning. They occupied Room 5 on the first floor at the front of the house at the stairs end where there were steps up to the second floor and down to the ground floor.

Five days later, on 11 August 1884, Rosina was sitting in the drawing room at dusk with the gas fire alight but the shutters still open. Her married sister was in the room at the time and also their two brothers and a friend who had just ceased playing tennis because of the light. Suddenly both Rosina and her sister saw the ghost figure on the balcony outside the window, apparently looking into the room. She stood there for some minutes and then walked to the end of the balcony, which ran the length of the house; she then returned to the window and there 'seemed to disappear'. Soon afterwards she was seen by Rosina within the drawing room although on this occasion she was not seen by Rosina's sister who was also present. The same evening the sister, who was a year younger than Rosina, saw the figure on the stairs as she came out of a room on the upper landing.

The following evening, 12th August, Rosina was walking up the garden towards the orchard when she saw the figure cross the orchard, walk across the top of the carriage drive in front of the house and disappear through the open side door.

Rosina hurriedly followed and was in time to see the figure cross the hall and enter the drawing room; still Rosina followed and watched the figure take up her usual position behind the couch in the bay window. Shortly afterwards Captain Despard came into the drawing room and Rosina told him the ghost figure was there. He said he could not see the ghost so Rosina went up to the figure to show him exactly where it was. As she approached the figure, it walked swiftly round behind Captain Despard, across the room, out of the door and along the hall, disappearing as usual near the garden door; both Rosina and her father followed. When she had gone they looked for her in the garden, having unlocked the garden door, which Captain Despard had locked as he had come in, but they saw nothing more of the figure on that occasion.

The same evening Rosina heard her younger sister playing the piano and singing in the drawing room; suddenly she heard the music and singing stop abruptly and her sister came out of the room into the hall and called for Rosina. She said she had seen the figure in the drawing room, close behind her as she sat at the piano. Together the two sisters entered the drawing room and both of them saw the figure standing in the bay in her usual place. Rosina spoke to her several times but received no reply. The figure remained motionless for ten or fifteen minutes, we are told, and then suddenly walked forward across the room to the door, passed along the hall and disappeared by the door into the garden. At this moment Rosina's youngest sister, then aged thirteen, came hurrying in from the garden, saying she had seen the figure coming up the kitchen steps outside. All three sisters then went out into the garden when their married sister called to them from her bedroom (Room 5) on the first floor, saying that she had just seen the figure pass across the lawn at the front of the house and along the carriage drive towards the orchard.

That evening, it would seem, the figure was seen by four people and from practically every angle. Here Rosina's report states 'my father was then away' although she has previously stated that during the evening of 12th August she and her father had been in the drawing room with the ghost; possibly there is a little confusion of dates at this point. She also says her youngest brother was out, implying that the only males of the family with the ability to see the figure were absent from the house.

During the morning of 14 August 1884, the parlourmaid walked into the dining room at the front of the house, at about 8.30 am, to open the shutters and there she saw the figure. Even with the shutters closed, we are told, the room was very light and sunny but the maid had opened one shutter when, on turning round, she saw the figure walk across the room and disappear. That evening everyone was on the look-out for the ghost but they did not see her. This parlourmaid, who afterwards married and left the Despard family, was interviewed by Myers at her home and the gist of her evidence is included in this re-examination later on.

Two days later, on 16 August 1884, Rosina saw the figure on the drawing room balcony at about 8.30 pm. This time the figure did not reappear inside the drawing room but on looking out at the side door, Rosina found that the figure had vanished. The gardener said he had seen the same figure in the same place early that morning, at about 6 o'clock.

Three days later, on 19th August, the whole family went on holiday and were away for a month, leaving three servants in the house. Back at 'Donore' after their holiday the Despards learned that footsteps and other noises had been heard frequently but, adds Rosina with — at last — a touch of scepticism: 'As the stair-carpets were up part of the time and the house was empty, many of these noises were doubtless due to natural causes', though attributed to the ghost by the servants. The cook, interestingly enough, spoke of seeing the figure in the garden at the back of the house, standing by a stone vase on the lawn but, sadly, Rosina does not seem to have obtained any details about this independent sighting.

During the rest of 1884 and the following year, 1885, the apparition, according to Rosina, 'was frequently seen' throughout the year but especially during July, August and September. The apparition was 'of exactly the same type, seen in the same places and by the same people, at varying intervals'. The noises, too, continued, it seems, with unexplained footsteps being heard by several visitors and new servants as well as by the five Despard sisters and little Willy, then nine — 'in all by about twenty people' — many of whom had not previously heard of the apparition or the mysterious sounds.

Other additional sounds began to be reported and to gradually increase in intensity: the noise of someone walking up and down on the second floor landing; of bumps against the bedroom doors; and of the handles of the doors turning. The bumps against the bedroom doors were so marked, distinct, sudden and unexpected that they were often the cause of considerable alarm. Indeed, they terrified one new servant who had heard nothing of the reputed haunting and consequently believed that burglars were breaking in, while another servant, after an attack of paralysis down one side, attributed it to terror caused by 'attempts at her door worse than usual one night'; the doctor however thought the attack was probably caused by coldness.

A second set of footsteps now seemed to join the first set, the new ones being quite different — heavy, irregular and constantly recurring, lasting the greater part of the night and often three or four nights a week. They seemed to be especially centred on the front right-hand room on the first floor, Room 5 — the room once occupied by Henry and Imogen Swinhoe. Here, during the summer months, and also on the upper landing heavy thuds and bumping sounds were continually heard; but these facts were kept quiet, at the request of the landlord, who feared that such stories might lead to the depreciation in value of his property. New servants were not told of the mysterious happenings although to anyone who had already heard of them, it was carefully explained that the apparitions and the noises were quite harmless. Some servants left, giving the disturbances as their reasons for doing so, and those who stayed, says

Rosina, could never be induced to leave their bedrooms once they had retired for the night.

During 1885, at Frederick Myers' suggestion, Rosina Despard kept a camera handy, always ready to try to photograph the ghost. On the few occasions when she tried to do so, however, she obtained no result, usually because, nearly a hundred years ago, a long exposure was necessary for such a dark figure to be photographed by candlelight and this was understandably impracticable. Rosina still endeavoured to communicate with the figure, constantly speaking to it whenever the opportunity arose, and asking it to make signs, if unable to speak, but with no result. She also tried to touch the figure again, but she never succeeded in doing so and on those rare occasions when she managed to corner the ghost, it 'disappeared'.

During the summer of 1886, Mrs Twining, the Despard's regular charwoman, saw the figure in the hall, at the door leading to the kitchen stairs, as she was waiting for her wages. Until the figure suddenly vanished, as no real person could have done, Mrs Twining took the figure to be a lady visitor who had lost her way. Frederick Myers interviewed Mrs Twining three years later and obtained her separate account of this event.

One night in July 1886, when Rosina and her father were away from home, Mrs Despard and her personal maid heard a loud noise in an unoccupied room over their heads. They went up to discover the cause of the noise but by the time they had climbed the stairs all was quiet and they found nothing to account for the sounds. They returned to Room 1 on the first storey. Shortly afterwards they heard loud noises from the direction of the morning room on the ground floor; they again set out to investigate but were no more than halfway down the stairs when they saw a bright light in the hall which alarmed them. They both scurried upstairs again where they called to Edith Despard, then aged twenty-two; she joined them and they all went downstairs together and examined the doors and windows, finding everything in order and fastened as it should be. Mrs Despard and her maid then went to bed and Edith went on to her room on the second storey, passing as she did so the room occupied by her younger sisters, then aged nineteen and seventeen. They opened their bedroom door, saying they had heard noises and had also seen what they described as 'the flame of a candle, without candle or hand visible' cross the room diagonally from corner to corner. Two of the maids also opened their doors, saying they had been disturbed by noises and all five stood talking about the strange happenings. Suddenly they all heard footsteps walking up and down the corridor between them! As the sounds passed they felt a sensation which they described as 'a cold wind' although their candles were not blown out and they saw nothing. The footsteps then sounded as though they descended the stairs, reascended and again descended, and this time they did not return.

That autumn Rosina collected evidence suggesting an earlier haunting, although in no instance was she able to obtain a first-hand account. She heard (as we have seen) about a jobbing gardener who had worked several times a week at a house on the opposite side of the road and had reported seeing a figure in the front garden of 'Donore' several times — before the Despards moved in; this figure, it is said, he knew to be a ghost but on seeking to trace this witness Rosina discovered that he had died and his widow, having left Cheltenham, could not be traced. Rosina met the lady who had lived in Cheltenham seven or eight years earlier and well remembered having frequently been told that the house and garden were haunted — but she could not remember the names of any of the people who were reported to have seen anything. Thirdly the apparition was mentioned by an uncle of Rosina, since dead, at an Army dinner in Halifax, Nova Scotia. An officer present remarked that when he had been at Cheltenham, seven or eight years earlier, he had been told that the house in question was haunted and he remembered looking up at the windows with interest as he rode past to see whether he could see anything.

Captain Despard did succeed in tracing a carpenter who had done various jobs at the house during the occupancy of the Swinhoes and he said he knew that Imogen Swinhoe wished to get possession of the jewellery that had once belonged to the first Mrs Swinhoe. Mr Henry Swinhoe had called him in to make a receptacle under the floorboards in the morning room where Mr Swinhoe had placed the jewellery, and the carpenter had then nailed down the floorboards and replaced the carpet. This man remembered the exact spot and Captain Despard made him take up the boards: they located the receptacle between the floorboards but the container was empty. Captain Despard thought that the jewellery might have been reburied near the garden door, where the ghost figure often disappeared, and he had some boards taken up but nothing was found.

Captain Despard also located the registration of

Imogen Swinhoe's death, at Clifton on 23 September 1878, with cause of death given as 'Dipsomania 3 months; subacute Gastritis 1 week' [The death certificate is reproduced in B. Abdy Collins, The Cheltenham Ghost (Psychic Press, 1948), pp. 250—1]. Captain Despard even traced the doctor who had attended Imogen Swinhoe and asked him whether there had been any disfigurement of the face which might account for its persistent concealment and the doctor recalled the case but said there had been no such disfigurement, although the face had become more full and round. It has been claimed [Andrew Mackenzie, Apparitions and Ghosts (Arthur Barker, 1971)] that Henry Swinhoe was encouraged to drink heavily by Imogen whom he found to be an extreme drinker during the course of their honeymoon.

During 1887 the reported appearances of the ghost became noticeably less frequent. On 4th February that year Edith Despard saw the figure as she walked downstairs at about 7.30 in the evening. It moved across the hall from the direction of the front door towards the drawing room, while Edith stood watching at the top of the first flight of stairs. The gas was alight in the hall at the time. During the course of an interview with Frederick Myers, Edith told him that she thought this was about the tenth time she had seen the figure. She went on into the dining room and reported the matter to her father and they called Rosina who was in the morning room at the time; all three of them went into the drawing room, opening the door to do so but inside there was no sign of the figure.

During the years from 1887 to 1889 Rosina says the figure was 'very seldom seen' although footsteps were heard, while the louder noises gradually ceased. Unfortunately no dated incidents are given; and from 1889 to 1892 when Rosina compiled the 'record' — quite by chance I am sure the actual date was 1st April! — she says that as far as she knew the figure had not been seen at all and, although the lighter footsteps lasted a little longer, 'they have now ceased'.

During the course of a subsidiary section headed 'Proofs of Immateriality' Rosina refers to her attempts to get the ghost to leave some kind of trace of its presence. Several times she fastened fine string across the stairs at various heights before going to bed herself, having made sure that the rest of the household had gone up to their rooms. She fastened the ends of the cord to the wall and bannisters by means of small pellets of marine glue. Such strings, stretched across the stairs, would be displaced by the lightest touch and would not be felt by anyone passing up or down the stairway, nor would they be seen by candlelight from above or below. Yet twice, at least, Rosina maintains that she saw the figure pass through the cords, leaving them intact. Her second proof of immateriality is the 'sudden and complete disappearance of the figure, while still in full view'; the third, the impossibility of touching the figure; the fourth, the appearance of the figure in a room where the doors are closed. It will have been noticed, indeed it could hardly have been missed, that we are totally dependent upon Rosina for the validity of each and every one of these proofs of immateriality. Under this heading Rosina also gives her reasons for believing that the figure is connected with the second Mrs (Imogen) Swinhoe.

1. The complete history of the house is known and if we are to connect the figure with any of the previous occupants, she is the only person who in any way resembled the figure.
2. The widow's garb excludes the first Mrs Swinhoe.
3. Although none of the Despard family had ever seen the second Mrs Swinhoe, several people who had known her identified her from the description of the figure supplied by Rosina and other members of the family. On being shown a photograph album containing a number of portraits, Rosina says she picked out one of Imogen's sister as being most like the figure and afterwards she was told that the sisters were much alike.
4. Imogen's step-daughter and others told the Despard family that she especially used the front drawing room, in which the figure continually appeared, and her habitual seat was on a couch placed in a similar position to the one belonging to the Despards.
5. The figure, says Rosina, is undoubtedly connected with the house, none of the percipients having seen it anywhere else, nor had any other hallucination.

Finally Rosina lists the 'Conduct of Animals in the

House', remarking at the outset that she and the family had strong grounds for believing that the apparition was seen by two dogs — firstly, by a retriever that slept in the kitchen being found, on several occasions, to be in a state of terror when the cook went into the kitchen first thing in the morning; he was also seen more than once coming from the orchard thoroughly cowed and terrified; and secondly, a Skye-terrier, being a smaller dog, was allowed the run of the house and habitually slept on Rosina's bed and 'undoubtedly heard the footsteps outside the door'. On one occasion, 27 October 1887 to be exact, this dog was suffering from an attack of rheumatism and was very disinclined to move, yet on hearing the footsteps it sprang up and sniffed at the door. Rosina states that this dog suddenly ran up to the mat at the foot of the stairs in the hall, wagging its tail and moving its back in the way dogs do when expecting to be caressed [his sounds a most unlikely reaction by a dog to paranormal activity *(Author)*]. It also jumped up, fawning as it would if a real person had been standing there, then suddenly shrank away with its tail between its legs and retreated, trembling, under a sofa. Everyone present believed that it had seen the figure and it does seem that, as related, the dog's performance was most peculiar and much more striking, probably, to an onlooker than it appears from a written description. The family cat, which lived in the kitchen, never showed any signs of seeing the ghost.

Rosina, in response to a request from Frederick Myers, attempted to describe her feelings in the presence of the ghost but this she says she found very difficult. On the first few occasions there was a feeling of awe at something unknown, mixed with a strong desire to know more about it. Later, when she was able to analyse her feelings more closely and the initial novelty had worn off, she felt conscious of a feeling of loss, as if she had lost power to the figure [A common experience, probably psychological in origin *(Author)*]. She mentioned the fact that most of the other percipients spoke of feeling a cold wind, but she had not experienced this herself. She acknowledged the assistance she had received in writing the account by reference to 'a set of journal letters written at the time', and from notes of interviews between Frederick Myers and her father and various members of the family.

The 'Report' is enhanced by separate accounts from Miss Catherine M. Campbell, the friend to whom Rosina first spoke of the apparition and to whom she wrote many letters with contemporary news of the disturbances; and Edith Despard, Willy Despard and others. At the time of her account, or later as far as we know, Miss Campbell never saw the ghost — except once, telepathically, more than a hundred miles from Cheltenham. But she did hear the footsteps and confirms that they were unlike any member of the Despard family, and the servants could be excluded since they were all changed during the period that footsteps were heard although the footsteps were 'unaltered in character'. Miss Campbell states that at the time (31 March 1892) she still had the all-important letters from Rosina in her possession but being in the nature of a diary they contained 'so many allusions to private matters' that neither Rosina nor Catherine Campbell herself could see their way to making them over to the Society for Psychical Research.

Edith Despard's account gives her first-hand testimony of seeing the figure three times, including the occasion when she was playing the piano and singing in the drawing room: 'Suddenly I felt a cold, icy shiver, and I saw the figure bend over me, as if to turn over the pages of my song . . .' She also describes the various noises and the figure in some detail: 'A tall woman in old-fashioned widow's weeds. . . the hands are long and very well shaped.'

Willy Despard's account includes three definite instances of seeing the figure and one possible sighting and of occasionally hearing noises suggesting a person walking about in soft slippers. The married sister's account tells of the three times that she saw the figure, including once 'in the spare room at night' and of the varied and 'very frightening' noises. The two last statements are from Mrs Brown, a parlourmaid at the house some seven years earlier and Mrs Twining, the Despard's charwoman for eight or nine years. Both accounts bear out what has already been stated by Rosina Despard but really contains nothing of importance except that Mrs Brown refers to the noises being worst on the top floor and Mrs Twining refers to the Despard family as 'very good, kind people'. It has to be said that such servants would obviously say anything to please such employers and would not say anything to displease them.

In his book on the case [The Cheltenham Ghost (Psychic Press, 1948), pp. 115—16] B. Abdy Collins was able to include the evidence of one living witness, an old solicitor friend of his who says, in 1944, that he saw the ghost a number of times over fifty years earlier, two occasions being very clear in his mind. He refers to the apparition as 'A harmless ghost — at any rate it did not appear to upset or affect people and those immediately concerned took little notice of it'. 'I remember, however,' he adds, 'the dogs disliked and apparently feared it.' 'It was a tall female figure dressed in black and with a handkerchief to her face as if crying. To the best of my recollection "she" was substantial and I have no impression of translucency.' This witness (who requested that his name should not be published) believed that the ghost was known in her lifetime to his godmother, with whose family he lived for a time when a boy, but she would never speak of her. 'If this is so (I have no reason to doubt it) the ghost's original could not when I saw her have long been dead.' He distinctly remembered seeing the figure in the garden in bright sunlight (when he was a small boy) and also in the drawing room, 'when we made a ring round her by joining hands, from which she appeared merely to walk out between two people and then disappeared'.

Andrew MacKenzie, in his book, The Unexplained [Arthur Barker, 1966, pp. 54—6] mentions the possibility of the strange sounds being the result of underground streams and postulates the somewhat preposterous idea that 'some real condensation of vapour' may have 'formed from time to time' and gave 'rise to the impression that it was a "ghost"' [ibid, p. 57]. Such an explanation is simply inadequate to meet the evidence, and so is Guy Lambert's suggestion that it was all due to subterranean flood water. The available evidence is that most of the occupants saw the distinct figure of a woman, a figure that was seen from many angles and close to, a figure that 'almost spoke' on one or two occasions and descriptions by those who say they saw the figure correspond to a very remarkable degree — not least in the emphasis on the 'real' appearance. It is quite impossible to reconcile such testimony with 'condensation of vapour' or movement and noise caused by underground water.

I feel there may be a much simpler and more convincing explanation for a figure that everyone who saw believed to be solid: perhaps the figure they saw may indeed have been as solid and as real as they were. Rats, mice and owls may have been eliminated but no one seems to have considered the possibility of the figure being a real person: a very simple, very plausible and very likely explanation. Could the vast majority of the sightings of the Cheltenham 'ghost' and the 'mysterious noises' attributed to it be evidence of a real person living in the house with the willing connivance of Captain Despard (and possibly Mrs Despard), but unbeknown to the rest of the household; an illicit lodger, in fact?

Captain Despard was, at first, unwilling to discuss the 'ghost', take the matter seriously or co-operate in any way and it was only after several conversations with Frederick Myers and faced with the combined testimony of his family and servants, that he agreed to collaborate and assist in the investigation of the 'ghost'. All this is readily understandable if, for reasons of his own, he had installed someone inside the house. Myers says that Despard's reluctance to allow the evidence to be collected until the haunting had ceased was based on consideration for the feelings of the owner of the house; it may not have been due to anything of the kind.

Mrs Despard has been described as being 'a great invalid' so it cannot be considered to be outside the bounds of possibility that the Captain might seek consolation, companionship and an intimate relationship with another woman. Perhaps such a liaison had been easier before the Despards moved to Cheltenham when the unknown lady may have lived conveniently near. But with the move and the large and growing-up Victorian-minded family to consider — what was to be done? In such a rambling and dark house as 'Donore' was in those days, it would probably not have been too difficult to secrete a person in one of the rooms, unbeknown to anyone; there was plenty of room, as we have seen, and any orders given by Captain Despard would have been obeyed implicitly and without question. The evident incapability of Mrs Despard would make such a deception that much easier than it might be in other circumstances, unless her husband was acting with her tacit approval.

The natural reluctance to be seen plainly or possibly recognized could well account for the 'figure' always holding a handkerchief to her face, a singular preoccupation of the Cheltenham ghost for which no satisfactory explanation has ever been discovered. Consider the detailed description of Rosina's first sighting of the 'ghost'; the invariable reaction of all those who saw it — that it was real and solid; the perpetual 'inability' of Captain Despard (and his wife who may have been in the secret) to see the figure; the reaction of the dogs; the really incredibly long period of time between when Rosina first saw the 'ghost' and when she spoke of the matter to her father. Could she have known or guessed the true explanation? Could this 'scandal' have been the 'private matter' so often alluded to in the personal letters between Rosina and her friend and confidant Catherine Campbell, letters that have conveniently 'disappeared'; could witness after witness really have seen a ghost when they saw a figure 'substantial and with no impression of translucency'; a figure that made sounds when it walked and needed doors to be opened to enable it to enter a room?

Such a solution would certainly account for the fact that the Captain and his wife were sometimes the only ones present in a room where others saw the figure, who said they could not see anything; a figure that was perhaps a real person, known to Captain Despard whose identity and presence in the house he wished to keep 'hidden'. It will be recalled that the first time the figure was seen by Rosina Despard was late at night. She had gone up to her room but was not in bed when she 'heard someone at the door, and went to it, thinking it might be' her mother; there was nothing 'ghostly' about the sounds, nothing frightening, no sense of apprehension or coldness; she simply thought her mother was there. In the passage she at first saw nothing unusual and then she saw the 'figure of a tall lady, dressed in black, standing at the head of the stairs'. Even the somewhat credulous Abdy Collins [The Cheltenham Ghost (Psychic Press, 1948), p. 19] remarks that it 'is a noticeable fact that at this, her first sight of the ghost, of which she says she had heard nothing', Rosina does not record the least alarm. 'Unless she at once apprehended the figure was abnormal, it was curious behaviour to leave a strange woman to roam about the house at night.'

It is surely significant that all who saw the figure 'say

that it was opaque and so life-like that at first they mistook it for a living person'. Several witnesses never had any doubt that it was a real person, possibly because that is just what it was. It is interesting, to say the least, that almost (but not quite) unique among ghost sightings the figure was observed from almost every angle — from the front, the back, both sides and even from above — and the observation that the figure 'reacted to its environment', if my theory is correct, assumes a new significance.

Assuming that the Cheltenham 'ghost' was a living female friend of Captain Despard who resided, secretly, in the house, it is entirely understandable that the figure was 'never seen when the members of the family and their friends waited for it'. Again, if it was indeed a real person who, not unnaturally perhaps, quickly tired of being secreted within the house, sought exercise inside the house and the occasional stroll in the garden — what could be more natural than that she should emerge from her room when she might least expect to meet anyone, after midnight, in the small hours of the morning and occasionally during daylight when she may have thought everyone was out or partaking of a meal.

Such a theory would presuppose that the footsteps were physical noises made by the woman on her perambulations and it is interesting to reflect that Rosina Despard says whenever she heard the footsteps and went out of her room, she saw the figure. On one occasion Rosina might almost have been writing of a living person when she says 'I spoke to her as she passed at the foot of the stairs, but she did not answer although as before she stopped and seemed as though about to speak'. This would be exactly what might happen if the figure were real and Rosina knew she was real but the woman could not bring herself to speak to Rosina. After all, what could she say? It certainly does not sound like the report of a ghostly experience. Or again, Edith, Rosina's sister, younger by a year, saw the figure her elder sister had seen and said afterwards 'It never struck me that the figure could be a ghost...'

It is true to say that in the whole annals of psychical research there is no clear record of a ghost which, after persistently haunting a house for a few years, gradually fades and is never seen or heard again. Logic surely points to a real person being mistaken for a ghost, or being passed off as a ghost, most probably an intimate friend of Captain Despard, who lived in the house for a period. Sightings by servants can often be dismissed as stories that they make up because they know it is the sort of thing their employers want to hear, already knowing what their employers think or say they have seen. Certainly some of the evidence from the servants strongly suggests such an explanation, such as the alleged sighting on 16 August 1884, when Rosina claimed to see the figure on the balcony during the evening and the gardener told her he had seen the same figure in the same place early that morning. If the servants became too inquisitive, perhaps they were dismissed: certainly there were lots of changes among the servants during the occupation of the Despards.

Earlier and later alleged sightings could easily be explained in terms of wishful thinking, malobservation, inexact reporting and idle gossip. Andrew MacKenzie has revealed [Apparitions and Ghosts (Arthur Barker, 1971)] that 'the figure of a woman in a long Victorian-type dress' was reportedly seen very briefly at another house in Pittsville Circus Road in 1958 and again in 1961, within sight of the house now known as 'St Anne's' but the story is unsatisfactory on several counts and it is difficult to see any good reason for connecting the narrative with the so-called 'Morton' case. There are reports of other, comparable, apparitions in the vicinity, including one of a female figure holding a handkerchief to her face and a 'nun-like' figure seen in 1939 and 1940 (a case I investigated in the company of Professor Henry Habberley Price [A Host of Hauntings (Leslie Frewin, 1973), p. 41]), but on the whole the evidence I have seen is conflicting, nebulous, unsatisfactory and quite unacceptable by serious psychical researchers.

The enormous credence given to the Cheltenham case is quite remarkable when one recalls that no first-hand contemporary evidence whatever is available for the haunting, only a record written more than ten years after Rosina Despard claimed she first saw the ghost and probably five years after the last time it was reportedly seen. The record was written from memory 'assisted by reference to a set of journal letters written at the time' but unfortunately never seen by anyone other than the writer and the recipient. Dumb animals are usually good witnesses of psychic activity and at 'Donore' the family cat never showed any signs of seeing a ghost while the dogs either sprang up and sniffed at the door or wagged their tails and seemed quite happy. Such reactions are not typical of animals in the presence of ghosts.

Much of the value of this case must be detracted by the fact that neither the Society for Psychical Research nor any responsible person was ever in possession of the original documents. Any unbiased re-examination of the evidence must reveal good reasons to treat the case with considerable reservations: for instance, several times Rosina remarks upon the quality of the footsteps, 'not at all like those of any of the people in the house... soft and rather slow, though decided and even...'; the footsteps, perhaps, of someone taking a little exercise but not wishing to be heard or disturbed. What in fact do we know about the subsequent history of Rosina Despard? Mrs Pamela Huby has discovered that after the Despards left Cheltenham Dr Despard lived at Virginia Water in 1900 and at Fleet, Hampshire, in 1914. In 1925 she was living at Yarmouth, Isle of Wight, where she had retired after having been Assistant Medical Officer at Holloway Sanatorium. There always seems to have been some mystery about Rosina's age but in August 1976 the rector of St James' Church, Yarmouth, at my request, checked the registers and found the record of Miss Despard's burial on 11 December 1930. The Revd Alan Daniels was also good enough to locate the grave and tell me the inscription: 'In Loving Memory of Rosina Clara Despard, MD, born 6 March 1863, died 8 December 1930. RIP.'

To my mind the Cheltenham ghost is one of the less convincing cases of haunting in the records of psychical research. It seems quite incredible that it has achieved the prominence that it has enjoyed for many years and there is little doubt in my mind that the explanation for most of the happenings can be found in terms of wilful and deliberate deception, malobservation, imagination lending colour to fact for the purpose of something interesting to write about each day and, perhaps, physical disturbances that it is no longer possible to determine.

THE MYSTERY OF VERSAILLES

The Grand Trianon, Versailles, explored by Annie Moberly and Eleanor Jourdain one hot August day immediately before they walked into a very strange adventure

THE MYSTERY OF VERSAILLES 267

The Petit Trianon, Versailles, where the two English ladies became convinced that they had stepped back in time. Their 'adventure' is probably the best known ghost story in the world

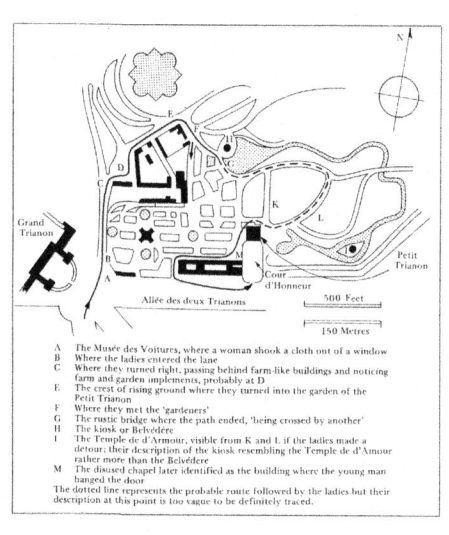

M. Sage's sketch map of the Petit Trianon gardens, Versailles, illustrating the probable route of Miss Moberly and Miss Jourdain when they had their 'adventure'

A The Musée des Voitures, where a woman shook a cloth out of a window
B Where the ladies entered the lane
C Where they turned right, passing behind farm-like buildings and noticing farm and garden implements, probably at D
E The crest of rising ground where they turned into the garden of the Petit Trianon
F Where they met the 'gardeners'
G The rustic bridge where the path ended, 'being crossed by another'
H The kiosk or Belvédère
I The Temple de d'Armour, visible from K and L if the ladies made a detour; their description of the kiosk resembling the Temple de d'Amour rather more than the Belvédère
M The disused chapel later identified as the building where the young man banged the door

The dotted line represents the probable route followed by the ladies but their description at this point is too vague to be definitely traced.

The 'adventure' of Miss Annie Moberly and Miss Eleanor Jourdain, when they apparently 'stepped back into the past' in the gardens of Versailles in 1901 has come to be regarded by many people as one of the best authenticated ghost stories of all time. Written in a scholarly, restrained and unemotional style by two ladies of high integrity — one the Principal and the other Vice-Principal-elect of St Hugh's College, Oxford — their book, entitled simply An Adventure attracted considerable attention when it appeared in 1911 and subsequently in a number of editions and reprints. It was a first-hand ghost story from two intelligent and healthy women who had spent ten years researching the experience, and for many years it was quoted in psychic circles and by the man in the street as the one ghost story that defies a logical explanation. That it is a fascinating story is beyond argument but can it really be possible that the two ladies met and talked with people, in long-vanished surroundings, who had been dead for over a hundred years?

In July 1976, Dr Joan Evans, the distinguished historian, archaeologist and copyright owner in An Adventure, told me that she would not permit any further publication of the book. Her reasons for this decision and her explanation of the mystery are exciting, plausible and novel; but first let us re-examine the story of an adventure that, whatever the explanation, is as strange as anything to be found in the annals of psychical research.

The gardens of the Palace of Versailles have been the scene of a number of apparently supernormal happenings over the years, including that of two young English ladies (Miss Bunow and Miss Lambert) who visited the gardens for the first time in 1928 and saw and spoke to people who disappeared [see the Society for Psychical Research Journal, Volume 38, number 683 (March 1955)]. But by far the best known are the experiences of Miss Moberly and Miss Jourdain who, they decided later, found themselves walking together in the Trianon of 1789 and meeting figures that had unaccountably arisen from that unfamiliar past. The ladies were unaware that each August the ghosts of Queen Marie Antoinette and her courtiers are said to relive the last days of the ancien regime.

The year before her visit to Paris with Miss Moberly (who was seventeen years her senior) Miss Jourdain had acquired a flat on the south side of the Seine and there, with a certain Mile Menegoz as partner, she ran a small finishing school for girls from her private school at Watford. Now, during the holidays, the flat was a convenient place to stay in Paris and she and her friend Annie Moberly were happily installed there early in August 1901.

After spending several days sight-seeing in Paris, a city they did not know at all well, they decided to visit Versailles where neither had been before. Accordingly, on 10th August, a hot, still afternoon, they went to Versailles and had the adventure of their lives.

They journeyed from Paris by train, walked through the rooms and galleries of the great Palace built by Louis XIV and, while resting beside some open windows in the Salle des Glaces, Miss Moberly suggested that it might be pleasant to walk in the gardens and visit the Petit Trianon. They had vaguely heard of it as a favourite spot of Marie Antoinette, who had a garden laid out in English style and built rustic villas in which she and her court ladies amused themselves by pretending to lead the lives of peasants. Indeed it should be remembered that the two ladies had with them Baedeker's guide to Paris and the 1900 edition contains the following advice: 'A visit should be paid to the Jardin du Petit Trianon which is laid out in the English style and contains some fine exotic trees, an artificial lake, a "Temple of Love" and a Hamlet (sic) of nine or ten rustic cottages, where the court ladies played a rustic life.' Miss Moberly says, 'My sole knowledge of it [the Petit Trianon] was from a magazine article read as a girl, from which I received a general impression that it was a farmhouse where the Queen had amused herself' and in the next paragraph she refers to 'looking in Baedeker's'. The following account is based on her report as published in the fourth edition of An Adventure (Faber and Faber, 1931).

Ascertaining the general direction of the Petit Trianon, they set off but they soon seem to have lost themselves. Before long they began to find the gardens depressing and they both felt tired and mildly unhappy. As they became aware of these feelings they noticed that the delightful and cooling breeze had dropped and the scenery, especially the trees, suddenly appeared to be flat and two-dimensional, 'as though painted on canvas' as they put it in their book. They walked up a deserted drive, green and broad, then 'crossed the drive' and reached a lake. At this point Miss Moberly expressed surprise in her account, written some time later, that her friend, who was leading, did not ask the way from a woman shaking a white cloth out of a window in a building at the corner of the lane. She supposed, however, that Miss Jourdain must know the way and she followed.

As they walked the two school teachers talked of mutual friends and acquaintances, of England, the weather and of their future plans; there was nothing strange, strained or unusual in their relationship and they chatted amicably as they wandered on, deeper and deeper into a mystery. They walked up a lane, made a sharp turn past some buildings, looked in at an open doorway and noticed the end of a carved staircase but no one seemed to be about and they did not like to go in. Resuming their walk, they discovered a choice of three paths ahead of them and seeing two men some way ahead on the centre path, they chose that one, caught up with the men, asked the way and were directed straight on. Afterwards the ladies spoke of these men as gardeners since they remembered a wheelbarrow of some kind nearby and a pointed spade; yet on recollection they seemed more like officials of some kind and were wearing long coats and small three-cornered hats. Both the ladies agreed that the gardeners replied to their inquiry in a 'casual and mechanical way' but Miss Jourdain alone (it later transpired) saw, as they talked, a detached cottage with a woman and a girl standing in the doorway, dressed in clothes quite different to those of French people of 1901.

The ladies walked briskly forward, talking together as before but from the moment they left the lane 'an extraordinary depression' settled on Miss Moberly and in spite of repeated efforts to shake off the feeling, it grew steadily worse. Looking back she could offer no reason for the gloom and despondency she felt; she was not unduly tired, the day was pleasant, she had enjoyable company and she was becoming more and more interested in the surroundings. She concentrated on hiding her depression from her companion and was distressed to find the gloom quite overpowering as they reached a point where the path ended, 'being crossed by another, right and left'.

Ahead of them they saw a wood and, just inside the wood and overshadowed by trees, a circular garden kiosk, like a small bandstand, with a man sitting close by. Miss Moberly noticed at the time that the ground in front of the kiosk was covered with rough grass and dead leaves and she took an instant dislike to the place; it was so shut in that they could not see beyond the kiosk and she suddenly realized that everything looked unnatural, the trees beyond the kiosk seemed flat and lifeless 'like a wood worked in tapestry'. There were also no effects of light and shade and no sign of any wind. The man, who wore a cloak and a large hat, turned and looked at the two ladies, and his countenance and whole appearance filled them with alarm. His dark face was pockmarked and he seemed to exude evil. His eyes were turned towards them but he seemed to be looking through them, beyond them, almost as though they were not there. The ladies were loath to approach the 'repulsive' figure in front of them, although they needed directions and they were therefore somewhat relieved to hear, from the way they had come, the sound of someone running towards them, breathless and obviously in a great hurry.

Miss Moberly turned round but could see no one and then, suddenly and unexpectedly, they found another man standing beside them, obviously a gentleman. He was tall, with large eyes, black curly hair, wore a large sombrero, and had 'apparently, just come either over or through the rock (or whatever it was) that shut out the view of the junction of the paths'. The sudden appearance of this man was something of a shock to the visitors but they noticed that he was red-faced and wore a dark cloak wrapped across him like a scarf before he exclaimed, 'Mesdames, mesdames, il ne faut pas passer par la... par ici... cherchez la maison.. He was young and excited and said a good deal more that the ladies did not catch but they gathered that he wished them to take the right-hand path. They immediately set off towards a little bridge on the right but, on turning to thank the young man, found that he had disappeared, and again they heard the sounds of someone running quite close to them.

Our two adventurers walked over a little rustic bridge which crossed a small ravine where a tiny waterfall cascaded down a green bank with ferns, so close they could have touched it. Beyond the bridge they followed a path through some trees, along the edge of a small meadow bounded by more trees and overshadowed by trees that grew in it. Next they came upon a house which they did not see until they were close to it, a square, solidly built small country house with long, shuttered windows that looked north towards an English garden (where they were). The north and west sides of the house boasted a terrace and on the grass, with her back to the terrace, a lady sat, sketching. She turned and looked full at the English ladies who noticed that she possessed a pretty face although she was not particularly young and she wore a shady white hat, a light summer dress that was long-waisted, low cut and rather old-fashioned looking. For some inexplicable reason Miss Moberly felt annoyed at the presence of this lady; Miss Jourdain didn't see her at all.

The two visitors stepped up on to the terrace of the house and at this point Miss Moberly remarks on the feeling that she was acting out a dream. The oppressiveness and silence seemed so unnatural, and then she again saw the sketching lady and noticed that the lace cape she wore about her neck and shoulders was pale green in colour. The two friends crossed the terrace towards the south-west corner of the garden and there they saw another house. A young man suddenly emerged from the door of this house, stepped out onto a terrace and banged the door behind him. He seemed to be some kind of footman, although he wasn't wearing livery, and he appeared to call to Miss Moberly and Miss Jourdain, saying he would show them the way into the house. Seeming distinctly amused, he led them to another entrance in the front drive.

Once inside this building, the Petit Trianon in fact, our two ladies were kept waiting until the arrival of a French wedding party, a gay affair in which the ladies gladly took part, walking arm in arm to form part of a long procession round the rooms under the leadership of a guide. The English visitors felt revived again; they were interested in the wedding and the contents of the Petit Trianon and they felt quite happy and lively as they took a carriage back to the Hotel des Reservoirs, in Versailles, where they had some tea, walked back to the station and then made their way back to Paris. Unfortunately for us and indeed for everyone seriously interested in the story, neither Miss Moberly nor Miss Jourdain 'felt inclined to talk' and, incredible as it may seem, they say they did not mention the events of that afternoon to each other for a whole week. When they did get round to discussing their trip to Versailles, they discovered something very strange for while some of the people and the surroundings had been seen by both ladies, certain of the figures and objects and surroundings had been seen by one of them and not by the other. The more they compared notes the more puzzled they became. Finally they reached the conclusion that they must have 'stepped back in time' and had walked through the gardens of Versailles during the French Revolution of 1789, 112 years earlier. But, as Harry Price points out, they wrote their reports a week too late for them to be of any real value [Harry Price, Fifty Years of Psychical Research (Longmans, Green, 1939), p. 280].

It is important to bear in mind that during the whole of their visit to Versailles Miss Moberly and Miss Jourdain did not see one thing strange enough to warrant comment upon at the time; later — a whole week later (and possibly more, for those initial notes have never been located) — Miss Moberly began to write a descriptive letter of the expedition and 'as the scenes came back, one by one', the same sensation of dreamy and unnatural oppression came over her so strongly that she stopped writing and said to Miss Jourdain, 'Do you think that the Petit Trianon is haunted?' Her friend's answer was a prompt and revealing, 'Yes, I do'. That brief conversation probably had a considerable effect on the subsequent researches and writing-up of the story of the 'adventure' for once the idea that the place might be haunted was firmly established in the minds of the 'adventurers', consciously and unconsciously they would lean towards an explanation of their experience that involved the paranormal.

Literally for years the strange adventure haunted the two friends and, as time and opportunity presented itself, they conducted extensive research into the whole period in an effort to solve the mystery. First they deposited records of their independent accounts at the Bodleian Library, enabling them later to establish a convincing case for the genuineness of their experience.

They soon found that the woods, the bridge, the ravine, the waterfall and the kiosk no longer existed in the garden of Versailles, although they had been there in the days of Marie Antoinette. The door in the Petit Trianon that had been slammed by the helpful young man had been blocked up for almost a century. Old maps were traced, old documents located, old plans discovered and everything seemed to bear out the accuracy of the descriptions and accounts prepared by the visiting school teachers of the gardens of Versailles as they were in the days of Marie Antoinette. Furthermore, certain details in the descriptions of the places the ladies said they had seen were flatly contradicted — even laughed at — by experts and students of the period. Yet Miss Moberly and Miss Jourdain stuck to their stories (although elaborating them here and there to fit the historical facts) and later documents were discovered that showed the ladies to have been correct in many details.

On the other hand there is so much confusion about the case that it must be considered unproven. One of the most obvious flaws in the case is the lapse of time before anything was written down about the experience. Although Miss Moberly talks of her 'descriptive letter' detailing the whole experience being compiled a week after the event, this document has never been found, which is a pity, for it would be valuable evidence, seemingly the only memorandum made by either of the ladies within three months of the experience.

The two later documents were compiled by the ladies more or less independently, although 'independently' is hardly an apt description, for they were compiled after discussion between the two people concerned and after reading each other's previous accounts. At all events it is all we have, and these accounts, the earliest as far as we know, in existence, were written on 25 November 1901 in the case of Miss Moberly (107 days after the experience) and on 28th November in the case of Miss Jourdain (110 days after the visit to Versailles). Written records of experiences should be made at the earliest moment possible after the event since this is the only way to prevent blurring of memory and risking the colouring of the experience by later knowledge and this is evident from a comparison between the description of the experience in the first edition of An Adventure [Macmillan, 1911] and subsequent editions [Macmillan, 1913; Guy Chapman, 1924; Faber and Faber, 1931; Faber and Faber, 1955]. Indeed, the extent to which false corroborative detail can become part of a personal experience is quite remarkable, as D.H. Rawcliffe points out [The Psychology of the Occult (Derricke Ridgway, 1952), p. 372], and the case under review is a perfect example of retrospective falsification. Although regarded by many people as a paranormal adventure beyond question, in fact the case is open to criticism at almost every point.

During the course of several conversations with the late William H. Salter, a council member of the Society for Psychical Research, from 1950 onwards, we discussed the case of An Adventure at some length and I always remember two things he said. Firstly, no one can say what persons, beside Miss Moberly and Miss Jourdain, were in the gardens of the Petit Trianon that August day in 1901 and, secondly, the narrative contains a mass of details and it is in the details that the whole point lies. W.H. Salter always believed that in cases of spontaneous paranormal perception it was necessary to have three 'scenes' clearly defined: the 'visionary' scene — the people and material objects that the percipient or percipients seemed to hear or see during the experience; the 'active' scene — the people and material objects that were or could have been perceived through the normal senses by other persons at the same time and place; and the 'distant' scene — the people and material objects that were, or may have been, perceived through the normal senses by other people at some different time or different place. Unless the 'visionary' scene materially differs from the 'active' scene and at the same time substantially resembles the 'distant' scene in details not normally known to the percipient, then no case for paranormality can be made out. Salter, an experienced and respected researcher, never felt that the Moberly/Jourdain case met this criteria whereas the two educated and intelligent English ladies, after further visits to Versailles and an enormous amount of research, came to the conclusion that they had seen the Petit Trianon and the gardens at Versailles as they had been in 1789.

Miss Moberly and Miss Jourdain pointed out that their initial visit had been on 10th August, a significant date, for on that day in the year 1792 the Tuileries was sacked, the Swiss Guard massacred, and the doomed royal family brought before the Assembly. The two ladies began to believe that Queen Marie Antoinette, during the agonizing hours that she was confined, before a messenger arrived with news of the approaching Paris mob, may have cast her mind back to her last afternoon at Trianon and that she and her friend had 'inadvertently entered within an act of the Queen's memory when alive'; that somehow they had become part of Marie Antoinette's memory through their being at the Petit Trianon on that particular day; 'that the Queen had gone back in such vivid memory to other Augusts spent at Trianon, that some impress of it was imparted to the place'.

Guy Lambert, a former president of the Society for Psychical Research, has produced evidence to suggest that both ladies may have been deeply hallucinated as to sight and hearing, practically all the way from the 'gardener's house', where they entered the garden, until they went into the house, and certainly some of the phrases used by the two ladies in their accounts of the experience bear out such a hypothesis. 'Yet we were not asleep, nor in a trance, nor even greatly surprised —everything was too natural' and again (in the case of Miss Jourdain) 'I began to feel as if I were walking in my sleep; the heavy dreaminess was oppressive.'

Other people claim to have had similar adventures at Versailles [[see Andrew MacKenzie's The Unexplained (Arthur Barker, 1966) and Apparitions and Ghosts (Arthur Barker, 1971)]] and Andrew MacKenzie [see his book The Unexplained (Arthur Barker, 1966), p. 88] has suggested that unusual atmospheric conditions in the vicinity of the Trianon may cause certain people to hallucinate the landscape and figures, or just the figures, of the past, the atmosphere presumably affecting the brain and resulting in localized hallucinations. Some of these theories seem to me to be more difficult to accept than the idea that the ladies did experience some unusual kind of psychic phenomenon.

There are on record many instances of people being genuinely puzzled by being unable to relocate a house or building or stretch of country. Usually these experiences can be explained in terms of mistakes being made in the place they thought they had seen the building or tract of land. This idea of 'mislocation' has been applied to the Versailles case and it has been suggested that the ladies (whose sense of direction was obviously poor since they failed at the outset of their experience to find the direct route to the Petit Trianon) may have taken a roundabout route, seeing objects and people visible to everyone, and later looked for them in the wrong places. Whatever the explanation for the adventure experienced by Miss Moberly and Miss Jourdain, it is possible to explain the whole of the experience in terms of mal-observation, confusion of memory and unconscious self-deception; indeed J.R. Sturge-Whiting did just that. He succeeded in actually proving, incident by incident, that there is a perfectly rational solution to the mystery [The Mystery of Versailles (Rider, 1938)].

It was William Salter who reminded me that nothing whatever is said by either of the two ladies as to what any of the five male people, four men and a lad, wore on their legs although one would have thought the very different apparel worn in 1792 and 1901 would leap to the eye of anyone, being the difference between breeches and trousers. In 1790 tight-fitting breeches were worn either knee-length or ankle-length, generally being buttoned up the outsides to below the knee or thigh level and either buttoned there or tied with strings. By 1901 trousers, usually fastened by a strap under the instep, had universally replaced breeches, except for sport and other special occasions. The silence of the two authors on this point cannot but suggest that they noticed nothing unusual about the clothing of the men they saw, below the waist; that in fact the leg-wear was appropriate to 1901. If this is so there must be a strong presumption that the males they saw were persons of the twentieth century and in that case it seems reasonable to assume that the females they saw were also of the present century.

In 1911, when the first publishers of An Adventure specifically asked the Society for Psychical Research to review the book, the society asked one of their French members, M. Sage, to explore the walk taken by the two ladies ten years earlier. (His excellent sketch-map is still the best guide for readers of An Adventure.) He was able to identify every material thing the ladies encountered during their adventure and he gave it as his opinion that all the supposed eighteenth-century persons described in the book might well have been met in the flesh in the Versailles of 1901.

Yet why do other visitors to the Petit Trianon gardens have similar experiences of seeing forms that appear to date from the time of the French Revolution? In 1938 Mrs Elizabeth Hatton saw the figures of a woman and a man 'in fustian clothes' drawing a little wooden cart loaded with logs. They passed quite close to Mrs Hatton (who was aged about fifty at the time) but no sound accompanied the experience. As Mrs Hatton turned to see where the figures went, they gradually vanished. According to Andrew MacKenzie [Apparitions and Ghosts (Arthur Barker, 1971), pp. 136—7] Mrs Hatton had no recollection of hearing about the famous 'adventure' of Miss Moberly and Miss Jourdain before her own experience but she admits that her memory is 'not so good', which is understandable in a woman then in her eighties.

Mrs Clair Hall told Andrew MacKenzie [ibid, p. 137] that she saw 'a tiny old woman, all in black' on a path near the Grand Trianon in 1937 but there is no evidence to suggest that this was not a real person. Jack and Clara Wilkinson, poultry farmers from Westmorland, and also their young son, saw the figure of a woman in a gold-coloured crinoline-type dress standing on the top step of the Grand Trianon in 1949. A moment later the figure had disappeared [ibid, p. 139]. They immediately went to the place where they had seen the figure and were satisfied that a real person could not have slipped away so quickly. Besides, there is no building near the balustrade and the nearest trees are about twenty yards away.

For its wealth of detail, scholarly interpretation and length of time that the experience lasted, then, the 'adventure' of the two maiden ladies in 1901 stands alone. Miss Moberly and Miss Jourdain, intelligent people in good health, certainly thought they had had a remarkable experience but, unfortunately for posterity, they recorded, investigated and published accounts of their experience in such a way as to leave the whole affair in an impenetrable fog of uncertainty. In doing so, however, they may have made a valuable contribution to the public attitude to these matters, demonstrating in no uncertain manner the value of properly dated, contemporary records, independent attestation and, most important of all, careful inquiry, before any research is begun, to ascertain the possibility of a normal explanation. If, in the future, anyone who is healthy in mind and body, intelligently believes that he or she has 'stepped back in time' or experienced a vision of the past or 'entered within an act of memory', it is to be hoped that they will remember An Adventure and do all those things that the two authors of that work failed to do. As William Salter once said to me, the two authors of An Adventure, starting out with the best of intentions, muddled their case at an early stage so completely as to make all the later labours useless. It is also interesting to know that both ladies were 'essentially credulous and would always prefer a picturesque and romantic explanation to one that was capable of scientific proof' [Dr Joan Evans in an article, 'An End to An

Adventure', published in Encounter, October 1976].

There seems little doubt that there is a perfectly normal explanation for all the material things that the two ladies saw that hot August day in 1901. M. Sage has proved beyond any shadow of doubt that there is insufficient evidence to warrant serious consideration of any supernormal happening as far as the physical and material objects and surroundings are concerned. But what about the people the ladies saw, met and talked with? Apart from the distinct possibility that they were real and normal people — a lady artist could well have been dressed in the manner described; a girl of thirteen or fourteen could well have been wearing a dress reaching her ankles in 1901; the 'gardeners' could easily have been some minor officials visiting the gardens — and so on, Dr Joan Evans has an ingenious and more than probable explanation for the whole adventure, or at any rate most of it.

Comte Robert de Montesquiou-Fezenzac was born in 1855, a member of one of the oldest great families of France; he lived an idle and aristocratic life and he had a passion for the eighteenth century. He and his friends wore eighteenth century clothes whenever they could and were in the habit of taking part in tableaux vivants and fancy dress balls in the galleries, parks and gardens of Versailles. Later he tired of such lavish amusements and preferred to organize smaller parties, sometimes for poetry reading and always in costumes of the eighteenth century, for his intimate friends.

According to Philippe Jullian [Robert de Montesquiou, un prince 1900 (Libraire, Academique Perrin, Paris,

1965)], Robert de Montesquiou had an Argentinian secretary, Gabriel Yturri, who was dark and handsome and these two often dressed alike. They sometimes wore long travelling cloaks and there was a touch of strangeness about their elegance. A photograph of the pair suggests that they may well have been the 'officials' or 'gardeners' seen by the two ladies in 1901.

During their later researches Miss Moberly and Miss Jourdain made careful inquiries as to whether any fete or similar event had been staged at Versailles during the afternoon of 10 August 1901, but they overlooked the possibility of a rehearsal. Dr Joan Evans believes that Robert de Montesquiou and his friends were in fact engaged in rehearsing a tableau vivant which the two English ladies inadvertently walked into. Indeed Miss Jourdain wrote at one point, regarding the 'gardeners': 'Both seemed to pause for an instant as in a tableau vivant, but we passed on, and I did not see the end.'

Dr Joan Evans believes that the 'full explanation' that the two ladies thought would one day 'become possible' has at last been found and she has decided that the only honourable course is to veto any further publication of the famous and possibly notorious book, An Adventure; although not everyone, even at the Society for Psychical Research, is convinced that such a hypothesis covers all the facts. Was the adventure a ghostly one? Perhaps we shall never know for sure but I think Dr Evans should have the last word. Writing to me from her home in Gloucestershire, in a letter dated 26 July 1976, she says: 'The bona fides of the ladies are impeccable but they did make a great fuss about very little.'

THE BORLEY HAUNTINGS

Borley Rectory: probably the earliest photograph in existence of 'the most haunted house in England' showing Mrs H.D.E. Bull, the Revd 'Harry' Bull and seven of his sisters

Borley Church, where many strange happenings have been reported in recent years

The interior of Borley Church; dominated by the massive Waldegrave tomb

The site of Borley Rectory from the roadway, 28 July 1975. Some people have commented on the figure of a wizened little old man with one arm pointing upwards, apparent in the light patch of foliage above the left-hand gate - an identical figure was reported by a former rector at the same place early in the 1920s

Borley Church - the bricked up north doorway

Plan of former grounds and present site of Borley Rectory

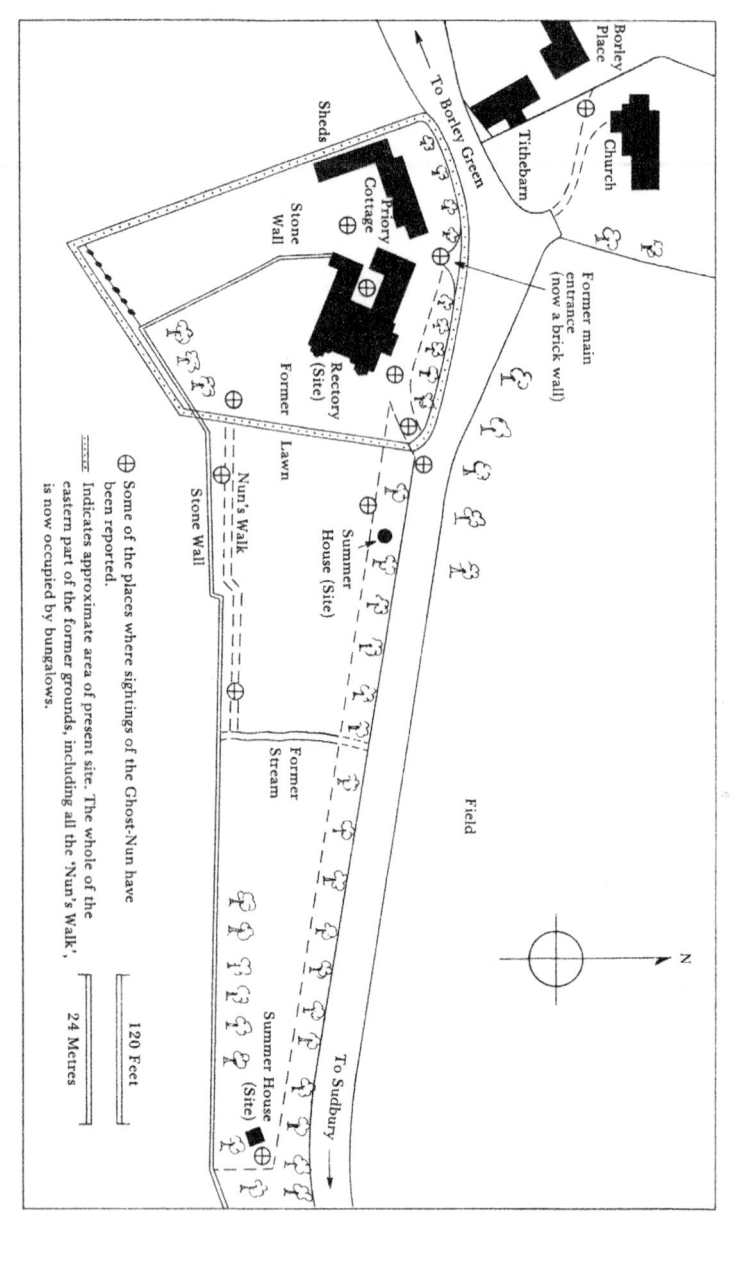

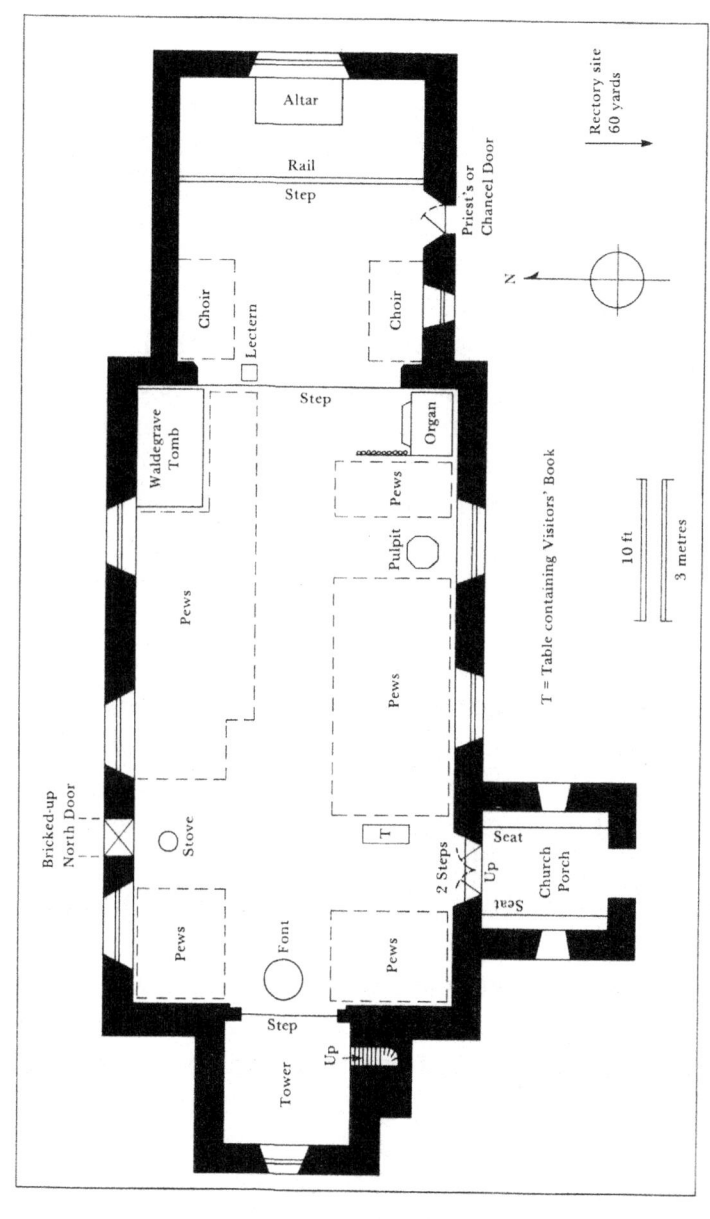

Borley Church, based on a plan by the Borderline Science Investigation Group, 1976

A couple of miles out of Sudbury, Suffolk, on the road to Long Melford, there is an easily-missed turning that runs in a westerly direction at Rodbridge Corner. A narrow road winds over the disused railway line, turns a sharp corner by the old school and then begins a long climb up a hill to a church, a farm, and a few cottages. Directly opposite the church with its clipped yew trees and low wooden fence, at the side of a recently modernized cottage, there is a forlorn patch of ground, overgrown with weeds and bramble, sprouting with wild bushes and young trees. Nature looks like fast reclaiming a spot where once stood a house that became famous as 'the most haunted house in England', for this is the site of Borley Rectory, the subject of four major books, scores of broadcasts, innumerable articles, endless discussion and not a little controversy. The ghosts of Borley seem to either fascinate or repel most of those who study the case and for every one person who seeks to dismiss the ghosts for one reason or another, there are a thousand who avidly read the books, study the evidence, discuss the pros and cons and as likely as not visit the site with notebook and camera, seeking to rebuild in their minds the gloomy, red-brick house on the hill that seems to have been the scene of much human misery and some human happiness and to have housed so many strange people that no one could find peace there.

Were the ghosts merely projections of the disordered minds of people who lived at Borley Rectory, the result of fraud, distortion of evidence, malobservation and wishful thinking or were the ghosts objective? Did the 'nun' really walk along the path beside the lawn? Did a phantom coach really race noiselessly alongside the church where once the old road ran? Did ghostly footsteps walk those rooms, and ghostly voices whisper, and ghostly hands play ghostly music? To answer these questions it is necessary to know something of the history of Borley Rectory and, perhaps just as important, something about its inhabitants. More than thirty years have passed since I first visited Borley, spending a night on the site where the great cellars still gaped at the wide skies and the outline of the vanished rectory easily discernible. Since then I have lost count of my visits—to carry out research and investigation, to visit successive owners of the site who had become friends, to call on the various incumbents or local people I had come to know, to make a film or take part in a television or radio programme, to lead a party of Ghost Club members, or simply to enjoy the peace of this pleasant corner of Essex with its delightful church—and always there are memories of the past, its intrigues and its ghosts.

There has long been talk of Borley Rectory being built on the site of a monastery but no evidence has ever been found for such an assumption. It may be that the rumour came into circulation in an attempt to establish the authenticity of the oldest ghost story from Borley, namely that a monk or lay brother from a religious house on the site of Borley Rectory fell in love with a young novice from a nearby nunnery (possibly at Bures). The two almost made good their escape in a coach one dark night but they were betrayed, chased, caught and speedily punished, the man being hanged and the girl bricked-up alive. It is a story that contains plausible reasons for most of the early ghostly manifestations — the spectral nun, the phantom coach and horses, the atmosphere of hopelessness, the impression of sadness, the footsteps, the dark figures, the sighs, whisperings and tolling bell. Unfortunately, for the romantically inclined, it is not only extremely unlikely that any kind of religious establishment existed before the Herringham rectory that preceded the Bull rectory, but there is very little evidence that a nunnery ever existed anywhere nearby. This is not to say, of course, that some aspects of the traditional story may not be based on fact, although most historical authorities agree that no nun was ever bricked-up alive in this country — as far as is known.

It is an undisputed fact that Borley Rectory was built in 1863 by the Revd H.D.E. Bull, rector of Borley from 1862 to 1892. As his family increased until he and his wife had fifteen children, he found it necessary to add a room here, build an extension there and reorganize the space somewhere else until the building became a rambling, rabbit-warren of a house, gaunt and ugly, isolated and irregular, and gloomy in the extreme. Yet the place held a certain fascination for most of its occupants and it is acknowledged that from the date of the first occupation, 1863, until its final disintegration in 1947, everyone who lived at the place — four successive rectors, their wives and families, and subsequently several laymen and their families — reported strange happenings for which they were unable to offer a satisfactory rational explanation. The happenings included apparitions, audible phenomena, temperature variations, touchings, movement of objects, unexplained fires — in fact just about every type of experience that has ever been reported from haunted houses.

During the occupancy of the Revd H.D.E. Bull there is considerable evidence that the ghost nun was seen on many occasions; certainly the rector and his wife knew all about the story that the nun 'always' appears on 28th July; that strange noises could often be heard in certain rooms of the house at night; that the curtains frequently billowed and moved when there was no breath of wind, in broad daylight; that objects appeared and disappeared and moved by themselves when no living person was anywhere near. Undoubtedly the rector and his wife knew all about these happenings but, understandably in a Victorian household, there was never any discussion on the subject in front of the children and they were not allowed to talk about the matter. An old friend of the Bull family told me of these happenings and of the measures that the Revd and Mrs Bull would go to in an effort to keep the stories of the haunting within the family, even, it has been supposed, to bricking-up a window because of the repeated appearances of the ghost nun on the pathway outside. More graciously, to avoid the likelihood of strangers experiencing peculiar happenings, visitors would be asked to lunch, or tea perhaps, but never to dinner, for that took place in the evening — and it was during the evenings and at night-time that the ghosts of Borley usually, but not always, manifested.

On 28 July 1901 four of the Bull daughters saw the ghost nun walking along the Nun's Walk, a path bordering the garden that ran parallel with the road, so called because this was where the ghost was most frequently seen. There is a theory that tragic and violent happenings leave some kind of impression on the atmosphere, an image that can be picked up and reappear under certain conditions. It is a theory that could account for those apparitions that are always seen in one particular place, doing one particular thing, and the figure of the nun in the garden at Borley may be an example of this type of ghost.

Three of the Bull daughters were returning from a garden party that sunny summer evening as one of them, Miss Ethel Bull, herself told me on several occasions. As she, Freda and Mabel entered the rectory garden they all saw the figure in a black robe, with bowed head, slowly walking or gliding along the Nun's Walk. They were suddenly very frightened; they had heard whispers of the ghosts and, indeed, Ethel and one of her sisters had several times glimpsed figures in the house and garden that could not be accounted for. But this was different. This was no possible figment of the imagination, no other member of the family, no shadow or trick of the light; the figure or form was seen simultaneously by three young ladies and it stopped them in their tracks, undecided what to do. Eventually one of them ran into the house and fetched another sister (frequently named as Elsie but there was no Elsie Bull, and it seems likely that it was Dodie) who, thinking the figure was a real nun who was on some charitable mission or seeking help of some kind, went towards the Nun's Walk. The figure stopped, looked towards the four girls, all intently watching her, and promptly vanished! There is no doubt that this daylight sighting by four independent witnesses of an apparently three-dimensional objective and solid figure that disappeared before their eyes, made a considerable impression on the Bull family. Whether their father and mother liked it or not, the story soon spread throughout the immediate neighbourhood and, doubtless, lost nothing in the telling. It is worth noting, however, that Miss Ethel Bull and her sisters told a consistent story of this experience for the remaining sixty years of their lives.

Other apparitions at this period included a tall, dark man who was seen from time to time in one of the passages on the first floor of the rectory and in one of the bedrooms; each time it was seen the figure is said to have vanished inexplicably. There were many reports of paranormal bell-ringing including the unmistakable 'ding-dong' of the great yard bell that hung high up in the central courtyard of Borley Rectory for almost eighty years and now hangs at my home in Hampshire; raps and taps that seemed to emanate from solid walls and isolated furniture; inexplicable footsteps that tramped up and down the stairways, along corridors and inside locked and empty rooms at all hours of the day and night.

Henry Dawson Ellis Bull (1833-92) was the first Bull to be connected with Borley although his brother Felix was rector of nearby Pentlow where the Bulls had been rectors for four generations: John Bull (1734-1802) was rector from 1756 to 1802; his son John (1767-1834) rector from 1802 until 1834; his son Edward (c. 1812-77) rector from 1834 to 1877 and his son Felix (1852-1927), rector from 1877 to 1927. Pentlow Rectory, during the incumbency of Felix Bull, was troubled by poltergeist phenomena [Harry Price, *Poltergeist*

Over England (Country Life, 1945), p. 282].

The Revd H.D.E. Bull was succeeded at Borley by his son the Revd Henry Foyster Bull, who was known as Harry Bull to avoid confusion with his father. Harry Bull held the living from the death of his father (in the Blue Room at Borley Rectory) in 1892 until his own death (also in the Blue Room at Borley Rectory) in 1927. He was a man who impressed different people in different ways, varying from the description of his school friend P. Shaw Jeffrey, 'An extraordinary man . . . always asleep . . . nine times out of ten he never turned up for his meals...' to another Oxford friend who, like Shaw Jeffrey often stayed at Borley Rectory during the incumbency of Harry Bull, but who went on to become a medical practitioner; he told me, 'He was one of the most normal men you could meet'. Yet another friend of Harry Bull told me 'He could hail a spectre as easily as most people hail a friend' and certainly Harry Bull claimed to see the ghost nun scores of times; having grown up with stories of 'her' as it were, he took 'her' for granted and often told his parishioners, 'The nun was busy again last night. . .'; he also said he saw and heard the phantom coach many times. It is even suggested that he built the summer house in the garden facing the Nun's Walk for the express purpose of watching for the ghost. Yet he was a lovable and easy-going man with a great sense of humour and he was much loved by his flock and his family (until he married a nurse against the wishes of his sisters).

One of his more curious experiences concerned the figure of a 'little old man'. One day Harry Bull was in his garden when he saw the arresting spectacle of a little wizened old man standing on the lawn with one arm pointing upwards; he thought the features resembled those of a former gardener who had died years before. As Harry Bull approached the strange little figure, it vanished. I mention this particular incident among Harry Bull's many odd experiences because of a curious photograph taken in 1975. On 28th July that year (reputedly the day for ghostly happenings at Borley) Mr Ray Armes of Norwich visited Borley and took several photographs, including one of the rectory site from the roadway. When this photograph was developed the figure of a 'wizened little old man' is plainly visible among the foliage in the centre of the picture — with one arm pointing upwards! Close scrutiny of the photograph suggests that the explanation (as with so many 'ghost' photographs) lies in the unusual lighting of an uncommon formation of foliage. It is none the less interesting, not least to speculate on the possibility that this may have been the explanation for what Harry Bull saw!

It really is necessary to keep one's sense of proportion in examining photographs for anything unusual and I always remember, years ago, photographing the excavation of one of the wells at Borley. One pile of earth, I thought, contained what could be taken for a face and to see how far I was deluding myself I showed the photograph to the late James Turner, who owned the rectory site at the time, asking him whether he could see a face. His reply was, 'Which face — I can see eight faces!'

Other apparent phenomena during the thirty-five year incumbency of Harry Bull included 'padding' noises, the sound of crashing crockery, footsteps and the unexplained shape of a man: all were experienced by the Coopers, who were employed by the Bulls and occupied the cottage that escaped the fire that later destroyed the rectory, and became the home of successive owners of the rectory site. Furthermore the Coopers, who told me their stories first hand, said they saw the ghost nun many times and one bright moonlit night, Mr Edward Cooper saw an old-fashioned black coach or square cab drawn by two horses and sporting two side lamps, in the yard below his bedroom window. Cooper told me that he called his wife but by the time she reached the window the coach, its trappings glittering in the moonlight, and with a rather dim figure or possibly two figures on the box seat, had, apparently, swept noiselessly out of the rectory gates, across the road and disappeared in the direction of the east side of the church. Neither the Coopers, nor the Bulls, nor Harry Price knew when this story was published that in fact an old road once ran precisely where the coach was said to have been seen.

Borley Rectory was by now known far and wide as 'the most haunted house in England' and when Harry Bull died in 1927 (to be buried, like his father in Borley churchyard, opposite the rectory) the reputation that the rectory had acquired made it difficult to find a successor. Indeed it was sixteen months later that the Revd G. Eric Smith, recently arrived from India and totally unaware of anything odd about the rectory, took the living. He moved in with his English wife, but they only stayed nine months.

Puzzled by 'sibilant whisperings', mysterious bell-ringing, slow and deliberate footsteps that paraded deserted rooms in the vast building (far too big for two people), appearances of the phantom nun perambulating along the Nun's Walk and elsewhere in the garden, sightings of the traditional coach-and-horses, various shadowy shapes, curious noises, movement of objects and rooms lighting-up inexplicably, Eric Smith, not knowing what to do for the best, wrote to the Daily Mirror. They contacted Harry Price, then at the zenith of his career as a ghost hunter, and he promptly visited Borley, little thinking that the case would preoccupy his attention for almost twenty years, in fact for the rest of his life; that it would become the most famous haunting in the world; and that, after his death, his considerable reputation as an impartial psychical researcher would be attacked on the basis of his handling of this remarkable case.

Harry Price, during the few years following his first visit to Borley, asked questions, explored the history of the rectory and its occupants, conducted research in the district and elsewhere and built up a formidable story of the haunting. He found a journeyman carpenter who had seen a pale-faced, sad-looking nun standing by the rectory gateposts four times during the autumn of 1927 (when the rectory was unoccupied) and always in the early morning when it was barely light; he obtained long statements from various members of the Bull family, the Coopers and other servants and past and present local residents and visitors. He even thought he experienced some paranormal activity himself when he seemed to glimpse a shadow on the Nun's Walk and was smothered with glass when a half-brick shattered part of the glass-topped veranda where he was standing with a reporter. He heard 'incessant' bell-ringing, saw showers of pebbles and discovered keys 'from nowhere' and he obtained phenomena at request when he asked for one of the house bells to be rung and it duly rang — 'under perfect control'.

The Smiths left Borley Rectory in July 1929 and for a while ran the parish from nearby Long Melford but, by the following April, Eric Smith had moved to Norfolk. He died in 1940 while his wife lived on for some years at Sheringham, her memory confused and totally unreliable. In 1945 she wrote to the Church Times stating that neither she nor her husband ever believed Borley Rectory to be haunted — a statement that is at complete variance with a wealth of contemporary evidence. Miss Ethel Bull told me, for example, in a letter, that Mrs Smith used to shriek with fright when she was at the rectory and Mrs E.E. Payne, still living at historic Borley Place, well recalls Mrs Smith pointing out the 'mysterious lights' in the rectory windows. Mrs Smith wrote a fictional account of the haunting which was never published.

After the Smiths left there was more difficulty in finding a new rector for the parish but eventually the Bulls, patrons of the living, persuaded a cousin, the Revd Lionel Foyster to take on the spiritual responsibility for Borley. He and his young wife Marianne with their little adopted daughter of two-and-a-half moved into the haunted rectory. They stayed for five years and during that time the reported phenomena reached a hitherto unparalleled variety, intensity and violence. In October 1931 the Bull sisters called on Harry Price in London and asked him to visit the rectory again. He did so in the company of Mrs Mollie Goldney (later to become a well-known member of the Society for Psychical Research but at that time a member of the Council of Price's National Laboratory of Psychical Research) and other responsible people. On this occasion Harry Price believed that Mrs Foyster, for reasons of her own, could have been responsible for all the curious things that he and his party witnessed during their visit, including wine turning into ink, and he told the rector of his suspicions. Mr Foyster always thought the world of his young wife, and in his eyes she could do no wrong. He was furious with Price who was not able to visit the rectory again until the Foysters had gone, although he continued to receive reports of strange happenings at Borley Rectory from many quarters.

During the Foyster period, October 1930 to October 1935, all of the reportedly paranormal phenomena previously witnessed were repeated — bells rang, footsteps sounded, apparitions were seen, objects were moved, noises were heard — but a wealth of new evidence suggested that such activity as physical violence, the materialization and dematerialization of bottles, doors locking and unlocking, strange smells, inexplicable outbreaks of fire and messages written on scraps of paper and on the walls of the rectory, were being experienced by the Rector and his family, friends, visitors and even strangers. Indeed Foyster wrote a manuscript, which he gave to Harry Price, detailing the experiences since he had come to Borley, which he called 'Fifteen Months in a Haunted House' [We await with interest Trevor Hall's projected book about Marianne Foyster].

Sir George and Lady Whitehouse and their nephew Richard were friends, and neighbours, of the Foysters. They were often at Borley Rectory and more than once they gave shelter to the Foysters who maintained that they were driven from their home by the violence of the activities. Richard Whitehouse, in particular, personally witnessed some remarkable happenings and he has himself told me of his experiences. He later became a Benedictine monk. Guy L'Estrange, later to become a Justice of the Peace and a local figure of some standing, talked with Lionel Foyster who told him of having seen a pencil raise itself into the air and write words on the wall. L'Estrange himself told me of seeing bottles suddenly appear out of nowhere, of hearing footsteps, bell-ringing that was totally inexplicable and of seeing a form that he could not explain. In 1932 Harry Price estimated that at least two thousand allegedly paranormal incidents had occurred at Borley Rectory during the Foyster incumbency. For the full story of this period of the haunting, and indeed for the complete story of the whole case (up to 1973), it is necessary to consult The Ghosts of Borley [Peter Underwood and Dr Paul Tabori, The Ghosts of Borley (David and Charles, 1973)].

After the Foysters left, the house was never lived in again. The Revd Lionel Foyster died in April 1945, Marianne Foyster (as was) now lives quietly in a small town in America, devoting her time to the care of the aged. The new Borley incumbent, the Revd Alfred C. Henning, served the combined parishes of Borley and Liston and he and his family moved into Liston Rectory. Both Mr and Mrs Henning became very interested in the haunting and both of them had many personal experiences to relate; I heard these during my visits to the Hennings. When he learned that 'the most haunted house in England' was not to be the home of the new rector of Borley, Harry Price hurried to Borley and succeeded in renting the property for twelve months. His aim was to introduce to the place a fresh set of people, sceptical, cultured and educated, who would report and record under scientific conditions anything of a paranormal nature that might take place in the house. With this aim in view he inserted an advertisement in The Times and from the scores of answers he selected about forty doctors, engineers, scientists and others who he felt were the right kind of people to form a rota of investigators. During the next twelve months an astonishing variety of 'phenomena' were reported, when the rectory was under strict control and every effort was made to eliminate fraud and inaccurate observation. Reported paranormal activity included movement of objects, unexplained noises of almost every description, pencil-markings, door-locking, cold draughts, the appearance and disappearance of objects, patches of luminous light and an overwhelming smell of incense.

During Price's tenancy one of his leading investigators, Sidney H. Glanville, took his daughter Helen to Borley and they tried out a planchette board. Sidney Glanville told me that he had been interested in psychic matters for many years and he had this planchette up in his loft; he had tried it out a number of times with members of his family and with friends but he had never succeeded in getting anything at all. When he was going to Borley he had suddenly remembered the planchette, found it and taken it along. At Borley, as soon as his daughter, using it for the first time, placed her finger on the board, it seemed alive and dozens of messages were obtained, purportedly emanating from the ghost nun who said her name was Marie Lairre. She also said she had been murdered at Borley and, among many other things, that she had come from France. A few months later, in March 1938, another communicator, 'Sunex Amures' threatened to burn down the rectory. In May 1938, Price's tenancy ended.

The rectory was now purchased for £500 by Captain W.H. Gregson who managed to insure the property for £10,000. At midnight on 27 February 1939, the rectory caught fire and was soon gutted, 'phantom figures' being seen by policemen and others during the fire. The captain's claim against the insurance company was eventually settled out of court for £750 and costs. While Captain Gregson and his family were at Borley all of them claimed to experience a number of incidents for which they could find no rational explanation. After Captain Gregson the ownership of the site changed hands several times. The remaining structure was demolished and the bricks sold: one person who purchased some Borley bricks to build a garage always maintained that the garage was haunted; and several visitors to the site who took away bricks and stones and fragments of the old rectory claimed afterwards that curious things happened to them that they attributed to the articles from Borley.

1940 saw publication of Harry Price's best-selling book, 'The Most Haunted House in England' (it should be noted that he put the title in inverted commas — he was using the name by which the house had long been known). Soon the case was attracting the attention of a great many people, some of whom visited Borley and claimed to experience strange happenings in the vicinity of the vanished rectory while others, like the Revd Dr W.J. Phythian-Adams, produced theories and ideas for Harry Price to work on. In the case of the Canon of Carlisle, it was suggested that digging and excavation on the site might well be rewarding. But by now the country was at war, Borley was an isolated hamlet and Harry Price's home was nearly 150 miles away. However, by 1943 many more clues and 'pointers' suggested that digging on the site might well be rewarding and by then East Anglia was a little healthier than it had been in 1941 when German air raids were a constant menace. Digging began with the rector and his wife, Harry Price and his secretary, a local historian and the site owner being present.

Among articles of interest a few human bones, including part of a jawbone, were unearthed. The jawbone, identified as belonging to a young female, showed signs of being attacked by a deep-seated abscess and it was felt that this was particularly interesting in view of the fact that so many people who had claimed to see the ghost nun said she was 'sad-faced', 'unhappy-looking', or 'looking as if she had been crying'. These bones were subsequently buried by the rector in nearby Liston churchyard. Reports of ghosts and ghostly happenings at Borley did not, however, cease with the fire, the total disappearance of the haunted rectory or with the burial of the human remains. Even today, more than thirty-five years after the fire and thirty years after the burial of the casket containing human bones, hardly a week goes by without a first-hand account of some strange happening at Borley reaching me.

After the fire the haunting entities seemed to transfer their activities to the cottage bordering the site and across the road to the church, and there exists a wealth of good evidence for paranormal activity at both places. At the cottage loud noises have been reported many times, dark shapes of people have been glimpsed where no living person has been, a phantom cat put in several appearances, unexplained footsteps have been repeatedly heard, voices have been reported, articles have appeared and disappeared and seances have produced startling results.

Within lovely little Borley church apparently paranormal music has been heard many times, tapping noises have repeatedly been reported by visitors in the vicinity of the Waldegrave monuments, objects have been moved, footsteps have been heard, figures have been seen, strange and strong odours have been noticed, chanting, singing and talking has been heard and odd things have happened to mechanical apparatus in the locality. For full details of the many and varied later happenings at Borley, as already stated, it is necessary to consult The Ghosts of Borley. Having related something of the history of the case, let us now examine for the first time in some detail the evidence of recent alleged appearances of the ghost nun and of ghost voices in the church.

One of the most curious and controversial stories to come out of Borley in recent years concerns the activities of Geoffrey Croom-Hollingsworth and his associates. I touched on this subject in The Ghosts of Borley [David and Charles, 1973, pp. 182—3, 216—19] and more details were included in the BBC television documentary, 'The Ghost Hunters', screened on 4 December 1975.

Mr Croom-Hollingsworth from Harlow became interested in Borley and its mysteries and during 1970, 1971, 1972 and 1973 he visited Borley many times, accompanied by friends. He carried out many experiments on the site of the rectory, inside the church and in the churchyard, sometimes using an infra-red camera, walkie-talkie sets and sound recording apparatus. As early as May 1970 he was able to tell me that he had recorded sounds, including voices and noises resembling gun shots that he was totally unable to account for. A month later, on 20th June, he and two of his friends claimed to see a shrouded figure walk down the church path soon after midnight and disappear behind one of the yew trees.

In January 1972, using a sound scanner that could pick up sounds over a radius of some five hundred yards, something registered on the scanner and they tracked it for a short time. Croom-Hollingsworth synchronized a movie camera with the scanner and at one time he thought he had obtained a moving picture of a ghost. Five months later Geoffrey Croom-Hollingsworth and his associate Roy Potter told me they had seen the Borley ghost from two different vantage points. Croom-Hollingsworth was keeping watch in the back garden of a bungalow that now occupies part of the old Nun's Walk, while his two companions were on the roadway between the church and rectory cottage. At 1.50 am Croom-Hollingsworth suddenly felt icy cold and at the same time he saw what he took to be the ghost nun, at the lower, south-east end of the Nun's Walk. She 'drifted' across the bungalow garden at a height of about a foot above ground level, passed through a fence bordering the old rectory site and disappeared in the direction of the main gateway, near the cottage.

Meanwhile Croom-Hollingsworth had contacted his companions by radio and they steeled themselves to see the apparition which they had been told was coming their way. One of them suddenly became aware that he too felt icy cold. Croom-Hollingsworth called again to say that the figure had reappeared, retracing 'her' path across the old lawn and had passed back through the fence and had disappeared between two bungalows — only to re-appear again and glide towards Croom-Hollingsworth! 'She' stopped about fifteen feet in front of him and he was able to study the figure in some detail [ibid., p. 218]. His associates Roy Potter and F. Connell now parted company, Connell remaining on watch on the roadway and Potter walking down the road and into the pathway of the nearest bungalow. After a moment he saw two figures at the bottom of the garden. One was Croom-Hollingsworth, the other, a grey form that seemed to be clothed in long drapery that covered the head and ended at the feet of the figure. When he was about twenty yards from this figure, it turned and walked straight through the fence, crossed a ditch and disappeared near a pile of rubbish on the south-west side of the site. Croom-Hollingsworth and his companion told me they saw the figure again in 1972. Once, Roy Potter says, he threw a brick at the figure and it went right through it! Each time, it seems, bright moonlight enabled the figure to be clearly seen.

By this time Croom-Hollingsworth had travelled many miles to talk to people about the Borley haunting and he had fortuitously acquired an exercise book that is in effect a diary that once belonged to Dodie Bull, one of the daughters of the Revd H.D.E. Bull and his wife; it covers several months of 1885 and, I am told, actually mentions the ghost nun. Croom-Hollingsworth and his friends had also obtained interesting tape recordings of various noises in the vicinity. During the course of the television film a number of details were mentioned that did not correspond with Mr Croom-Hollingsworth's original reports to me and these included the time he saw the figure, the objects it walked through, the duration of time it was under observation, the route the figure took, the reaction of his associates and several other incidents, but doubtless this is understandable in all the circumstances; at the time of the interview with Hugh Burnett for the television programme Geoffrey Croom-Hollingsworth was working on the Mil motorway extension at Epping.

Mr Croom-Hollingsworth tells me that the results of his investigations at Borley interested David Ellis, a young researcher at Cambridge and a member of the Society for Psychical Research, and he suggested that experimentation inside Borley Church with a tape recorder might prove interesting. Here Denny Densham comes into the picture. He is experienced in the use of sound recording apparatus and with some friends and relatives made a number of visits to Borley Church and produced a combined recording that is certainly interesting.

At first the two recording machines were left running

on their own inside the locked building after the whole church and its immediate area had been searched. The resulting tape carries what the investigators 'firmly believe' to be the 'sound of a ghost stepping forward and opening something that sounds like a door'. At first they thought they had recorded the sound of the chancel door being opened but they were satisfied that this was not the answer and they could find nothing inside the church that could have made the 'ghostly' sounds. A few days later a party that included Denny Densham spent an entire night in the church, after again making a thorough search. This time they noticed a change in the atmosphere and experienced the feeling of being watched (which is perhaps not unexpected in the circumstances and is likely to be a purely subjective and natural experience). However, they heard and recorded a number of odd noises including something that sounded like a human sigh.

During the course of later investigations they again spent a night inside Borley Church and this time they drew a complete blank until, at 1.45 am, they all experienced a tingling sensation and some of them felt that a presence was pressing against their backs. They all felt certain that they were then going to get some interesting results and they were right. (It must be faced that the visitors had in some respects prepared themselves for some kind of experience — keyed themselves up to a pitch when 'something' was almost bound to happen. Hours of waiting in darkness at a reputedly haunted locality has this effect, I have seen it and experienced it many times.) They then heard and recorded, apparently from the direction of the altar rails, the sound of footsteps, followed by the noise of something being dragged along the floor, and then more footsteps. Later they heard, and recorded, faint rapping sounds.

During the course of a fourth visit all the party kept watch on the chancel door and after a long time they saw a kind of glow around this door 'as though a phosphorescent aura was emanating'. Again they recorded the sound of footsteps, raps of varying intensity and a more frightening sigh. (It may be thought that no further explanation than extended concentration in near total darkness could account for the 'aura', but what of the recorded sounds?)

During a fifth visit, the church was occupied by the investigating team throughout the night and just after four o'clock in the morning the watchers heard odd clicks and taps from the direction of the font (I am sure the visitors realized that these sounds almost certainly had a natural explanation and were only to be expected). Then those present began to see tiny patches of light moving on the curtain behind the font and on one of the pews. (I would have thought this 'phenomenon' might well have been accounted for in terms of moonlight shining through the church windows and being the result of reflection but, oddly enough, this possibility does not seem to have been explored.) Then the watchers heard, and recorded, a loud crash which startled them and suggested to everyone that something had been thrown down. (The team should have carefully searched for evidence of anything that may have fallen from the roof or been disturbed by a rodent or bird, but I have no record of this being done.) Now the party noticed that it seemed colder (this might have been subjective and could easily have been established one way or the other by the simple use of a thermometer) and then the lights seemed to advance. There were no further sounds and eventually the lights vanished. The watchers felt that the microphone proved that the lights were physical but of course the sounds proved nothing of the kind.

During the course of the television programme in which these recordings were broadcast the producer, Hugh Burnett, specifically told me that he had understood that every effort had been made to find a physical cause for the noises but those concerned were satisfied that there was nothing inside the church that could be responsible for the varied sounds and noises that they had recorded. I can only say that I took Hugh Burnett round the church and within a very few moments I had located objects that made it possible for every noise to have a natural explanation; I do not say that the recorded noises were made naturally, only that a very brief examination of the interior of the church enabled me to reproduce all the 'psychical' noises.

Other investigators have been unhappy about some of the recordings made in Borley Church — and indeed elsewhere and claimed to be voices from the dead — for it does seem possible that the recordings may have a perfectly normal explanation. On 28/29 May 1976, four members of The Ghost Club, led by Tony Broughall, spent a night in Borley Church with three objects in view, and I quote from his official report which is preserved in the Borley Dossier:

'The object of this exercise in Borley Church was three-fold:

1. To obtain recordings of various paranormal sounds similar to those recorded in the early 1970s.

2. To observe any paranormal lights or glows as also reported previously.

3. To study the acoustics of the building in relationship to the afore-mentioned recordings and make an analysis of the possible source and origin of the sounds.

'The party of investigators was led by Tony Broughall and comprised Mrs Georgina Broughall, Mr Alan Roper and Mr Charles Doerrer; all members of The Ghost Club.

'Mr Roper was at the church by 7.45 pm and whilst awaiting the arrival of other members of the party, he met the Rector, the Revd K.A. Finnimore and chatted to him outside the church gates. The remaining members of the group arrived at 9.10 pm, their late arrival being due to the heavy Whitsun holiday traffic. The weather was dull and dry with a heavy cloud cover which limited the light to only fair for the time of year. Throughout the night there was no moonlight. Two photographs were taken inside the church, showing the group with the Rector, and after his departure the main recorder was placed by the chancel steps behind the organ. The microphone was suspended from one of the choir-stall pillars, and positioned facing the altar. Mr Doerrer with a portable recorder remained mobile, ready to commence recording at the first hint of any unusual sound.

'At 10.17 pm thermometers were placed at opposite ends of the nave of the church. The first was laid on the book ledge of the small front pew at the side of the Waldegrave tomb, the second was placed on the table used for the Visitors' Book. Nineteen minutes were allowed to pass before the first readings were taken to enable the instruments to settle at accurate readings. Detailed herewith are the results of the readings through the main part of the night, and it will be apparent that there were no significant temperature variations. All readings quoted are in degrees Fahrenheit and all times quoted are British Summer Time.

Time	Thermometer at tomb	Thermometer on table
10.26 pm	60	58
10.38 pm	59	57.5
11.08 pm	58	57.5
11.42 pm	60	57
11.55 pm	59	57
12.34 am	59	57.5
1.00 am	58	57
1.39 am	59	57
2.20 am	59	57
2.53 am	59	57
3.17 am	58	57

'After the 3.17 am readings were taken both doors were opened several times in the course of other pursuits and no further readings were noted as it was felt that the influx of cold air into the building would falsify such readings. Furthermore unanimous opinion also upheld the view that with dawn breaking the most advantageous time for the production of any auditory type of phenomena had, in effect, passed uneventfully.

'Six recordings were made between 11.08 pm and 5.11 am with breaks in between for consultations and refreshment. The times and durations of these recordings are given herewith:

Recording started	Duration	Recording stopped	Remarks
11.08 pm	34 mins	11.42 pm	—
11.55 pm	39 mins	12.34 pm	-
1.00 am	39 mins	1.39 am	-

2.20 am animal cries heard	33 mins	2.53 am	Owls and
3.17 am and dawn chorus	26 mins	3.43 am	Dawn
4.55 am left running in locked and empty church	16 mins	5.11 am	Recorder

Total time recorded on tape: 3 hrs 7 mins

'Subsequent careful analysis of the recordings has confirmed the opinion of those present that no paranormal sounds were heard in Borley Church during the investigations. Before the last period of recording was commenced it was decided that the church should be vacated and the recorder left running on the off-chance that whilst the party were viewing the alterations to the Rectory cottage there might be sounds produced in the church whilst it was empty. On arrival back at the church the recorder was stopped at 5.11 am. In order to immediately ascertain the result of this recording it was played back to the party. The sounds of the group's footsteps, the opening, closing, bolting and locking of the two doors were clearly reproduced as the party first vacated the building and later returned. All present at once noticed the distinct similarity between the alleged paranormal sound of a door opening as claimed on the 'ghost' recording and the actual recorded sound of the Porch Door being opened, even down to a squeak of a hinge. It may be recalled that in a BBC television programme Mr Peter Underwood was shown trying and opening the Priest's Door in the chancel, from which area it was claimed some paranormal sounds originated, and it was stated that this was not the door heard in the 'paranormal' recording. A recording of the television programme was located on the tape and played to the group as a check, but again those present agreed that the alleged paranormal recording seemed to be nothing more than a straightforward recording of the Porch Door opening.

'In view of the serious implications that it is possible to draw from this comparison it was decided to move the recorder up to the Porch Door and make a deliberate recording of the door being opened and closed. On playback the similarity was even more pronounced — sufficient, in the unanimous opinion of the group present, to cast considerable doubt on previous claims to recordings of paranormal noises in Borley Church.

'With this in mind it was suggested that the sounds of sighs and footsteps should also be deliberately recorded by the group in order to make a further comparison with the allegedly paranormal sounds. Once more the results were closely similar. Bearing these possibilities and revelations in mind, plus the fact that daylight was now strong and 6.0 am fast approaching, it was decided to bring the night's proceedings to a close. Accordingly the equipment was packed away, the electricity was turned off at the mains, and after a careful check to ensure that the building was secured and as it had been found on entry, the party set off for their respective homes. The members of my group and myself would like to acknowledge the kind co-operation that we received from Peter Underwood for his help and recommendations made to the Revd Keith Finnimore on our behalf; the practical help and warm welcome of the rector himself who showed a keen interest in our researches as well as granting permission for the venture; and Mrs B. Payne, who as Churchwarden made available the facilities for picking up and returning the church key.

'CONCLUSIONS. The initial feelings of the group were that the 'ghost' recordings must be looked at from an entirely different angle, due mainly to the ease with which they were duplicated in just a few moments. It is known that some investigators of the Borley saga have been dubious from the outset as to the paranormal validity of these sounds. According to reports several nights, spread over a period of more than a year, were spent recording inside Borley Church and perhaps it might be thought somewhat unfair to dismiss such extended efforts on the strength of one uneventful night, but counteracting this is the incredible ease with which the recordings were duplicated. Is it beyond the bounds of possibility that what was actually recorded were the team's own footsteps and their own opening and closing of the door, by accident? Could they have mistaken the positions of these sounds on the tapes when they entered or left the church? The only point which we were all in complete agreement about with regard to the claims of previous recordings made in the church is the fact that they were made in Borley Church. Other than that it is perhaps not wise to speculate.'

During the course of a letter, dated 16 June 1976, Mr Tony Broughall refers to Mr Croom-Hollingsworth's encounter with the ghost nun. He says:

'For weeks I kept replaying the the tape of the TV broadcast and the Croom-Hollingsworth interview because something "bugged" me about it. When the penny finally dropped it was so simple that I could have kicked myself for not seeing it sooner. Croom-Hollingsworth stated that the nun "doesn't see you . . . she is living in her own time . . .". If this is so why did she stop in front of him? Surely if she was living in her own time she would have either carried on and passed him, passed through him, or vanished immediately that she encountered his auric field or atmospheric vibrations? Then we have the "hard-headed" investigator who, we are told, threw a brick at her!!! Hardly the type of scientific response I would expect a serious investigator to employ when presented with such a unique opportunity. With the apparition in view for "nine to eleven" minutes I should have thought it far more scientific to have waited until it became clear that the apparition did not intend to proceed further and then, having fully noted everything possible about "her", perhaps risk losing her by trying to obtain a flash photograph, although I would be somewhat doubtful about doing even that.'

On the other hand in April 1976, I received independent reports of a visit to Borley by Paul deVos, a member of the Society for Psychical Research, Steven White, Michael Phillip Oakes and Nigel Nettlefield, on the night of 26-27 March 1976, together with a tape recording that contains some curious noises.

On this occasion the microphone was placed in the pulpit, the long flex trailing across the floor and through a chink in the door to the tape recording machine which was situated in the porch. The church was then locked by Mrs Payne, the Churchwarden, who retained the key.

The subsequent recording included noises that can be described as a loud bang and peculiar dragging noises. While playing their tape over inside the church the following morning all four visitors heard the handle of the Priest's Door bang and rattle and 'about six footsteps walked across the front of the church, by the altar'. An immediate search outside and inside failed to suggest any possible explanation.

During the course of an article that appeared in the American National Enquirer it is reported that 'veterinary surgeon Gordon Dobbs and his wife Catherine of London' saw the ghost nun at Borley in 1958. Mr Dobbs is quoted as saying: 'I saw a figure walking across the path in front of me. I was about to call out a greeting when I realized that it made no sound, nor did it disturb the puddles of water over which it passed. I knew of the legend and when I realized that the figure was that of a nun, my heart froze ... I wondered what a nun was doing strolling around at that time of night ... until I realized it was not a human figure in front of us. One moment it was there. The next it was gone. It could only have been a ghost.' Every effort has been made to trace Mr Gordon Dobbs to obtain a first-hand account of this experience but none of the appropriate organizations are able to help, the relevant Gordon Dobbs in the London telephone directory brought no success and I am left with the suspicion that Mr Dobbs may be a ghost himself! If, by any chance, he should read this report of his experience I would be delighted to hear from him in the hope that he will supply me with a full account for it is most important that all experiences at Borley reported by responsible people are preserved with the enormous quantity of good evidence for this remarkable case of haunting.

During the early summer of 1976 I was invited to take part in a BBC Overseas hour-long feature on 'Ghosts' (subsequently broadcast on 31st July and again on 1st August); accordingly I had several conversations with the scriptwriter John Pickford and suggested that the Borley haunting ought to be included. I introduced the producer to several possible contributors and, in the event, John Pickford went to Borley with John Taylor, Professor of Mathematics at London University, who is interested in scientifically recording paranormal activity. Accompanied by a technical assistant, they endeavoured to conduct a number of experiments with some quite sophisticated equipment, both inside and outside the church, to see whether they could obtain evidence of anything comparable to the strange sounds that have been recorded. Their equipment included a magnetometer for measuring ordinary magnetic fields and electric field measuring devices that would indicate television type waves and those of long wave radio.

During the course of examination of the interior of the church, at nine o'clock in the evening, John Taylor felt 'some slightly strange sensation' in one particular part of the church — a sensation of coldness in the vicinity of the Waldegrave monuments — 'a feeling of strength' that seemed to emanate from that quarter. After spending half an hour quietly in the somewhat melancholy churchyard, they again went into the church. There they positioned themselves a few yards in front of the altar, ready to measure any changes in electrical magnetic fields and to see whether these changes were related to any sounds they might hear or sights they might see. After about thirty minutes they left the church and discussed their conclusions so far in the churchyard.

John Taylor was satisfied that his equipment was performing perfectly but nothing unusual had been heard or seen and therefore there was nothing to work on. They decided to have another session inside the church. John Pickford, just before they left the church, began to feel cold and experienced a feeling of unease that seemed to be coming from the tower end of the church, the area farthest away from the equipment.

After a further two hours in the church John Taylor was asked to report on his feelings and opinions so far. He said he thought there seemed to be some slight movements in the area of the font (at the tower end of the church) which he thought may have been due to movement of the church foundations but when the three experimentors tried to duplicate these movements by stamping on the floor and banging on the font, they found that only reasonably strong attacks would actually cause the same level of movement; otherwise, apart from one or two blips in the electric field, they only heard a number of sounds that were rather odd. However they did establish that there was at least one bat inside the church although it was impossible to tell whether bats might be responsible for the noises or moths, also seen in the church, for they could make a noise that would register when they banged against windows or other parts of the church structure.

At the end of this visit it was agreed that no psychic force or presence manifested itself but it was felt that more work in this particular area might well be rewarding, and possibly with different people present who might unconsciously produce the right atmosphere.

During the course of a chapter on 'The Borley Haunt' in The Ghost Hunter's Companion [Leslie Frewin, 1977] I referred briefly to the remarkable experience of Mr Charles F.W. Chilton, MBE, at Borley in 1956. Since then Mr Chilton has been good enough to enlarge on the 'happening' and I quote verbatim from his letter of 17 May 1976:

> 'My experience at Borley was in the church, not in the churchyard, and it took place in the summer of 1956. I had spent a few weeks of that summer in Great Yarmouth producing seaside shows for the BBC. When after the last show my secretary, Sheila Anderson (now Mrs Wright) and I left Great Yarmouth for London I suggested that on the way home we make a detour and visit Borley. I had read Harry Price's accounts of the hauntings at that place and had met Price but I had never visited Borley. Passing so close to it seemed too good an opportunity to miss. We arrived at the church in the late evening. Dusk was falling. I cannot remember exactly what the weather was like. I think there had been a few showers earlier in the day but it was a calm, soft evening by the time we arrived at Borley.
>
> 'We inspected the church, outside and inside, and lingered a fair while over the Waldegrave tomb while I told my secretary of the Catholic persecutions, the suspected underground tunnel — the nun who had haunted the Rectory garden and of the young Waldegrave who might have raped and killed her.
>
> 'By now it was growing dark but there was sufficient daylight for us to see well. It was then we first heard the wind. It seemed to come from up in the roof above the Waldegrave tomb. Sheila remarked that it sounded as though a storm was getting up and perhaps we should think of leaving. We turned from the tomb and headed towards the door.

'The moment my back was turned to the altar there was a great crash immediately behind me. I can only describe the sound as that which would have been made by somebody throwing a large wooden form onto a hollow wooden floor. That was the immediate image that came to mind. Then it occurred to me that somehow I must have knocked over the heavy lectern. Meanwhile the wind reached a high-pitched howling, not unlike the sound made by wind blowing through a keyhole but heavier and louder.

'I remember seeing Sheila standing halfway down the aisle, her hands covering her face, not knowing whether to stay or run. Meanwhile the north and south doors on either side of the altar were rattling away as though by a strong wind from outside [The present bricked-up north door is at the west end of the church opposite the main entrance *(Author)*]. It got noticeably cooler (though this might have been from the chills now running up and down my back!)

'Nothing had been knocked over. Then I thought somebody must be playing a joke, somebody down in the crypt maybe. Probably because of the rain there might have been earlier in the day (or all week come to that — I do not remember the weather in Great Yarmouth being very summery) a long strip of protective coconut matting had been laid along the aisle and up the chancel steps.

'As I could see nobody nor anything that could account for the sudden and startling crash I lifted the matting, expecting to see a wooden floor. It was of stone. What kind of stone I cannot remember. It may have been ordinary paving or marble. The one thing I am sure about was that the floor was not wood.

'Meanwhile the wind (which I believed was blowing outside) howled and the north and south doors in the chancel walls rattled away. At this point I noticed that the altar stood well forward from the east wall, supplying a good place for any practical joker to hide. I walked between the wall and the altar — nothing. I tried to open the south door. It was locked. So was the north door. Unable to clear up the mystery of the big bang and affected somewhat by the noise of the wind, I decided to leave the church. Sheila had already gone.

'I don't suppose the time that passed between our hearing the crash and my deciding to leave could have been more than a few minutes. When I got outside (it was almost dark now) I was surprised to find the evening as calm and peaceful as when we went in — no wind — no storm — I don't think there was a cloud in the sky. I found Sheila by the car looking pretty pale and shaken. We discussed the incident, especially the wind. I suggested we should go back into the church to check whether the wind was still howling. Whether we both went back I cannot remember but I am sure *I* stood on the threshold of the main door and looked in. It was much darker now. I could just make out the features of the tomb and a few other things. All was still and calm. No noise of any kind.

'I returned to the car and we continued our journey home. I did not go back to Borley Church for more than ten years after that. When I did return I saw that the altar had been moved back to the east wall and it was no longer possible to walk behind the altar. I saw too that my memory had played me tricks with regard to the number of chancel doors there were. There is only one — in the south wall. I also noticed that the church had electric light. During my first visit the place had been lit by oil lamps.

'Although I hung about the church most of the evening until it was totally dark, half hoping for another phenomenon, nothing happened. I visited the church again two years ago (1974). This time I made a somewhat closer inspection of the area where the sound of the crash occurred; there is a large wooden trap-door set into it which, I presume, leads down into the crypt. None-the-less there was still only one chancel door.

'On the way out I saw a typewritten, short history of the church had been pinned on the inside of the main door. Naturally, I read it. Among other things it stated that although there is now only one door to the chancel there used to be two; the northern one being bricked up some two hundred years ago.' [In his Short History of Borley and Liston Churches (March 1973), J.M. Bull speaks of a 'priest's door, now covered with modern cement' and says 'a blocked-up doorway can be seen in the north wall']

Other, previously unpublished, evidence pertaining to the Borley haunting that has come to me include footsteps, heard by Mr Charles Hunter of Haverhill, Suffolk, as he stood with a friend at the gate of the churchyard one evening in July 1973. The footsteps, 'distinct and clear', seemed to come first from the direction of the rectory site and then from the church path behind the visitors, but then the footsteps were 'faster, as if someone was in a hurry'; then suddenly they were no longer heard.

Other visitors, in November 1975, experienced door-jamming, cold draughts, a sudden loud bang on the church door that seemed to come from inside, and a strange smell in the churchyard; no explanation could be discovered for any of these happenings, all of which have of course been reported many times over the years. Some may well have a natural explanation but there are a remarkable number of curious incidents which those who have experienced them are satisfied are inexplicable and cannot be lightly dismissed.

Alan Bestic, the writer and author, told me in August 1976 that he planned to visit Borley to see whether he could discover any new evidence. During the course of his subsequent article [News of the World, 25 August 1976] he recounted a meeting with Miss Meg Barton, whose father is a churchwarden, and she told him that she believed she had once spoken to the ghost nun: 'While I was riding my pony I saw a figure about five feet tall and wearing long robes. I said "Good afternoon", but she never looked up and I thought "what a rude person". My pony shied and snorted and when I looked back, the figure had gone.'

Other correspondents inform me of incidents that happen in their own homes when they, for example, watch a television programme about Borley. Mrs Dorothy Collyer is one such person who had a curious experience while watching a programme when Michael Bentine visited Borley Church. As he walked down the aisle, approaching the altar, he said he felt very cold and at this point Mrs Collyer, watching the programme at her home in Heathfield, Sussex, found her attention drawn to the corner of the church, by the existing Priest's Door, where she noticed that black and white shapes seemed to be moving. She rubbed her eyes but when she looked again the shapes were still there and as she watched they seemed to form themselves into the heads and shoulders of people, a crowd of people, seemingly watching the television cameras. The forms were completely faceless, at different heights, and constantly moving. Other people who saw the same programme saw nothing unusual but there was nothing wrong with Mrs Collyer's television set or with her eyes. As with so many of the reported happenings at Borley and elsewhere strange things happen at the least expected moment and only to certain people, yet not to any particular type of person as far as can be established. One thing is important: every incident of a possibly paranormal or psychic nature or anything that cannot be explained in rational terms must be carefully preserved, studied in conjunction with other evidence and examined in relation to new theories and new thoughts on this fascinating subject.

What is the answer to the mysteries of Borley? Some of the hundreds of reports of curious happenings can certainly be dismissed; perhaps some of the recorded noises have perfectly normal explanations; perhaps some of the sightings of the nun are the result of inaccurate observation, imagination or wishful thinking. But it does seem to me that of all the celebrated cases of haunting that we have considered this remarkable and lengthy story has so many unanswerable problems, innumerable puzzles and strange incidents reported by responsible, independent, unbiased, sane and sensible witnesses that it stands alone in the annals of psychical research as a continuing problem for the materialist and an exciting challenge for the psychical researcher.

SELECT BIBLIOGRAPHY

Britton, John, The Beauties of England and Wales, Vol. XV, London (1814).

Bull, J.M., A Short History of Borley and Liston Churches, privately printed (1937).

Carrington, Hereward, Personal Experiences of Spiritualism, T. Werner Laurie (1913).

Carrington, Hereward and Fodor, Nandor, The Story of the Poltergeist Down the Centuries, Rider (1953).

Collins, B. Abdy, The Cheltenham Ghost, Psychic Press (1948).

Coxe, Antony D. Hippisley, Haunted Britain, Hutchinson (1973).

Darwin, G.H., The Tides, John Murray (1898).

Day, James Wentworth, The Queen Mother's Family Story, Robert Hale (1967).

Dutton, Ralph Stawell, Hinton Ampner, A Hampshire Manor, Batsford (1968).

Edwards, W. Le Cato, Epworth, the Home of the Wesleys, privately printed (n.d.).

Fenwick, Hubert, Scotland's Historic Buildings, Robert Hale (1974).

Fodor, Nandor, Encyclopaedia of Psychic Science, Arthurs Press (1934).

Glanvill, Joseph, Saducismus Triumphatus, London (1681). Hadfield, A.J., Psychology and Mental Health, George Allen & Unwin (1950).

Halifax, Lord, Lord Halifax's Ghost Book, Geoffrey Bles (1936).

Hallam, Jack, Ghosts of London, Wolfe (1975).

Harper, Charles G., Haunted Houses, Chapman and Hall (1907).

Hole, Christina, Haunted England, Batsford (1940).

Hubbell, Walter, The Haunted House... The Great Amherst Mystery, Saint John, N.B. (1879).

Ingram, John H., The Haunted Houses and Family Traditions of Great Britain, Reeves and Turner (1912).

Iremonger, Lucille, The Ghosts of Versailles, Faber and Faber (1957).

Jullian, Philippe, Robert de Montesquiou, un prince 1900, Librarie, Academique Perrin, Paris (1965).

Knight, David C., Poltergeists: Hauntings and the Haunted, Lippincott, Philadelphia and New York (1972).

Lambert, R.S., Exploring the Supernatural, Arthur Barker (n.d.).

Law, Ernest, History of Hampton Court, Bell (1891).

Lindsay, Philip, Hampton Court — a history, Meridian Books (1948).

MacKenzie, Andrew, Apparitions and Ghosts, Arthur Barker (1971) and The Unexplained, Arthur Barker (1966).

Mee, Arthur, Wiltshire (The King's England Series), Hodder and Stoughton (1939).

Moberly, C.A.E. and Jourdain, Eleanor F., An Adventure (Fourth Edition) Faber and Faber (1931).

Podmore, Frank, Modern Spiritualism, Methuen (1902).

Price, Harry, Poltergeist Over England, Country Life (1945), The End of Borley Rectory, Harrap (1946) and 'The Most Haunted House in England', Longmans, Green (1940).

Rawcliffe, D.H., The Psychology of the Occult, Derricke Ridgway (1952).

Sitwell, Sacheverell, Poltergeists, Faber and Faber (1940).

Squiers, Granville, Secret Hiding Places, Stanley Paul (1934).

Sturge-Whiting, J.R., The Mystery of Versailles, Rider (1938).

Toy, Sidney, The Castles of Great Britain, Heinemann (1953).

Tyerman, L., The Life and Times of the Revd Samuel Wesley MA, Rector of Epworth, Simpkin, Marshall (1866).

Underwood, Peter, A Gazetteer of British Ghosts, Souvenir Press (1971), A Gazetteer of Scottish and Irish Ghosts, Souvenir Press (1973), The Ghost

Hunter's Companion, Leslie Frewin (1977), The Ghosts of Borley (with Dr Paul Tabori), David and Charles (1973), Haunted London, Harrap (1973) and Nights in Haunted Houses, (1994).

Journals and Proceedings of the British and American Societies for Psychical Research; Notes and Queries; Queen; Encounter; etc.

ABOUT THE AUTHOR

Peter Underwood

Peter Underwood was President of the Ghost Club (founded 1862) from 1960-1993 and probably heard more first-hand ghost stories than any man alive. He was a long-standing member of The Society of Psychical Research, Vice-President of the Unitarian Society for Psychical Studies, a member of The Folklore Society, The Dracula Society and the Research Committee of the Psychic Research Organization, he wrote extensively, and was a seasoned lecturer and broadcaster. He took part in the first official investigation into a haunting; sat with physical and mental mediums and conducted investigations at seances. He was present at exorcisms, experiments at dowsing, precognition, clairvoyance, hypnotism, regression; he conducted world-wide tests in telepathy and extra-sensory perception, and personally investigated scores of haunted houses across the country. He possessed comprehensive files of alleged hauntings in every county of the British Isles and many foreign countries, and his knowledge and experience resulted in his being consulted on psychic and occult matters by the BBC and ITV. His many books include the first two comprehensive gazetteers of ghosts and hauntings in England, Scotland and Ireland and two books that deal with twenty different occult subjects. Highlights from his published work include 'Nights in Haunted Houses' (1993), which collects together the results of group investigations, 'The Ghosts of Borley' (1973), his classic account of the history of 'the most haunted house in England', 'Hauntings' (1977), which re-examines ten classic cases of haunting in the light of modern knowledge, 'No Common Task' (1983), which reflects back upon his life as a 'ghost hunter', and 'The Ghost Hunter's Guide' (1986), which gives the reader all the advice necessary to become one. Born at Letchworth Garden City in Hertfordshire, he lived for many years in a small village in Hampshire.

BOOKS BY THIS AUTHOR

Ghosts Of North West England

The ghostly little monk of Foulridge and the giant apparition from Heaton Norris are just two of the denizens of the North-West you might not care to meet on a dark, stormy evening. But for those intrepid souls whose hearts quicken at the thought of eerie footsteps and muffled groans Peter Underwood has assembled an impressive collection of traditional legends.

Ghosts Of Kent

The first expert exploration of the haunted houses and authentic ghosts of Kent by the [former] President of the Ghost Club, Peter Underwood.

Karloff: The Life Of Boris Karloff

Boris Karloff was the most famous of all horror actors. His memorable portrayal of the Frankenstein monster added a new word to English dictionaries.

This Haunted Isle

Peter Underwood has personally visited the historic buildings and sites of Britain, and here presents a wealth of intriguing legends and new stories of ghostly encounters from more than a hundred such throughout the United Kingdom.

From Abbey House in Cambridge to Zennor in Cornwall, this is an A to Z of the haunted houses of Britain. At Bramshill in Hampshire — now a police training college — there have been so many sightings that even sceptical police officers have had to admit that the place is haunted. Beautiful Leeds Castle in Kent has a large, phantom black dog; there is an Elizabethan gentleman (seen by a Canon of the Church of England!) at Croft Castle; a Pink Lady at Coughton Court; a prancing ghost jester at Gawsworth; a spectre in green velvet at Hoghton Tower; six ghosts at East Riddlesden Hall; a headless apparition at Westwood Manor; and then there are some little-known ghosts in Windsor Castle, Hampton Court Palace and the Tower of London, and the strange ghosts of Chingle Hall, perhaps the most haunted house in England.

Exorcism!

Throughout history, the practice of exorcism has been used for the purpose of driving out evil spirits and demons though to possess human beings and the places they inhabit. But there are more startling instances where exorcism has been used: to cure a trawler that seemed to be cursed; to expel demons from Bram Stoker's black 'vampire' dog' even to rid Loch Ness and the Bermuda Triangle of their evil ambience. Peter Underwood explores this frightening ritual in relation to witches, vampires and animals, while his far-flung researches have unearthed dramatic cases in Morocco, Egypt, South Africa and the United States, as well as the British Isles.

Death In Hollywood

The Hollywood way of life has long been a potent mix of scandal, secrecy and sensation: exactly like the Hollywood way of death...

In this unique study, Peter Underwood charts the lives, loves and deaths of thirty of Tinseltown's most glittering stars. Many deaths were sad or senseless; some were tragic; others were the revenge of old age, while a few were the revenge of something altogether more sinister...

Peter Underwood's Guide To Ghosts & Haunted Places

Based on 50 years' expert study and investigation, this collection of cases from the files of Peter Underwood - an acknowledged expert and experienced investigator of haunted houses - represents a unique exploration of the world of ghosts, apparitions and psychic phenomena. If you want to satisfy your curiosity about the subject or simply enjoy a riveting read, this guide is for you.

No Common Task: The Autobiography Of A Ghost-Hunter

This is the autobiography of a man who has spent

thirty-five years of his life covering scientific psychical research, with detailed investigations into all kinds of manifestation that might be supernatural or paranormal in origin, including spiritualism, ESP, telepathy, hauntings and other occult phenomena. Many of the true experiences from the author's casebook are published here for the first time.

Dictionary Of The Supernatural

An A to Z of Hauntings, Possession, Witchcraft, Demonology and Other Occult Phenomena...

The entries cover all known (and some very little known) organisations, individuals, periodicals, terms of reference, and significant cases, events and incidents relevant to the subject. Under each entry there are notes on other appropriate books and further reading.

The Ghost Hunter's Guide

What are the qualities which make an ideal ghost hunter? You need to be part detective, part investigative reporter, a scientist, with a measure of the psychologist thrown in...

In this book, which is the first real guide to the hunting of ghosts, Peter Underwood manages to cover just about every aspect of this intriguing and mystifying subject.

Ghosts Of Hampshire And The Isle Of Wight

Peter Underwood, an acknowledged expert and experienced investigator of haunted houses, presents a selection of hauntings throughout Hampshire and the Isle of Wight. A formidable collection of ghoulies and things that go bump in the night.

This edition includes a foreword by author Alan Williams, as well as an interview Williams conducted with Underwood in 1997.

Jack The Ripper: One Hundred Years Of Mystery

Jack the Ripper still causes a shudder, synonymous as it is with violent murder and mutilation. But also of mystery and speculation - for the gruesome series of killings in London's East End in that horrific Autumn of 1888 have never been finally solved.

The Ghosts Of Borley: Annals Of The Haunted Rectory

'The Ghosts of Borley' (1973) was the first complete record of the unique Borley Rectory hauntings, detailing all the evidence known about this notorious haunted house from the early days of the Rev. H. D. E. Bull who built Borley Rectory in 1863, through the incumbencies of the Rev. Harry Bull, the Rev. Guy Eric Smith and the Rev. Lionel Foyster, to the investigations by Harry Price and other members of the Society for Psychical Research (SPR).

The Complete Book Of Dowsing And Divining

This comprehensive volume on dowsing and divining - from the twig and the pendulum to motorscopes and bare hands - traces the story of these fascinating and enigmatic phenomena from its origins in the world of fairy tales and mythology to recent theories that the enigma can be explained in terms of present-day psychology.

Into The Occult

Despite all the answers that conventional science can provide to the earth's mysteries, there remain certain phenomena for which no explanation can yet be found outside the occult. For this reason exploration of the occult and paranormal provides endless fascination.

Here is a survey of all the different aspects of this complex and intriguing subject, including an entire chapter on the relationship between sex and psychic phenomena, a subject on which, until recently, there has been an unwillingness to talk.

Deeper Into The Occult

'In an age when voodoo dancers have appeared in London, when Robert Williams, chief psychologist at Kansas State Industrial Reformatory admits to being a practising war-lock; when moon-astronaut Edgar Mitchell conducts extra sensory experiments in space;

when the course of a £1,000,000 road is altered to save a 'fairy tree'; when a ghost is officially registered on a census form; when Americans can 'dial-a-horoscope' for a twenty-four hour prophesy; and when the complete skeleton of a cyclops is unearthed by archaeologists — is it surprising that there is a growing interest in the occult, for research in many fields simply proves that things are not what they seem?'

Nights In Haunted Houses

For over thirty years, in his position as President and Chief Investigator of the Ghost Club of Great Britain, Peter Underwood was actively involved in undertaking night vigils and carrying out research into ghosts and paranormal activity in controlled, scientific conditions.

Queen Victoria's Other World

There have been many books about Queen Victoria but there has never been one that has explored her 'other world' - the world of the strange and unusual, the world of death and her fascination for it, and the world of the unseen and the paranormal that she could never resist.

The Vampire's Bedside Companion: The Amazing World Of Vampires In Fact And Fiction

The Vampire's Bedside Companion is a riveting compendium of new facts and fiction on the 'undying' theme of vampirism.

Here is a new theory on the genesis of Dracula (surely literature's most compelling and macabre figure?); thoughts on allusions to vampirism in Wuthering Heights; first-hand experience of Vampires in Hampstead, London; publication for the first time of the story of a fifteenth-century Vampire Protection medallion that Montague Summers presented to the author; an account by a professer of English at Dalhousie University of a visit to 'Castle Dracula' in Transylvania - The Vampire's Bedside Companion contains these and a wealth of other hitherto unpublished material on a subject that is of enduring interest: The Vampire Legend.

The Ghost Hunters: Who They Are And What They Do

A leading psychical researcher takes an in-depth look at ghost hunters, both past and present. Who are these intrepid explorers of the unknown? How do they probe and examine the realms of the seemingly inexplicable? What are their conclusions? In fascinating detail, Peter Underwood profiles the lives and adventures of some of the most famous names in psychical investigation.

Printed in Great Britain
by Amazon